DATE DUE			

Junior Worldmark Encyclopedia of the States

Junior Worldmark Encyclopedia of the

States

Third Edition

VOLUME 4

Tennessee to Wyoming,
Washington D.C.,
Puerto Rico, U.S. Pacific and
Caribbean dependencies, and
U.S. overview

GALE GROUP

★

THOMSON LEARNING

Detroit • New York • San Diego • San Francisco
Boston • New Haven, Conn. • Waterville, Maine
London • Munich

JUNIOR WORLDMARK ENCYCLOPEDIA OF THE STATES, THIRD EDITION

Timothy L. Gall and Susan Bevan Gall, *Editors*
Karen Hanson, *Associate Editor*
Barbara Dickinson, Jennifer Jackson, Sarah Kunz, and Jennifer Wallace, *Assistant Editors*
Brian Rajewski, Deborah Rutti, and Bram Lambrecht, *Graphics and Layout*
Janet Fenn and Matthew Markovich, *Proofreaders*
University of Akron Laboratory for Cartographic and
    Spatial Analysis, Joseph W. Stoll, Supervisor;
    Scott Raypholtz, Mike Meger, *Cartographers*

U•X•L Staff

Allison McNeill, *U•X•L Senior Editor*
Carol DeKane Nagel, *U•X•L Managing Editor*
Thomas L. Romig, *U•X•L Publisher*
Evi Seoud, *Assistant Manager, Composition Purchasing and Electronic Prepress*
Rita Wimberley, *Senior Buyer*
Mary Krzewinski, *Art Director*
Mike Logusz, *Graphic Artist*

Library of Congress Cataloging-in-Publication Data

Junior Worldmark encyclopedia of the states / [Timothy L. Gall and Susan Bevan Gall, editors]. -- 3rd ed.
        p. cm.
    Includes bibliographical references and index.
    Contents : v. 1. Alabama to Illinois -- v. 2. Indiana to Nebraska -- v. 3. Nevada to South Dakota -- v. 4. Tennessee to Wyoming
    ISBN 0-7876-5376-4 (set) -- ISBN 0-7876-5377-2 (v. l) -- ISBN 0-7876-5378-0 (v. 2) -- ISBN 0-7876-5379-9 (v. 3) -- ISBN 0-7876-5380-2 (v. 4)
    1. United States--Encyclopedias, Juvenile. 2. U.S. states--Encyclopedias, Juvenile.
    [1. United States--Encyclopedias.] I. Gall, Timothy L. II. Gall, Susan B.

E156.J86 2001
973'.03--dc21
                                                                        2010041056

CONTENTS

READER'S GUIDE

Junior Worldmark Encyclopedia of the States, Third Edition, presents profiles of the 50 states of the nation, the District of Columbia, Puerto Rico, and the U.S. dependencies, arranged alphabetically in four volumes. *Junior Worldmark* is based on the fifth edition of the reference work, *Worldmark Encyclopedia of the States.* The *Worldmark* design organizes facts and data about every state in a common structure. Every profile contains a map, showing the state and its location in the nation.

For this third edition of *Junior Worldmark,* facts were updated and many new photographs were added. While the second edition photographs were chosen to illustrate economic activity in the state, new photographs for this edition were selected to feature notable citizens. In addition, a Population Profile was added to each state entry giving the breakdown of the state's population by race as enumerated by Census 2000. For the first time in history, respondents to Census 2000 were given the opportunity to select one or more race categories to indicate their racial identity. The U.S. Census Bureau reported data for each state in seven race categories: White *alone;* Black or African American *alone;* American Indian and Alaska Native *alone;* Asian *alone;* Native Hawaiian and Other Pacific Islander *alone;* Some other race *alone;* and Two or more races. About 98% of all respondents reported only one race. The population

profile gives users of *Junior Worldmark* access to the latest population data for the states.

Each state's political history is documented in the updated table listing the governors who have served the state since the founding of the nation. As with the first and second editions, recognition is due to the many professional photographers, tourist bureaus, convention centers, press offices, and state agencies that contributed the photographs that illustrate this encyclopedia.

Web sites listed at the end of the Bibliography for each state article have been verified and updated. An extensive survey of available sites was undertaken in May 2001 and only those with information relevant to the needs of students were chosen for inclusion.

Attention is also drawn to the many article reviewers listed at the end of this Reader's Guide. The reviewers contributed insights, updates, and substantive additions that were instrumental to the creation of this work. The editors are extremely grateful for the time and effort these distinguished reviewers devoted to improving the quality of this encyclopedia.

Sources

Due to the broad scope of this encyclopedia many sources were consulted in compiling the information and statistics presented in these volumes. Of primary importance were the publications of the U.S. Bureau of the Census. The most recent agricultural statistics on crops and livestock were obtained from files posted by the U.S. Department of Agriculture on its gopher server and its world-wide web site at http://www.econ.ag.gov. Finally, many fact sheets, booklets, and state statistical abstracts were used to update data not collected by the federal government.

Profile Features

The *Junior Worldmark* structure—40 numbered headings—allows student researchers to compare two or more states in a variety of ways.

Each state profile begins by listing the origin of the state name, its nickname, the capital, the date it entered the union, the state song and motto, and a description of the state coat of arms. The profile also presents a picture and textual description of both the state seal and the state flag (a key to the flag color symbols appears on page xii of each volume). Next, a listing of the official state animal, bird, fish, flower, tree, gem, etc. is given. The introductory information ends with the standard time given by time zone in relation to Greenwich mean time (GMT). The world is divided into 24 time zones, each one hour apart. The Greenwich meridian, which is 0 degrees, passes through Greenwich, England, a suburb of London. Greenwich is at the center of the initial time zone, known as Greenwich mean time (GMT). All times given are converted from noon in this zone. The time reported for the state is the official time zone.

The body of each country's profile is arranged in 40 numbered headings as follows:

1 LOCATION AND SIZE. The state is located on the North American continent. Statistics are given on area and boundary length. Size comparisons are made to the other 50 states of the United States.

2 TOPOGRAPHY. Dominant geographic features including terrain and major rivers and lakes are described.

3 CLIMATE. Temperature and rainfall are given for the various regions of the state in both English and metric units.

4 PLANTS AND ANIMALS. Described here are the plants and animals native to the state.

5 ENVIRONMENTAL PROTECTION. Destruction of natural resources—forests, water supply, air—is described here. Statistics on solid waste production, hazardous waste sites, and endangered and extinct species are also included.

6 POPULATION. Census 2000 statistics, including the seven categories identifying race introduced with the 2000 census of population, are provided. Population density and major urban populations are summarized.

7 ETHNIC GROUPS. The major ethnic groups are ranked in percentages. Where appropriate, some description of the influence or history of ethnicity is provided.

8 LANGUAGES. The regional dialects of the state are summarized as well as the number of people speaking languages other than English at home.

9 **RELIGIONS.** The population is broken down according to religion and/or denominations.

10 **TRANSPORTATION.** Statistics on roads, railways, waterways, and air traffic, along with a listing of key ports for trade and travel, are provided.

11 **HISTORY.** Includes a concise summary of the state's history from ancient times (where appropriate) to the present.

12 **STATE GOVERNMENT.** The form of government is described, and the process of governing is summarized. A table listing the state governors, updated to 2000, accompanies each entry.

13 **POLITICAL PARTIES.** Describes the significant political parties through history, where appropriate, and the influential parties in the mid-1990s.

14 **LOCAL GOVERNMENT.** The system of local government structure is summarized.

15 **JUDICIAL SYSTEM.** Structure of the court system and the jurisdiction of courts in each category is provided. Crime rates as reported by the Federal Bureau of Investigation (FBI) are also included.

16 **MIGRATION.** Population shifts since the end of World War II are summarized.

17 **ECONOMY.** This section presents the key elements of the economy. Major industries and employment figures are also summarized.

18 **INCOME.** Personal income and the poverty level are given as is the state's ranking among the 50 states in per person income.

19 **INDUSTRY.** Key industries are listed, and important aspects of industrial development are described.

20 **LABOR.** Statistics are given on the civilian labor force, including numbers of workers, leading areas of employment, and unemployment figures.

21 **AGRICULTURE.** Statistics on key agricultural crops, market share, and total farm income are provided.

22 **DOMESTICATED ANIMALS.** Statistics on livestock—cattle, hogs, sheep, etc.—and the land area devoted to raising them are given.

23 **FISHING.** The relative significance of fishing to the state is provided, with statistics on fish and seafood products.

24 **FORESTRY.** Land area classified as forest is given, along with a listing of key forest products and a description of government policy toward forest land.

25 **MINING.** Description of mineral deposits and statistics on related mining activity and export are provided.

26 **ENERGY AND POWER.** Description of the state's power resources, including electricity produced and oil reserves and production, are provided.

27 **COMMERCE.** A summary of the amount of wholesale trade, retail trade, and receipts of service establishments is given.

28 PUBLIC FINANCE. Revenues, expenditures, and total and per person debt are provided.

29 TAXATION. The state's tax system is explained.

30 HEALTH. Statistics on and description of such public health factors as disease and suicide rates, principal causes of death, numbers of hospitals and medical facilities appear here. Information is also provided on the percentage of citizens without health insurance within each state.

31 HOUSING. Housing shortages and government programs to build housing are described. Statistics on numbers of dwellings and median home values are provided.

32 EDUCATION. Statistical data on educational achievement and primary and secondary schools is given. Per person state spending on primary and secondary education is also given. Major universities are listed, and government programs to foster education are described.

33 ARTS. A summary of the state's major cultural institutions is provided together with the amount of federal and state funds designated to the arts.

34 LIBRARIES AND MUSEUMS. The number of libraries, their holdings, and their yearly circulation is provided. Major museums are listed.

35 COMMUNICATIONS. The state of telecommunications (television, radio, and telephone) is summarized. Activity related to the Internet is reported where available.

36 PRESS. Major daily and Sunday newspapers are listed together with data on their circulations.

37 TOURISM, TRAVEL, AND RECREATION. Under this heading, the student will find a summary of the importance of tourism to the state, and factors affecting the tourism industry. Key tourist attractions are listed.

38 SPORTS. The major sports teams in the state, both professional and collegiate, are summarized.

39 FAMOUS PEOPLE. In this section, some of the best-known citizens of the state are listed. When a person is noted in a state that is not the state of his of her birth, the birthplace is given.

40 BIBLIOGRAPHY. The bibliographic and web site listings at the end of each profile are provided as a guide for further reading.

Because many terms used in this encyclopedia will be new to students, each volume includes a glossary and a list of abbreviations and acronyms. A keyword index to all four volumes appears in Volume 4.

Acknowledgments

Junior Worldmark Encyclopedia of the States, Third Edition, draws on the fifth edition of the *Worldmark Encyclopedia of the States.* Readers are directed to that work for a complete list of contributors, too numerous to list here. Special acknowledgment goes to the government officials throughout the nation who gave their cooperation to this project.

Reviewers

The following individuals reviewed state articles for this or previous editions. In all cases the reviewers added important information and updated facts that might have gone unnoticed. The reviewers were also instrumental in suggesting changes and improvements.

Patricia L. Harris, Executive Director, Alabama Public Library Service

Patience Frederiksen, Head, Government Publications, Alaska State Library

Jacqueline L. Miller, Curator of Education, Arizona State Capitol Museum

John A. Murphey, Jr., State Librarian, Arkansas State Library

Eugene Hainer, School Library Media Consultant, Colorado State Library

Susan Cormier, Connecticut State Library

Dr. Annette Woolard, Director of Development, Historical Society of Delaware

Reference Staff, State Library of Florida

Cheryl Rogers, Consultant, Georgia Department of Education, Public Library Services

Lorna J. T. Peck, School Library Services, Specialist, State of Hawaii Department of Education

Marcia J. Beckwith, Director, Information Services/Library, Centennial High School, Boise, Idaho

Karen McIlrath-Muskopf, Youth Services Consultant, Illinois State Library

Cordell Svengalis, Social Science Consultant, Iowa Department of Education

Marc Galbraith, Director of Reference Services, Kansas State Library

James C. Klotter, State Historian, Kentucky Historical Society

Virginia R. Smith, Head, Louisiana Section, State Library of Louisiana

Ben Keating, Division Director, Maine State Library

Patricia V. Melville, Director of Reference Services, Maryland State Archives

Brian Donoghue, Reference Librarian, Massachusetts Board of Library Commissioners

Denise E. Carlson, Head of Reference, Minnesota Historical Society

Ronnie Smith, Reference Specialist, Mississippi Library Commission

Darlene Staffeldt, Director, Statewide Library Resources, Montana State Library

Rod Wagner, Director, Nebraska Library Commission

Reference Services and Archives Staff, Nevada State Library & Archives

Kendall F. Wiggin, State Librarian, New Hampshire State Library

John H. Livingstone, Acting Assistant Commissioner and State Librarian, New Jersey State Library

Robert J. Torrez, State Historian, New Mexico State Records and Archives

R. Allan Carter, Senior Librarian, New York State Library

Staff, Information Services and State Archives Research, State Library of North Carolina

Doris Daugherty, Assistant State Librarian, North Dakota State Library

Carol Brieck and Audrey Hall, Reference Librarians, State Library of Ohio

Audrey Wolfe-Clark, Edmond, Oklahoma

Paul Gregorio, Assistant Professor of Education, Portland State University, Portland, Oregon

Alice L. Lubrecht, Acting Bureau Director, State Library of Pennsylvania

Barbara Weaver, Director, Department of State Library Services, Rhode Island

Michele M. Reid, Director of Public Services, South Dakota State Library

Dr. Wayne C. Moore, Archivist, Tennessee State Library and Archives

Douglas E. Barnett, Managing Editor, New Handbook of Texas, Texas State Historical Association

Lou Reinwand, Director of Information Services, Utah State Library

Paul J. Donovan, Senior Reference Librarian, Vermont Department of Libraries

Catherine Mishler, Head, Reference, Library of Virginia

Gayle Palmer, Senior Library Information Specialist, Washington/Northwest Collections, Washington State Library

Karen Goff, Head of Reference, West Virginia Library Commission

Richard L. Roe, Research Analyst, Wisconsin Legislative Reference Bureau

Priscilla Golden, Principal Librarian, Wyoming State Library

Staff, Washingtoniana Division, Martin Luther King Memorial Library, Washington, D.C.

Jean Hanson, MLS, Consultant, web sites.

Advisors

The following persons were consulted on the content and structure of this encyclopedia. Their insights, opinions, and suggestions led to many enhancements and improvements in the presentation of the material.

Mary Alice Anderson, Media Specialist, Winona Middle School, Winona, Minnesota

Pat Baird, Library Media Specialist and Department Chair, Shaker Heights Middle School, Shaker Heights, Ohio

Pat Fagel, Library Media Specialist, Shaker Heights Middle School, Shaker Heights, Ohio

Nancy Guidry, Young Adult Librarian, Santa Monica Public Library, Santa Monica, California

Ann West LaPrise, Children's Librarian, Redford Branch, Detroit Public Library, Detroit, Michigan

Nancy C. Nieman, Teacher, U.S. History, Social Studies, Journalism, Delta Middle School, Muncie, Indiana

Madeleine Obrock, Library Media Specialist, Woodbury Elementary School, Shaker Heights, Ohio

Ernest L. O'Roark, Teacher, Social Studies, Martin Luther King Middle School, Germantown, Maryland

Ellen Stepanian, Director of Library Services, Shaker Heights Board of Education, Shaker Heights, Ohio

Mary Strouse, Library Media Specialist, Woodbury Elementary School, Shaker Heights, Ohio

Comments and Suggestions

We welcome your comments on the *Junior Worldmark Encyclopedia of the States, Third Edition,* as well as your suggestions for features to be included in future editions. Please write to: Editors, *Junior Worldmark Encyclopedia of the States,* U•X•L, 27500 Drake Road, Farmington Hills, Michigan 48331-3535; or call toll-free: 1-800-877-4253.

Guide to State Articles

All information contained within a state article is uniformly keyed by means of a boxed number to the left of the subject headings. A heading such as "Population," for example, carries the same key numeral (6) in every article. Therefore, to find information about the population of Alabama, consult the table of contents for the page number where the Alabama article begins and look for section 6.

Introductory matter for each state includes: Origin of state name
Nickname
Capital
Date and order of statehood
Song
Motto
Flag
Official seal
Symbols (animal, tree, flower, etc.)
Time zone.

Flag color symbols

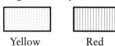 Yellow   Red   Green   Blue   Orange   Brown   White   Black

Sections listed numerically

1 Location and Size
2 Topography
3 Climate
4 Plants and Animals
5 Environmental Protection
6 Population
7 Ethnic Groups
8 Languages
9 Religions
10 Transportation
11 History
12 State Government
13 Political Parties
14 Local Government
15 Judicial System
16 Migration
17 Economy
18 Income
19 Industry
20 Labor
21 Agriculture
22 Domesticated Animals
23 Fishing
24 Forestry
25 Mining
26 Energy and Power
27 Commerce
28 Public Finance
29 Taxation
30 Health
31 Housing
32 Education
33 Arts
34 Libraries and Museums
35 Communications
36 Press
37 Tourism, Travel, and
      Recreation
38 Sports
39 Famous Persons
40 Bibliography

Alphabetical listing of sections

Agriculture	21	Labor	20
Arts	33	Languages	8
Bibliography	40	Libraries and Museums	34
Climate	3	Local Government	14
Commerce	27	Location and Size	1
Communications	35	Migration	16
Domesticated Animals	22	Mining	25
Economy	17	Plants and Animals	4
Education	32	Political Parties	13
Energy and Power	26	Population	6
Environmental Protection	5	Press	36
Ethnic Groups	7	Public Finance	28
Famous Persons	39	Religions	9
Fishing	23	Sports	38
Forestry	24	State Government	12
Health	30	Taxation	29
History	11	Topography	2
Housing	31	Tourism, Travel, and	
Income	18	Recreation	37
Industry	19	Transportation	10
Judicial System	15		

Explanation of symbols

A fiscal split year is indicated by a stroke (e.g. 1999/00).
Note that 1 billion = 1,000 million = 10^9.
The use of a small dash (e.g., 1998–99) normally signifies the
   full period of calendar years covered (including the end year indicated).

TENNESSEE

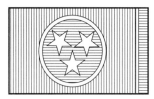

State of Tennessee

ORIGIN OF STATE NAME: Probably derived from Indian name *Tenase,* which was the principal village of the Cherokee.

NICKNAME: The Volunteer State.

CAPITAL: Nashville.

ENTERED UNION: 1 June 1796 (16th).

SONGS: "When It's Iris Time in Tennessee"; "The Tennessee Waltz"; "My Homeland, Tennessee"; "Rocky Top"; "My Tennessee"; "Tennessee"; "The Pride of Tennessee."

PUBLIC SCHOOL SONG: "My Tennessee."

POEM: "Oh Tennessee, My Tennessee."

FOLK DANCE: Square dance.

MOTTO: Agriculture and Commerce.

SLOGAN: Tennessee—America at Its Best.

FLAG: On a crimson field separated by a white border from a blue bar at the fly, three white stars on a blue circle edged in white represent the state's three main general divisions—East, Middle, and West Tennessee.

OFFICIAL SEAL: The upper half consists of the word "Agriculture," a plow, a sheaf of wheat, a cotton plant, and the roman numeral XVI, signifying the order of entry into the Union. The lower half comprises the word "Commerce" and a boat. The words "The Great Seal of the State of Tennessee 1796" surround the whole. The date commemorates the passage of the state constitution.

WILD ANIMAL: Raccoon.

BIRD: Mockingbird.

CULTIVATED FLOWER: Iris.

WILDFLOWER: Passion flower.

TREE: Tulip poplar.

GEM: Tennessee pearl.

ROCKS: Limestone, agate.

INSECTS: Ladybug, firefly.

TIME: 7 AM EST = noon GMT; 6 AM CST = noon GMT.

1 LOCATION AND SIZE

Situated in the eastern south-central US, Tennessee ranks 34th in size among the 50 states. The total area of the state is 42,144 square miles (109,152 square kilometers).

Tennessee extends about 430 miles (690 kilometers) east-west and 110 miles (180 kilometers) north-south. The boundary length of Tennessee totals 1,306 miles (2,102 kilometers).

[2] TOPOGRAPHY

Tennessee is divided into six major physical regions. The easternmost region is the Unaka Mountains, part of the Appalachian chain. The Unakas actually include several ranges, notably the Great Smoky Mountains. Clingmans Dome in the Great Smokies, which rises to 6,643 feet (2,025 meters), is the highest point in the state. Lying due west of the Unakas is the Great Valley of East Tennessee. Since the coming of the Tennessee Valley Authority (TVA) in 1933, the area has been dotted with artificial lakes and dams, which supply electric power and aid in flood control.

The Cumberland Plateau in Middle Tennessee includes both the Cumberland Mountains and the Sequatchie Valley. The Highland Rim, also in Middle Tennessee, encircles the Central Basin and is the state's largest natural region. With its rich soil, the Central Basin is more densely populated than any other area in the state. The westernmost of the major regions is the Gulf Coastal Plain, which slopes gradually westward until it ends abruptly at the bluffs overlooking the Mississippi Flood Plains.

Most of the state is drained by the Mississippi River system. The two longest rivers are the Tennessee, with a total length of 652 miles (1,049 kilometers); and the Cumberland, which is 687 miles (1,106 kilometers) long. Both flow into the Ohio River in Kentucky.

[3] CLIMATE

Generally, Tennessee has a temperate climate, with warm summers and mild winters. The warmest parts of the state are the

Tennessee Population Profile

Total population in 2000:	5,689,283
Population change, 1990–2000:	16.7%
Hispanic or Latino†:	2.2%
Population by race	
One race:	98.9%
White:	80.2%
Black or African American:	16.4%
American Indian/Alaska Native:	0.3%
Asian:	1.0%
Native Hawaiian/Pacific Islander:	—
Some other race:	1.0%
Two or more races:	1.1%

Population by Age Group

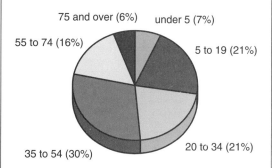

75 and over (6%) under 5 (7%)
55 to 74 (16%) 5 to 19 (21%)
35 to 54 (30%) 20 to 34 (21%)

Top Cities by Population

City	Population	% change 1990–2000
Memphis	650,100	6.5
Nashville-Davidson	569,891	11.6
Knoxville	173,890	5.3
Chattanooga	155,554	2.0
Clarksville	103,455	37.0
Murfreesboro	68,816	53.2
Jackson	59,643	21.8
Johnson City	55,469	12.3
Kingsport	44,905	23.5
Franklin	41,842	108.2

Notes: †A person of Hispanic or Latino origin may be of any race. NA indicates that data are not available.
Sources: U.S. Census Bureau. Public Information Office. *Demographic Profiles.* [Online] Available http://www.census.gov/Press-Release/www/2001/demoprofile.html. Accessed June 1, 2001. U.S. Census Bureau. *Census 2000: Redistricting Data.* Press release issued by the Redistricting Data Office. Washington, D.C., March, 2001.

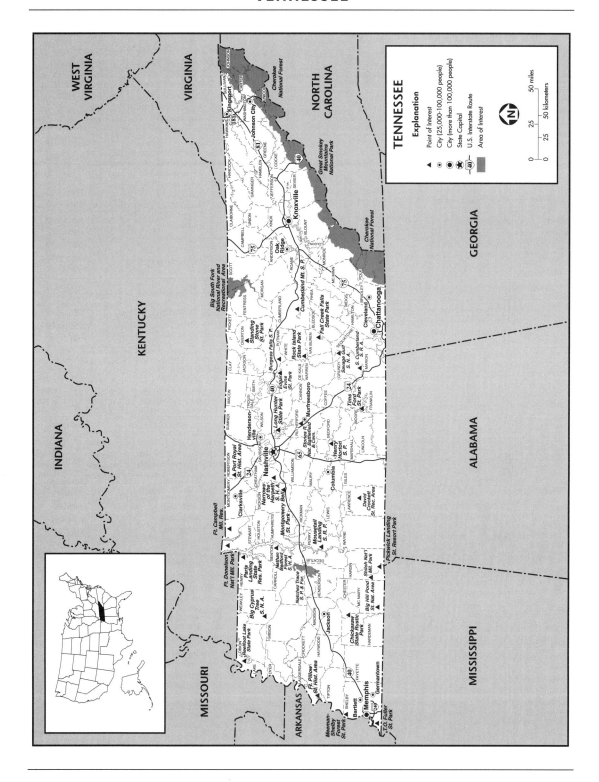

Photo credit: Tennessee Tourism.

Chimney Tops, 16 peaks soaring above 6,000 feet in the Great Smoky Mountains National Park, Gatlinburg.

Gulf Coastal Plain, the Central Basin, and the Sequatchie Valley. Annual mean temperatures are around 60°F (16°C) in most parts of the state. The record high temperature for the state is 113°F (45°C), set in 1930; the record low, –32°F (–36°C), was registered in 1917. Average annual precipitation is 49 inches (124 centimeters) in Memphis and 46 inches (117 centimeters) in Nashville.

4 PLANTS AND ANIMALS

With its varied terrain and soils, Tennessee has an abundance of native plants. Tree species include tulip poplar (the state tree) and shortleaf pine in the eastern part of the state; oak, hickory, and ash in the Highland Rim; gum maple, black walnut, and sycamore in the west; and cypress in the Reelfoot Lake area. In East Tennessee, rhododendron, mountain laurel, and wild azalea blossoms create a blaze of color in the mountains.

Tennessee mammals include the raccoon (the state animal), white-tailed deer, black bear, and bobcat. Ruffed grouse and mourning dove are among the most common game birds. Of the 186 fish species in Tennessee's lakes and streams, catfish, bream, and largemouth bass are some of the leading game fish.

The snail darter, cited by opponents of the Tellico Dam, is probably Tennessee's most famous threatened species. The bald eagle, red wolf, and American peregrine falcon are among the 63 animal species on the state's endangered list.

5 ENVIRONMENTAL PROTECTION

In the late 1800s, a system of channels was cut into the streams in western Tennessee to control flooding. However, there was a negative environmental impact on both habitat and cropland. The state is now in the process of restoring the natural meandering flow to the tributaries of the Mississippi River. The Department of Environment and Conservation is responsible for air, soil, and water protection. The Division of Pollution Prevention Assistance supports industries trying to reduce their pollution and waste. Tennessee had 15 hazardous waste sites as of 1998.

6 POPULATION

Tennessee, with a population of nearly 5,689,283, surpassed Missouri to rank 16th among the 50 states at the 2000 census. That year, the state had a density of 138 persons per square mile (53.3 persons per square kilometer). Projections to 2005 foresee a population of 5.97 million. In 1990, 67.7% of all Tennesseans lived in metropolitan areas. Memphis is the state's largest city; in 2000 it had a population of 650,100 (ranked 18th in the country). Nashville-Davidson had 569,891, followed by Knoxville, 173,890, and Chattanooga, 155,554. Approximately 28% of the population is 19 years of age and younger.

7 ETHNIC GROUPS

Descendants of European immigrants make up about half the population of Tennessee, the largest groups being of Irish, German, and English descent. In 1997, there were an estimated 884,500 blacks in Tennessee, 16.5% of the total population. In the same year, there were only about 49,500 Asians and Pacific Islanders (0.9%) and 12,000 Native Americans (0.2%) in the state.

8 LANGUAGES

Tennessee English represents a mixture of North Midland and South Midland features brought into the northeastern and northcentral areas; of South Midland and Southern features introduced by settlers from Virginia and the Carolinas; and of a few additional Southern dialects in the extreme western fringe. In 1990, 4,413,193 Tennesseans five years old and over—97% of the population in that age group—spoke only English at home. Speakers of other languages included the following: Spanish, 49,661; French, 20,444; and German, 17,716.

9 RELIGIONS

Baptist and Presbyterian churches were organized on the frontier soon after permanent settlements were made, and many divisions have occurred in both groups. Tennessee has long been considered part of the Bible Belt because of the influence of fundamentalist Protestant groups that believe in a literal accuracy of the Bible.

Protestant groups had a total of 2,830,239 known members in 1990. By far the largest group was the Southern

Tennessee Population by Race

Census 2000 was the first national census in which the instructions to respondents said, "Mark one or more races." This table shows the number of people who are of one, two, or three or more races. For those claiming two races, the number of people belonging to the various categories is listed. The U.S. government conducts a census of the population every ten years.

	Number	Percent
Total population	5,689,283	100.0
One race	5,626,174	98.9
Two races	59,476	1.0
White *and* Black or African American	12,273	0.2
White *and* American Indian/Alaska Native	19,006	0.3
White *and* Asian	7,793	0.1
White *and* Native Hawaiian/Pacific Islander	808	—
White *and* some other race	11,056	0.2
Black or African American *and* American Indian/Alaska Native	2,149	—
Black or African American *and* Asian	1,038	—
Black or African American *and* Native Hawaiian/Pacific Islander	243	—
Black or African American *and* some other race	2,421	—
American Indian/Alaska Native *and* Asian	303	—
American Indian/Alaska Native *and* Native Hawaiian/Pacific Islander	37	—
American Indian/Alaska Native *and* some other race	461	—
Asian *and* Native Hawaiian/Pacific Islander	396	—
Asian *and* some other race	1,289	—
Native Hawaiian/Pacific Islander *and* some other race	203	—
Three or more races	3,633	0.1

Source: U.S. Census Bureau. *Census 2000: Redistricting Data.* Press release issued by the Redistricting Data Office. Washington, D.C., March, 2001. A dash (—) indicates that the percent is less than 0.1.

Baptist Church, with 1,343,312 members. The United Methodists were second with 396,862, followed by the Churches of Christ, 219,996 and the Presbyterian Church, 71,129. There were 137,203 Roman Catholics in 1990 and an estimated 18,000 Jews in 1994.

10 TRANSPORTATION

Memphis, Nashville, Knoxville, and Chattanooga are the focal points for rail, highway, water, and air transportation. In 1998, Tennessee had 2,961 route miles (4,764 kilometers) of railroad track. Tennessee had 68,705 miles (110,546 kilometers) of rural roads and 17,321 miles (27,869 kilometers) of urban roads in 1997, when 4.53 million motor vehicles were registered in the state.

Tennessee has about 1,000 miles (1,600 kilometers) of navigable waterways. The completion in 1985 of the 234-mile (377-kilometer) Tennessee-Tombigbee Waterway gave Tennessee shippers a direct north-south route for all vessels between the Tennessee River and the Gulf of Mexico. In 1998, the ports of Nashville and Memphis handled 4.0 million and 17.2 million tons of freight, respectively. Nashville Metropolitan Airport is the state's major air terminal, with 47,770 air-

Photo credit: Tennessee Tourism.

The Nashville skyline and the General Jackson Showboat on the Cumberland River.

craft departures and 3.25 million boarded passengers in 1996.

11 HISTORY

When the first Spanish explorers arrived in the early 16th century, the Creek tribe was living in what is now East Tennessee, along with the Yuchi. About 200 years later, the powerful Cherokee drove them out of the area and established themselves as the dominant tribe. The Cherokee retained their tribal dominance until they were forced out by the federal government in the 1830s. Other tribes were the Chickasaw in West Tennessee, and the Shawnee, who occupied the Cumberland Valley in Middle Tennessee.

Explorers and traders from continental Europe and the British Isles were in Tennessee for well over 100 years before permanent settlements were established in the 1760s. By the mid-1700s, hundreds—perhaps thousands—of English adventurers had crossed the Appalachian barrier and explored the country beyond, claimed first by the colony of Virginia and later assigned to North Carolina. Perhaps the best known was Daniel Boone, who by 1760 had found his way into present-day Washington County, Tennessee.

With the conclusion of the French and Indian War in 1763, many people from North Carolina and Virginia began to cross the Alleghenies. Elisha Walden was among those who first led groups of "long hunters" into the wilderness. Two major areas of settlement developed. The larger one, in the northeast, was organized as the Watauga Association in the 1770s. The second major area was in the Cumberland Basin, where James Robertson established a settlement he called Nashborough (now Nashville) in 1779.

Statehood

The Revolutionary War did not reach as far west as Tennessee, but many of the early settlers there fought in the Carolinas and Virginia. Hardly was the Revolution over when Tennesseans began to think about statehood for themselves. In 1790, North Carolina ceded its western lands to the US. Tennessee became known as the Southwest Territory. The population doubled to more than 70,000 in 1795, and steps were taken to obtain statehood for the territory. On 1 June 1796, President George Washington signed a bill admitting Tennessee as the 16th state. Andrew Jackson became the state's first US representative.

By 1809, Nashville, Knoxville, and other early settlements became thriving frontier towns. Churches and schools were established, industry and agriculture developed, and Tennessee became a leading iron producer.

Andrew Jackson's rise to prominence came as a result of his successful leadership at the Battle of New Orleans, fought at the conclusion of the War of 1812. He returned to Nashville a hero, and was elected to the US Senate in 1823. Although

Jackson received the most votes, the 1824 presidential election was decided by the House of Representatives, which chose John Quincy Adams as president. Jackson ran again in 1828 and won, serving then as president of the US for eight years.

Early 19th Century

Social reform and cultural growth characterized the first half of the 19th century. A prison was built, and the penal code was reformed. Temperance newspapers were published and laws passed to limit the consumption of alcoholic beverages. In 1834 a few women, embracing the feminist cause, were influential in giving the courts, rather than the legislature, the right to grant divorces.

More than most other southern states, Tennessee was divided over the issue of slavery. Slaveholders predominated in the west, where cotton was grown profitably, as well as in Middle Tennessee. But in East Tennessee, where blacks made up less than 10% of the population, antislavery sentiment thrived. Supporters of emancipation urged that it be accomplished peacefully, gradually, and with compensation to the slave owners. At the constitutional convention of 1834, hundreds of petitions were presented asking that the legislature be empowered to free the slaves, while at the same time the convention sought to take away from free blacks the right to vote.

Considerable economic growth took place during this period. West Tennessee became a major cotton-growing area. The counties of the Highland Rim produced tobacco in such abundance that, by 1840,

Photo credit: Memphis Convention & Visitors Bureau.

The Lorraine Motel, the site of Dr. Martin Luther King's assassination in Memphis in 1968,
is now the National Civil Rights Museum.

Tennessee ranked just behind Kentucky and Virginia in total production. East Tennessee farmers grew fruits and vegetables for market.

Civil War

Tennessee became a major battleground during the Civil War, as armies from both North and South crossed the state. Many Tennesseans favored secession, but the eastern counties remained staunchly Unionist, and many East Tennesseans crossed over into Kentucky to enlist in the Union Army. In February 1862, Fort Donelson and Fort Henry were taken by General Ulysses S. Grant and naval Captain Andrew H. Foote, thereby opening the state to Union armies. Within two weeks Nashville was under Union army control, and both sides suffered tremendous losses at the Battle of Shiloh, two months later.

President Abraham Lincoln established a military government for the conquered state and appointed Andrew Johnson to head it. Johnson, who had been elected to the US Senate in 1858, remained there in 1861, the only southern senator to do so, refusing to follow his state into the Confederacy. In 1864, he was elected vice-president under Lincoln.

Confederate forces launched two major campaigns—both unsuccessful—to re-take the state, threatening Nashville in December 1862 and attacking Union forces at Franklin and Nashville two years later. In between, the Battle of Chickamauga, in which the Confederates drove Union troops back to Chattanooga in September 1863, was one of the bloodiest engagements of the war.

Post–Civil War

Returning to the Union in 1866, Tennessee was the only former Confederate state not to have a military government during Reconstruction. Economic readjustment was not as difficult as elsewhere in the South, and within a few years agricultural production recovered, but it did not exceed prewar levels until 1900. By the early 1880s, flour, wool, and paper mills were established in all the urban areas. By the late 1890s, Memphis was a leading cotton market and the nation's foremost producer of cottonseed oil.

As the 20th century dawned, the major issue in Tennessee was the crusade against alcohol, a movement with deep roots in the 19th century. In 1909, after the shooting of a prominent prohibitionist, "dry" forces enacted legislation that, in effect, imposed prohibition on the entire state. The prohibition movement helped promote the cause of women's suffrage, and in 1919, women were granted the right to vote in municipal elections. One year later, Tennessee became the 36th state to ratify the 19th Amendment to the US Constitution, thereby granting women the right to vote nationwide.

1920s–1940s

The 1920s brought a resurgence of religious fundamentalism. Nationwide attention was brought to the state with the trial and conviction of a high school teacher named John T. Scopes, who challenged a 1925 law prohibiting the teaching of the theory of evolution in the public schools.

The 1930s brought depression, but they also brought the Tennessee Valley Authority (TVA), established a few weeks after Franklin Delano Roosevelt's inauguration in 1933. By the late 1930s, power lines were being strung into remote areas bringing electricity to practically everyone. Inexpensive power became a magnet for industry, and industrial employment in the region nearly doubled in two decades. The building of a plant for the production of atomic weapons at Oak Ridge in 1942 was due in large measure to the availability of TVA power.

The Depression hurt many manufacturers, and farm prices declined drastically. The state still was in the grip of financial depression when World War II began. Tennessee firms received defense contracts amounting to $1.25 billion and employed more than 200,000 people during the war, and industrial growth continued during the postwar period, while agriculture recovered and diversified. The chemical industry, spurred by high demand during and after World War II, became a leading sector, along with textiles, apparel, and food processing.

Tennessee Governors: 1796–2001

1796–1801	John Sevier	Dem-Rep	1893–1897	Peter Turney	Democrat
1801–1803	Archibald Roane	Dem-Rep	1897–1899	Robert Love Taylor	Democrat
1803–1809	John Sevier	Dem-Rep	1899–1903	Benton McMillin	Democrat
1809–1815	Willie Blount	Dem-Rep	1903–1905	James Beriah Frazier	Democrat
1815–1821	Joseph McMinn	Dem-Rep	1905–1907	John Isaac Cox	Democrat
1821–1827	William Carroll	Dem-Rep	1907–1911	Malcolm Rice Patterson	Democrat
1827–1829	Samuel Houston	Democrat	1911–1915	Ben Walker Hooper	Republican
1829	William Hall	Dem-Rep	1915–1919	Thomas Clark Rye	Democrat
1829–1835	William Carroll	Democrat	1919–1921	Albert Houston Roberts	Democrat
1835–1839	Newton Cannon	Whig	1921–1923	Alfred Alexander Taylor	Republican
1839–1841	James Knox Polke	Democrat	1923–1927	Austin Peay III	Democrat
1841–1845	James Chamberlain Jones	Whig	1927–1933	Henry Hollis Horton	Democrat
1845–1847	Aaron Venable Brown	Democrat	1933–1937	Harry Hill McAlister	Democrat
1847–1849	Neill Smith Brown	Whig	1937–1939	Gordon Weaver Browning	Democrat
1849–1851	William Trousdale	Democrat	1939–1945	William Prentice Cooper	Democrat
1851–1853	William Bowen Campbell	Whig	1945–1949	James Nance McCord	Democrat
1853–1857	Andrew Johnson	Democrat	1949–1953	Gordon Weaver Browning	Democrat
1857–1861	Isham Green Harris	Democrat	1953–1959	Frank Goad Clement	Democrat
1862–1865	Andrew Johnson	Republican	1959–1963	Earl Buford Ellington	Democrat
1865	Edward Hazzard East	Prohibitionist	1963–1967	Frank Goad Clement	Democrat
1865–1869	William Gannaway Brownlow	Whig-Rep	1967–1971	Earl Buford Ellington	Democrat
1869–1871	DeWitt Clinton Senter	Conserv-Rep	1971–1975	Bryant Winfield Dunn	Republican
1871–1875	John Calvin Brown	Democrat	1975–1979	Leonard Ray Blanton	Democrat
1875–1879	James Davis Porter, Jr.	Democrat	1979–1987	Lamar Alexander	Republican
1879–1881	Albert Smith Marks	Democrat	1987–1995	Ned Ray McWherter	Democrat
1881–1883	Alvin Hawkins	Republican	1995–	Don Sundquist	Republican
1883–1887	William Brimage Bate	Democrat			
1887–1891	Robert Love Taylor	Democrat	Conservative Democrat – Conserv-Rep		
1891–1893	John Price Buchanan	Democrat	Democratic Republican – Dem-Rep		

1950s–1990s

Considerable progress was made toward ending racial discrimination during the postwar years, although the desegregation of public schools was accomplished only after outbursts of violence at Clinton, Nashville, and Memphis. The killing of civil-rights leader Martin Luther King, Jr., in Memphis in 1968 resulted in rioting by blacks in that city. The most notable political development during the 1970s was the resurgence of the Republican Party.

The early 1980s saw the exposure of corruption in high places: former governor Ray Blanton and several aides were convicted for conspiracy to sell liquor licenses, and banker and former gubernatorial candidate Jacob F. "Jake" Butcher was convicted of fraud following the collapse of his banking empire. On the brighter side, there was a successful World's Fair in 1982, as well as the Knoxville International Energy Exposition. The state economy also was bolstered by the arrival of both Nissan and General Motors plants.

12 STATE GOVERNMENT

Tennessee's constitution vests executive authority in a governor, elected for two years, who can approve or veto bills adopted by the legislature. Legislative power is placed in a general assembly, consisting of a house and senate, whose members serve terms of two years. The basic governmental structure established in 1796 remains the fundamental law today. Membership of the house was fixed at 99; and of the senate, at 33.

The governor appoints a cabinet of 21 members. The speaker of the state senate automatically becomes lieutenant governor. The secretary of state, treasurer, and comptroller of the treasury are chosen by the legislature.

Legislation is enacted after bills are read and approved three times in each house and signed by the governor. If the governor vetoes a measure, the legislature may override the veto by majority vote of both houses. Once every six years the legislature may submit to the voters the question of calling a convention to amend the constitution.

13 POLITICAL PARTIES

After the Civil War and Reconstruction, Tennessee primarily elected Democratic candidates for nearly a century, although East Tennessee remained a Republican stronghold. Although the 1920s saw a tendency away from one-party domination, Franklin D. Roosevelt and the government programs of the New Deal persuaded voters to elect more Democrats. Tennesseans voted overwhelmingly Democratic in the four elections that Roosevelt won (1932–44).

After World War II, the one-party dominance in Tennessee was tested again. Between 1948 and 1976, the only Demo-

Tennessee Presidential Vote by Political Parties, 1948–2000

YEAR	TENNESSEE WINNER	DEMOCRAT	REPUBLICAN	STATES' RIGHTS DEMOCRAT	PROGRESSIVE	PROHIBITION
1948	*Truman (D)	270,402	202,914	73,815	1,864	—
				CONSTITUTION		
1952	*Eisenhower (R)	443,710	446,147	379	887	1,432
1956	*Eisenhower (R)	456,507	462,288	19,820	—	789
				NATL. STATES' RIGHTS		
1960	Nixon (R)	481,453	556,577	11,298	—	2,450
1964	*Johnson (D)	635,047	508,965	—	—	—
				AMERICAN IND.		
1968	*Nixon (R)	351,233	472,592	424,792	—	—
					AMERICAN	
1972	*Nixon (R)	357,293	813,147	—	30,373	—
						LIBERTARIAN
1976	*Carter (D)	825,897	633,969	2,303	5,769	1,375
				NATL. STATESMAN	CITIZENS	
1980	*Reagan (R)	783,051	787,761	5,0211	1,112	7,116
1984	*Reagan (R)	711,714	990,212	—	978	3,072
1988	*Bush (R)	679,794	947,233	—	1,334	2,041
				IND. (Perot)		
1992	*Clinton (D)	933,521	841,300	199,968	727	1,847
1996	*Clinton (D)	909,146	863,530	105,918	—	5,020
				LIBERTARIAN		REFORM
2000	*Bush (R)	981,720	1,061,949	4,284	19,781	4,250

*Won US presidential election.

cratic nominees to carry the state came from the South (Lyndon Johnson and Jimmy Carter) or from a border state (Harry Truman). In state elections, the Republicans made deep inroads into Democratic power during the 1960s and 1970s.

Republican Don Sundquist became governor in 1994. In 1994, Dr. Bill Frist, a heart surgeon, was elected a US Senator on the Republican ticket, defeating the Democrat James Sasser. He was reelected in 2000. In 1994, Republican Fred Thompson defeated Jim Cooper for the remaining two years of Vice-President Al Gore's term. US Representatives included five Republicans and four Democrats in 2001. There are 18 Democrats and 15 Republicans in the state senate, and 58 Democrats and 41 Republicans in the state house in the same year. Tennessee voters, who gave Republican George Bush 57.4% of the vote in 1988, chose Bill Clinton in 1992 and 1996 with his Tennessee running mate, Al Gore. In the 2000 election, Republican George W. Bush received 51% of the vote to Democrat Al Gore's 47%.

14 LOCAL GOVERNMENT

Local government in Tennessee is exercised by 93 counties and 343 municipalities. The constitution specifies that county officials must include at least a registrar, trustee (the custodian of county funds), sheriff, and county clerk. Other officials have been added by legislative enactment. There are three forms of municipal government: mayor-council (or mayor-alderman), council-manager, and commission.

The mayor-council system is the oldest and by far the most widely employed. There were 14 school districts in 1997, as well as 491 special districts.

15 JUDICIAL SYSTEM

The five-member supreme court is the highest court in the state. The court has appeals jurisdiction only, holding sessions in Nashville, Knoxville, and Jackson.

Immediately below the supreme court are two appeals courts established by the legislature to relieve the crowded high court schedule. Circuit courts hear both civil and criminal cases. Tennessee also has chancery courts, which settle disputes regarding property ownership, hear divorce cases, and rule on a variety of other matters. At the bottom of the judicial structure are general sessions courts.

In 1996, Tennessee's crime rate ranked slightly above the national rate, at 5,034.4 reported crimes per 100,000 inhabitants. As of 1999, federal and state prisons in Tennessee had 18,317 inmates.

16 MIGRATION

There was a steady out-migration of blacks to industrial centers in the North during the 20th century. The state suffered a net loss through migration of 462,000 between 1940 and 1970, but gained over 465,000 between 1970 and 1990. During 1990–98, the state gained 337,600 from interstate migration, and 27,300 from abroad. The major in-state migration has been away from rural areas and into towns and cities. Blacks, especially, have tended to cluster in large urban centers.

17 ECONOMY

Tennessee's economy is based primarily on industry. Since the 1930s, the number of people employed in industry has grown at a rapid rate, while the number of farmers has declined. Wage rates and average weekly earnings are well below the national average. The principal manufacturing areas are Memphis, Nashville, Chattanooga, Knoxville, and Kingsport-Bristol. With the construction in the 1980s of a Nissan automobile and truck plant and a General Motors automobile facility, Tennessee is becoming an important producer of transportation equipment. Tourism is the third major contributor to the state's economy.

18 INCOME

With a per capita (per person) income of $24,437 in 1998, Tennessee ranked 34th in the US. Total personal income was $132.8 billion in the same year. In 1998, about 14.5% of all Tennesseans were living below the federal poverty level.

19 INDUSTRY

On the eve of the Civil War, only 1% of Tennessee's population was employed in manufacturing. Rapid industrial growth took place during the 20th century, however, and by 1981, Tennessee ranked third among the southeastern states and 15th in the US in value of shipments. In 1996, Tennessee's four major metropolitan areas, Memphis, Nashville, Knoxville, and Chattanooga, employed 48% of all the state's industrial workers. The number of jobs in the automotive indus-try increased from 3,000 in the mid-1980s to 22,000 by the mid- 1990s.

20 LABOR

In mid-1998, Tennessee had a total civilian labor force of 2.76 million. The overall unemployment rate then was 4.2%. In 1998, 7.9% of the state's workers were union members.

21 AGRICULTURE

Tennessee ranked 31st among the 50 states in 1999 with farm receipts of over $2 billion. There were 95,000 farms in 1998. From the pre-Civil War period to the 1950s, cotton was the leading crop, followed by corn and tobacco. During the early 1960s, soybeans surpassed cotton as the principal source of income. In 1998, 35.1 million bushels of soybeans, valued at about $196.5 million, were harvested. Tennessee ranked fourth among the tobacco-producing states in 1996 with a total crop production of 114 million pounds (51.7 million kilograms). In 1998, cotton production was 545,000 bales, valued at about $166.4 million. The corn harvest in 1998 was 99.5 million bushels, valued at $122 million.

22 DOMESTICATED ANIMALS

Livestock and livestock products account for about 41% of Tennessee's agricultural income, and meat animals are the state's most important commodity. In 1999, there were 2.2 million head of cattle, and production was valued at $1.02 billion.

The number of hogs produced has declined during the past 50 years, but their value has increased considerably. In 1997, there were 300,000 hogs. Poultry farmers produced 624 million pounds (259 million kilograms) of broilers in 1997.

23 FISHING

Fishing is a major attraction for sport but plays a relatively small role in the economic life of Tennessee. In 1996, Tennessee issued 968,807 sport-fishing licenses.

24 FORESTRY

Forests cover 13.6 million acres (5.5 million hectares), over half the state's total land area. About 95% of Tennessee's timber is in hardwoods, and more than one-half of that is in white and red oak. Of the softwoods, pine—shortleaf, loblolly, Virginia, pitch, and white—accounts for 80%; Red cedar accounting for 5% of the softwood supply.

Wood products manufacturing is Tennessee's fourth-largest basic industry. The state produces about $4.8 billion worth of wood products each year. The wood products industry in Tennessee falls into three main categories: paper and paper products, lumber, and furniture. Tennessee leads the nation in the production of hardwood flooring, log homes, and pencils, and is among the top three hardwood lumber-producing states.

25 MINING

The 1998 value of nonfuel mineral production in Tennessee was $709 million. Also in 1998, Tennessee led the nation in the value of natural gemstones, consisting almost entirely of cultured freshwater pearls and mother-of-pearl derived from freshwater mussel shells. Crushed stone

has been the leading nonfuel mineral commodity produced in Tennessee since 1981. In 1998, production was 64 million metric tons, valued at $384 million.

26 ENERGY AND POWER

The Tennessee Valley Authority (TVA) is the principal supplier of power in the state, providing electricity to more than 100 cities and 50 rural cooperatives. In 1998, Tennessee's electrical output totaled 94.1 billion kilowatt hours. There was one nuclear power facility in operation as of 1999.

Between 1978 and 1998, declining demand for coal, conservationist opposition to surface mining, and other factors led to a drop in coal production from 10 million tons to 2.7 million tons. Reserves in 1998 totaled 27 million recoverable tons. Tennessee produced 345,000 barrels of crude oil in 1999. Natural gas reserves were negligible.

27 COMMERCE

Tennessee has been an important inland commercial center for some 60 years. Wholesale sales totaled $86 billion in 1997; retail sales were $53 billion. Tennessee's foreign exports totaled nearly $9.6 billion in goods in 1998.

28 PUBLIC FINANCE

The revenues for 1997 were $15.7 billion; state-funded appropriations were $14.28 billion. The state's outstanding debt totaled $3.31 billion as of 1997, or $618 per capita (per person), the 3d lowest ratio among the states.

Photo credit: Tennessee Tourism.

The Grand Ole Opry, the longest continuously running live show in the world, in Nashville.

29 TAXATION

The major source of general state revenue is a sales and use tax; in 1996, the maximum rate was 6% (municipalities can impose an additional tax of up to 2.75%). Other taxes include a levy on dividend and interest income, a corporate income tax, and levies on inheritances, alcoholic beverages, tobacco, gross receipts, motor vehicle registration, and other items. Tennessee is one of a few states that does not impose a tax on salaries and wages. Counties and municipalities depend on real property taxes as their major source of income. Tennessee's state tax burden in 1997 was over $6.6 billion, or about $1,233 per person (47th among the states). In 1995, Tennessee paid about $9.5 billion in federal income taxes.

30 HEALTH

The major causes of death in Tennessee in 1998 were heart disease, cancer, cerebrovascular diseases, accidents, and diabetes mellitus. There were 122 community hospitals, with 20,682 beds in 1998. The average hospital expense in the same year was $963 per inpatient day, or $5,557 for an average cost per stay. The state had a rate of 13% uninsured adults in 1998.

31 HOUSING

In 1999, there were an estimated 2.3 million occupied housing units in the state.

The median monthly cost for owners with a mortgage payment in 1990 was $594; the median value of a home in 1990 was $58,400, up 3.4% from 1980. The median monthly apartment rent in 1990 was $357. In 1998, 34,100 new privately owned units worth over $3.4 billion were authorized.

32 EDUCATION

The 21st Century Schools Program adopted by the Tennessee General Assembly in 1992 gives communities wide discretion over education decision-making, makes local school systems more accountable for results, and is funding 5,450 high-technology classrooms in Tennessee's public schools. More than two of three adult Tennesseans hold a high school diploma. The state's public schools enrolled 893,020 students in 1998. Expenditures for public elementary and secondary schools amounted to $5,255 per student in 1999/2000.

The University of Tennessee system, with principal campuses at Knoxville, Memphis, Martin, and Chattanooga, enrolled some 32,400 students in 1992. The State University and Community College System of Tennessee includes 6 universities and 14 two-year community colleges throughout the state. Well-known private colleges are Vanderbilt University at Nashville, the University of the South at Sewanee, and Rhodes College at Memphis.

33 ARTS

Each of Tennessee's major cities has a symphony orchestra. The best known are the Memphis Symphony and the Nashville Symphony, the latter of which makes its home in the James K. Polk Cultural Center. Included in this complex are three performing arts centers and the State Museum. The major operatic troupe is Opera Memphis. Nashville is a center for country music. The Grand Ole Opry, Country Music Hall of Fame, and numerous recording studios are located there. Summer Lights, an annual music and art show, is held in Nashville the weekend following Memorial Day. Among the leading art galleries are the Dixon Gallery and the Brooks Memorial Art Gallery in Memphis. Tennessee has more than 300 arts groups.

34 LIBRARIES AND MUSEUMS

In all, there are more than 190 public libraries and 82 academic libraries in Tennessee. Their combined book stock exceeded 9.6 million, and their total circulation surpassed 21 million volumes. The largest libraries include the Vanderbilt University Library at Nashville, Memphis-Shelby County Library, and University of Tennessee at Knoxville Library.

Tennessee has 128 museums and historic sites. The Museum of Appalachia, near Norris, attempts an authentic replica of early Appalachian life, with more than 20,000 pioneer relics on display in several log cabins. A new Country Music Hall of Fame and Museum opened in Nashville in May 2001; it is four times the size of the original Hall of Fame.

35 COMMUNICATIONS

As of 1999, 94.5% of Tennessee's occupied housing units had telephones. Tennessee had 186 AM stations and 205FM stations in 1999. There were 42 television stations in operation in 2000. In total, there were 81,858 domain names registered for the Internet.

36 PRESS

In 1998 there were 12 morning newspapers, 13 evening dailies, and 16 Sunday papers. Leading Tennessee newspapers, with their daily circulations in 1998, are the *Memphis Commercial Appeal* (163,603); the *Nashville Tennessean* (184,979); the *Knoxville News-Sentinel* (115,248); and the *Chattanooga News–Free Press* (81,348).

37 TOURISM, TRAVEL, AND RECREATION

The natural beauty of Tennessee, combined with the activity of the Department of Tourist Development, has made tourism a large industry in the state.

Leading tourist attractions include the American Museum of Science and Energy at Oak Ridge; the Beale Street Historic District in Memphis, home of W. C. Handy, the "father of the blues;" Graceland, the Memphis estate of singer Elvis Presley; and Opryland USA and the Grand Ole Opry at Nashville. There are three presidential homes—Andrew Johnson's at Greeneville; Andrew Jackson's Hermitage near Nashville; and James K. Polk's at Columbia. Pinson Mounds, near Jackson, offers outstanding archaeological treasures and the remains of an Indian city. Reservoirs and lakes attract thousands of anglers and water sports enthusiasts.

There are 33 state parks, almost all of which have camping facilities. Extending into North Carolina, the Great Smoky Mountains National Park covers 241,207 acres (97,613 hectares) in Tennessee and drew nearly 10 million visitors in 1998.

38 SPORTS

Tennessee has two major league professional sports teams, both in Nashville: the Titans (formerly the Oilers) of the National Football League, and the Predators of the National Hockey League, who began play in 1999. Minor league baseball teams that compete in the Class-AAA Southern League are the Knoxville Vols, Chattanooga Lookouts, and Memphis Chicks. Tennessee's colleges and universities provide the major fall and winter sports. The University of Tennessee Volunteers and Vanderbilt University Commodores, both in the Southeastern Conference, compete in football, basketball, and baseball. Austin Peay and Tennessee Technological universities belong to the Ohio Valley Conference.

39 FAMOUS TENNESSEANS

Andrew Jackson (b.South Carolina, 1767–1845), the seventh president, moved to Tennessee as a young man. He won renown in the War of 1812 and became the first Democratic president in 1828. Jackson's close friend and associate, James Knox Polk (b.North Carolina, 1795–1849), was elected the nation's 11th president in 1844 and served one term. Andrew Johnson (b.North Carolina, 1808–75), also a Democrat, remained loyal to the Union during the Civil War and was elected vice-president with Abraham Lincoln in 1864. He became president upon Lincoln's assassination in 1865 and served out his predecessor's second term. Impeached because of a dispute over Reconstruction policies and presidential power, Johnson escaped conviction by one vote in 1868.

Albert Arnold Gore, Jr. (b. Washington, D.C., 1948) was a senator from Tennessee before being elected to the vice-presidency in 1992. Supreme Court justices from Tennessee include James C. McReynolds (b.Kentucky, 1862–1946), and Edward T. Sanford (1865–1930). Tennesseans who became cabinet officials include Secretary of State Cordell Hull (1871–1955) and Secretary of War John Eaton (1790–1856). Other nationally prominent political figures from Tennessee are Cary Estes Kefauver (1903–63), two-term US senator who ran unsuccessfully for vice-president in 1956 on the Democratic ticket; Albert Arnold Gore (1907–98), three-term member of the US Senate; and Howard Baker (b.1925), who in 1966 became the first popularly elected Republican senator in Tennessee history. Nancy Ward (1738–1822) was an outstanding Cherokee leader, and Sue Shelton White (1887–1943) played a major role in the campaign for women's suffrage.

Tennessee history features several military leaders and combat heroes. John Sevier (b.Virginia, 1745–1815), the first governor of the state, defeated British troops at Kings Mountain in the Revolution. David "Davy" Crockett (1786–1836) was a frontiersman who fought the British with Jackson in the War of 1812 and later became a congressman. Nathan

Photo credit: © Hampton House Studios/EPD Photos.

Nancy Ward (Nanye-Hi) as depicted by Tennessee artist Ben Hampton. She acted as a negotiator for the Cherokee with the white government, only to become disillusioned as treaty after treaty was broken. When the Cherokee land was forcibly taken, she escaped the Trail of Tears and fled into Tennessee.

Bedford Forrest (1821–77) and Sam Davis (1842–63) were heroes of the Civil War.

Cordell Hull was awarded the Nobel Peace Prize in 1945 for his work on behalf of the United Nations. In 1971, Earl W. Sutherland, Jr. (b.Kansas 1915–75), a biomedical scientist at Vanderbilt University, won a Nobel Prize for his discoveries concerning the mechanisms of hormones.

Stanley Cohen (b.New York, 1922) of Vanderbilt University won the Nobel Prize in medicine in 1986.

Sequoya (1770–1843) created an alphabet for the Cherokee language and promoted literacy. Famous Tennessee writers are the influential poet and critic John Crowe Ransom (1888–1974); author and critic James Agee (1909–55), posthumously awarded a Pulitzer Prize for his novel *A Death in the Family;* poet Randall Jarrell (1914–65), winner of two National Book Awards; and Wilma Dykeman (b.1920), novelist and historian. Sportswriter Grantland Rice (1880–1954) was born in Murfreesboro.

Tennessee has long been a center of popular music. Musician and songwriter William C. Handy (1873–1958) wrote "St. Louis Blues" and "Memphis Blues," among other classics. Bessie Smith (1898?–1937) was a leading blues singer. Elvis Presley (b.Mississippi, 1935–77) fused rhythm-and-blues with country-and-western styles to become one of the most popular entertainers who ever lived. Other Tennessee-born singers are Tina Turner (b.1938), Aretha Franklin (b.1942), and Dolly Parton (b.1946). Actor Morgan Freeman (b.1937) was born in Memphis.

40 BIBLIOGRAPHY

Aylesworth, Thomas G. *The Southeast: Georgia, Kentucky, Tennessee.* New York: Chelsea House, 1996.

Barrett, Tracy. *Tennessee.* New York: Benchmark Books, 1998.

Connelly, T. L. *Civil War Tennessee: Battles and Leaders.* Knoxville: University of Tennessee Press, 1979.

Corlew, Robert E. *Tennessee: A Short History.* 2d ed. Knoxville: University of Tennessee Press, 1981.

Joseph, Paul. *Tennessee.* Edina, MN: Abdo & Daughters, 1998.

Kent, Deborah. *Tennessee.* New York: Children's Press, 2001.

Kummer, Patricia K. *Tennessee.* Mankato, MN: Capstone Press, 1998.

Thompson, Kathleen. *Tennessee.* Austin, TX: Raintree Steck-Vaughn, 1996.

Weatherly, Myra. *Tennessee.* New York: Children's Press, 2001.

Web sites

Department of Education. Tennessee, Sounds Good to Me: Tennessee Facts. [Online] Available http://www.state.tn.us/education/webfacts.htm Accessed May 31, 2001.

Secretary of State. [Online] Available http://www.state.tn.us/sos/ Accessed May 31, 2001.

State of Tennessee. About Tennessee. [Online] Available http://www.state.tn.us/aboutt.html Accessed May 31, 2001.

TEXAS

State of Texas

ORIGIN OF STATE NAME: Derived from the Caddo word *tayshas,* meaning "allies" or "friends."

NICKNAME: The Lone Star State.

CAPITAL: Austin.

ENTERED UNION: 29 December 1845 (28th).

SONG: "Texas, Our Texas." Also: "The Eyes of Texas."

MOTTO: Friendship.

FLAG: At the hoist is a vertical bar of blue with a single white five-pointed star; two horizontal bars of white and red cover the remainder of the flag.

OFFICIAL SEAL: A five-pointed star is encircled by olive and live oak branches, surrounded with the words "The State of Texas."

BIRD: Mockingbird.

FLOWER: Bluebonnet.

TREE: Pecan.

GEM: Topaz.

STONE: Palmwood.

GRASS: Sideoats grama.

DISH: Chili.

TIME: 6 AM CST = noon GMT.

1 LOCATION AND SIZE

Located in the west south-central US, Texas is the largest of the 48 continental states. The total area of Texas is 266,807 square miles (691,030 square kilometers). The state's land area represents 8.8% of the US mainland and 7.4% of the nation as a whole. The state's maximum east-west extension is 801 miles (1,289 kilometers). Its extreme north-south distance is 773 miles (1,244 kilometers). The boundary length of the state totals 3,029 miles (4,875 kilometers). Large islands in the Gulf of Mexico belonging to Texas are Galveston, Matagorda, and Padre.

2 TOPOGRAPHY

Texas's major regions are the Gulf Coastal Plain in the east and southeast; the North Central Plains, covering most of central Texas; the Great Plains, extending from west-central Texas up into the panhandle; and the mountainous trans-Pecos area in the extreme west. The Balcones Escarpment, a geological fault line running across central Texas, separates the Gulf Coastal and Rio Grande plains from the North Central Plains and south-central Hill Country. This fault line divides East Texas from West Texas, or watered Texas from dry Texas.

Much of the North Central Plains is rolling prairie, but the dude ranches of the Hill Country and the mineral-rich Burnet-Llano Basin are also found here. West of the Cap Rock Escarpment are the Great Plains, which stretch north–south from the Panhandle Plains to the Edwards Plateau, and which are just north of the Balcones Escarpment. The trans-Pecos region, between the Pecos River and the Rio Grande, contains the highest point in the state: Guadalupe Peak, with an altitude of 8,751 feet (2,667 meters).

For its vast expanse, Texas boasts few natural lakes, the largest being Caddo Lake, which lies in both Texas and Louisiana. All together, the state contains close to 200 major reservoirs, 8 of which can store more than one million acre-feet of water. From the air, Texas looks as well-watered as Minnesota, but the lakes are artificial and much of the soil is dry.

One reason Texas has so many reservoirs is that it is blessed with a number of major river systems, although none is navigable for more than 50 miles (80 kilometers) inland. Starting from the west, the Rio Grande, a majestic stream in some places but a trickling trough in others, imparts life to the Texas desert and serves as the international boundary with Mexico. Its total length of 1,896 miles (3,051 kilometers), including segments in Colorado and New Mexico, makes the Rio Grande the nation's second-longest river. It is exceeded only by the Missouri-Mississippi river system.

The Colorado River is the longest river wholly within the state, extending about

Texas Population Profile

Total population in 2000:	20,851,820
Population change, 1990–2000:	22.8%
Hispanic or Latino†:	32.0%
Population by race	
One race:	97.5%
White:	71.0%
Black or African American:	11.5%
American Indian/Alaska Native:	0.6%
Asian:	2.7%
Native Hawaiian/Pacific Islander:	0.1%
Some other race:	11.7%
Two or more races:	2.5%

Population by Age Group

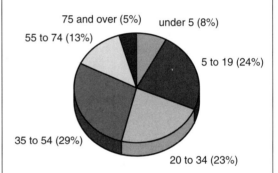

75 and over (5%)
under 5 (8%)
55 to 74 (13%)
5 to 19 (24%)
35 to 54 (29%)
20 to 34 (23%)

Top Cities by Population

City	Population	% change 1990–2000
Houston	1,953,631	19.8
Dallas	1,188,580	18.0
San Antonio	1,144,646	22.3
Austin	656,562	41.0
El Paso	563,662	9.4
Fort Worth	534,694	19.5
Arlington	332,969	27.2
Corpus Christi	277,454	7.8
Plano	222,030	72.5
Garland	215,768	19.4

Notes: †A person of Hispanic or Latino origin may be of any race. NA indicates that data are not available.
Sources: U.S. Census Bureau. Public Information Office. *Demographic Profiles.* [Online] Available http://www.census.gov/Press-Release/www/2001/demoprofile.html. Accessed June 1, 2001. U.S. Census Bureau. *Census 2000: Redistricting Data.* Press release issued by the Redistricting Data Office. Washington, D.C., March, 2001.

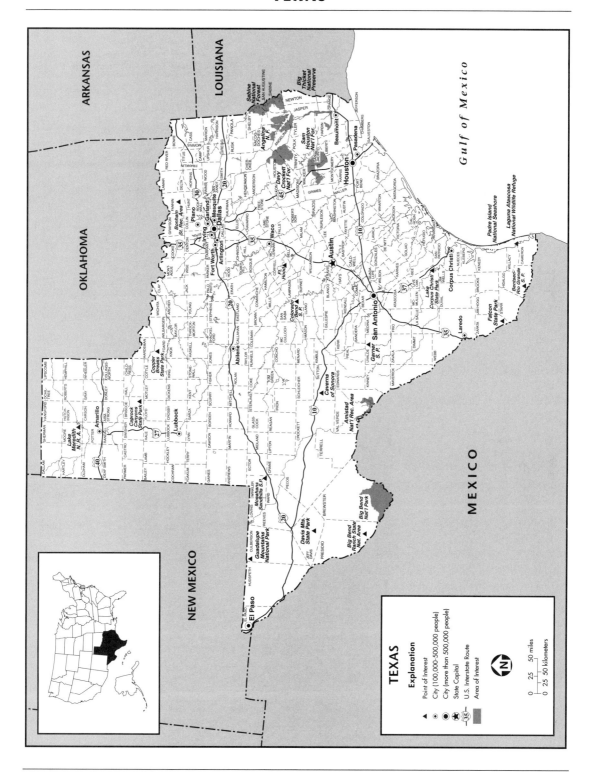

600 miles (970 kilometers) on its journey across central and southeastern Texas to the Gulf of Mexico. Other important rivers include the Nueces, the San Antonio, the Brazos, the Trinity, the San Jacinto, the Neches, the Sabine, the Red, and the Canadian.

Because of its extensive outcroppings of limestone, extending westward from the Balcones Escarpment, Texas contains a maze of caverns. Jack Pit Cave, in Menard County, with 19,000 feet (5,800 meters) of passages, is the most extensive cave yet mapped in the state.

3 CLIMATE

Texas's great size and topographic variety make its climate highly diverse. Brownsville, at the mouth of the Rio Grande, has had no measurable snowfall during all the years that records have been kept, but Vega, in the panhandle, averages 23 inches (58 centimeters) of snowfall a year. Near the Louisiana border, rainfall exceeds 56 inches (142 centimeters) annually, while in parts of extreme West Texas, rainfall averages less than 8 inches (20 centimeters).

Generally, a maritime climate prevails along the Gulf coast, with continental conditions inland. Texas has two basic seasons—a hot summer that may last from April through October, and a winter that starts in November and usually lasts until March. When summer ends, the state is too dry for autumn foliage, except in East Texas.

Temperatures in El Paso, in the southwest, range from a mean January minimum of 30°F (–1°C) to a mean July maximum of 95°F (35°C). At Amarillo, in the panhandle, temperatures range from 23°F (–5°C) in January to 91°F (33°C) in July. At Galveston, on the Gulf, the range is from 48°F (9°C) in January to 88°F (31°C) in August.

Perhaps the most startling contrast is in relative humidity, averaging 34% at noon in El Paso, 44% in Amarillo, and 72% in Galveston.

Record temperatures range from –23°F (–31°C) at Julia, on 12 February 1899, to 120°F (49°C) at Seymour in north-central Texas on 12 August 1936. The highest sustained wind velocity in Texas history, 145 miles per hour (233 kilometers/hour), occurred when Hurricane Carla hit Matagorda and Port Lavaca along the Gulf coast on 11 September 1961.

Hurricanes strike the Gulf coast about once every decade, usually in September or October. One hurricane that struck Galveston in 1900 caused over 6,000 deaths. Texas also lies in the path of "Tornado Alley," stretching across the Great Plains to Canada. The worst tornado in recent decades struck downtown Waco on 11 May 1953, killing 114 persons, injuring another 597, and destroying or damaging some 1,050 homes. Floods and droughts have also taken their toll in Texas. The worst flood occurred on 26–28 June 1954, when Hurricane Alice moved inland up the Rio Grande. That river rose 50 to 60 feet (15 to 18 meters) within 48 hours, as a wall of water 86 feet (26 meters) high in the Pecos River canyon streamed into it from the north.

4 PLANTS AND ANIMALS

Grassy pastureland covers about two-thirds of the state. Bermuda grass is a favorite ground cover. Texas has more than 20 native trees, of which several, including the catclaw, flowering mimosa, and weeping juniper are common only in Texas. Cottonwood grows along streams in almost every part of the state, while cypress inhabits the swamps. The flowering dogwood in East Texas draws tourists to that region every spring. Probably the most popular shade tree is the American (white) elm, and the magnolia is treasured for its grace and beauty. The pecan is the state tree. Pines grow in East Texas and the trans-Pecos region. Gonzales County, in south-central Texas, is the home of palmettos, orchids, and other semitropical plants not found anywhere else in the state.

The red wolf is steadily disappearing despite efforts throughout the US to save it. On the other hand, Texans claim to have the largest number of white-tailed deer of any state in the Union, an estimated 3 million. The nine–banded armadillo has gradually spread northward and eastward, crossing the Red and Mississippi rivers into the Deep South by sucking in air until it becomes buoyant and then swimming across the water. The armadillo is also notable for always having its young in litters of identical quadruplets. The chief mammalian predators are the coyote, bobcat, and mountain lion.

Texas attracts more than 825 different kinds of birds, with bird life most abundant in the lower Rio Grande Valley and coastal plains. Characteristic birds include

Photo credit: Courtesy of Austin Convention & Visitors Bureau, Regina Hill.

The National Wildflower Research Center in Austin.

the scissor-tailed flycatcher; Attwater's greater prairie chicken; the mockingbird, which is the state bird; and the roadrunner. The Gulf Coast is the winter nesting ground for the whooping crane. Controversy surrounds the golden eagle, protected by federal law, but despised by ranchers for allegedly preying on lambs and other young livestock.

Texas has its fair share of reptiles, including more than 100 species of snakes, 16 of them poisonous, notably the deadly Texas coral snake. There are ten kinds of rattlesnake, and some parts of West Texas hold annual rattlesnake roundups. Endangered species include, among others, the Mexican spotted owl and ocelot. Texas has 15 National Wildlife Refuges, with a total of 302,731 acres (122,511 hectares).

5 ENVIRONMENTAL PROTECTION

With the exception of eastern Texas, water is scarce in the state, especially in the arid west. Much of the state has absorbent soils, a high evaporation rate, vast areas without trees to hold moisture, and a rolling terrain susceptible to rapid runoff. The Texas Water Commission and Water Development Board direct the state's water supply and conservation programs. Various county and regional water authorities have been constituted, as have several water commissions for river systems.

The most powerful conservation agency in Texas is the Railroad Commission. Originally established to regulate railroads, the Commission extended its power to regulate oil and natural gas by virtue of its jurisdiction over the transportation of those products by rail and pipeline. The Commission acts to eliminate wasteful drilling procedures and decides which equipment and techniques are permissible.

As in other states, hazardous wastes have become an environmental concern in Texas. The agency that oversees compliance with hazardous-waste statutes is the Hazardous and Solid Waste Division of the Texas Water Commission. Texas had 32 hazardous waste sites as of 1998.

6 POPULATION

According to 2000 census figures, Texas ranked second behind California, with a population of over 20.8 million, yielding a density of just 79.6 persons per square mile (30.7 persons per square kilometer), identical to the national density average. The U.S. Census Bureau projects a population of 28.49 million in 2005. The population growth rate was 22.8% between 1990 and 2000.

Surprisingly, for a state whose population has grown so fast, about 65% of all state residents were born in Texas. In 1990, about 82% of all Texans lived in metropolitan areas. The largest, Houston, had nearly 2 million people (fourth in the US) in 2000. Close behind was Dallas, with nearly 1.2 million residents (eighth). San Antonio ranked ninth nationally at 1.14 million. Austin ranked 16th in the country with 656,562, and El Paso followed with 563,662 residents. Other cities and their 2000 populations were Fort Worth, 534,694; Arlington, 332,969; and Corpus Christi, 277,454. Plano, with 222,030 residents, grew by 72.5% between 1990 and 2000 alone. Texas has a relatively young population, with a median age of 32.3 (compared with the national average of 35.3). Approximately 32% of the population is 19 years of age and younger.

7 ETHNIC GROUPS

Hispanic Americans, who may be of any race, constitute the largest ethnic minority in Texas, about 29.4% of the population in 1997. Black Americans accounted for 12.2%. Some 56.2% were of European

Texas Population by Race

Census 2000 was the first national census in which the instructions to respondents said, "Mark one or more races." This table shows the number of people who are of one, two, or three or more races. For those claiming two races, the number of people belonging to the various categories is listed. The U.S. government conducts a census of the population every ten years.

	Number	Percent
Total population	20,851,820	100.0
One race	20,337,187	97.5
Two races	494,972	2.4
White *and* Black or African American	40,094	0.2
White *and* American Indian/Alaska Native	67,407	0.3
White *and* Asian	44,486	0.2
White *and* Native Hawaiian/Pacific Islander	3,498	—
White *and* some other race	267,739	1.3
Black or African American *and* American Indian/Alaska Native	7,563	—
Black or African American *and* Asian	5,348	—
Black or African American *and* Native Hawaiian/Pacific Islander	1,137	—
Black or African American *and* some other race	23,062	0.1
American Indian/Alaska Native *and* Asian	2,847	—
American Indian/Alaska Native *and* Native Hawaiian/Pacific Islander	228	—
American Indian/Alaska Native *and* some other race	8,579	—
Asian *and* Native Hawaiian/Pacific Islander	3,418	—
Asian *and* some other race	17,067	0.1
Native Hawaiian/Pacific Islander *and* some other race	2,499	—
Three or more races	19,661	0.1

Source: U.S. Census Bureau. *Census 2000: Redistricting Data*. Press release issued by the Redistricting Data Office. Washington, D.C., March, 2001. A dash (—) indicates that the percent is less than 0.1.

(non-Hispanic) ancestry, while 28.4% had Hispanic and European origins. Hispanic Americans numbered 5.7 million in 1997 (second only to California). Mostly of Mexican ancestry, they are a diverse group, divided by history, geography, and economic circumstances. Although many Native American groups have lived in Texas, few of their members remain. Overall, in the 1997 federal estimate, there were 93,300 Native Americans living in Texas. However, over 815,000 residents claimed some Native American ancestry in the 1990 Census.

In 1997, an estimated 10.9 million blacks lived in the state, ranking third behind New York and California. Houston and Dallas are, respectively, about 28% and 29% black.

All together, Texas has nearly 30 identifiable ethnic groups. Certain areas of central Texas are heavily Germanic and Czech. Significant numbers of Danes, Swedes, and Norwegians have also settled in Texas. As of 1996, about 11.1% of all Texans were foreign-born. Mexico was the country of birth for about 65% of the foreign-born. India, Vietnam, El Salvador, the Philippines, Germany, and the Dominican Republic are other leading countries of origin.

Pennybacker Bridge in Austin.

The 1997 federal estimate included 524,000 Asians and Pacific Islanders (2.7%). Vietnamese, Chinese, Filipinos, Asian Indians, Koreans, and Japanese are the most numerous Asian groups. Many of the Vietnamese were refugees who resettled in Texas beginning in 1975.

8 LANGUAGES

Most of the regional features in Texas English derive from the influx of South Midland and Southern speakers. There is a noticeable Spanish flavor from older as well as more recent word-borrowing. Texas pronunciation is largely South Midland.

Spanish has been the major foreign-language influence. In areas like Laredo and Brownsville, along the Rio Grande, as many as 90% of the people may be bilingual. In northeast Texas, however, Spanish is as foreign as French. In the days of the early Spanish ranchers, standard English adopted *hacienda, ranch, burro, canyon,* and *lariat.* The presence of the large Spanish-speaking population was a major factor in the passage of the state's bilingual education law, which requires that numerous school programs be offered in both English and Spanish.

In 1990, 11,635,518 Texans—74.6% of the population five years old or older—spoke only English at home. Other languages most commonly spoken at home included Spanish, 3,443,106; German, 90,659; and Vietnamese, 57,736.

9 RELIGIONS

Texas tends to be heavily Protestant in the north and east and Catholic in the south and southwest. Leading Protestant denominations and their known members in 1990 were Southern Baptist Convention, 3,259,395; United Methodist Church, 1,004,318; Churches of Christ, 380,948; Episcopal Church, 169,112; Assembly of God, 162,232; Presbyterian Church, 200,969; Christian Church (Disciples of Christ), 105,495; Baptists Missionary Association of America, 125,323; Lutheran Church-Missouri Synod, 134,280; and Evangelical Lutheran Church in America, 155,276. Roman Catholics numbered 3,574,728 in 1990, and there were an estimated 109,000 Jews in 1994.

10 TRANSPORTATION

Transportation has been a severe problem for Texas because of the state's extraordinary size and sometimes difficult terrain. Nevertheless, Texas ranks first among the 50 states in total railroad mileage, highway mileage, and number of airports. Texas is second only to California in motor vehicle registrations and in number of general aviation aircraft.

Three rail carriers—Burlington Northern/Santa Fe; Kansas City Southern; and Union Pacific—control about 85% of the mileage. The only rail passenger service in Texas is provided by Amtrak, which runs only two routes.

Dallas is constructing the Dallas Area Rapid Transit system (DART), to serve the city and 13 suburbs. Fort Worth has the state's only true subway, although Dallas-Fort Worth Regional Airport has its own rail shuttle system.

In 1997, Texas had 296,651 miles (477,311 kilometers) of public roadways, 72% of them rural. Texas has by far the most mileage of any state. In 1997, expenditures on roads and highways by federal state and local governments came to over $7.5 billion, second only to California. There were 12.8 million registered vehicles in 1997, including 7.08 million automobiles, 5.75 million trucks, and 77,864 buses. Trucking is vital to the Texas economy, because more than 1,800 communities are served by no other freight carrier.

With 13 major seaports and many shallow-water ports, Texas has been a major factor in waterborne commerce since the early 1950s. Port of Houston is the nation's second-most active harbor, with over 169.1 million tons of cargo handled in 1998. The Gulf Intracoastal Waterway begins in Brownsville, at the mouth of the Rio Grande, and extends across Texas for 423 miles (681 kilometers) on its way to Florida. In 1995, the waterway transported 78.3 million tons of cargo.

After American entry into World War I, Texas began to build airfields for training grounds. When the war ended, many US fliers returned to Texas and became civilian commercial pilots, carrying air mail, dusting crops, and mapping potential oil fields. In 1997, the state had 1,684 aircraft facilities, including 1,280 airports and 396 heliports. The Dallas-Fort Worth Regional Airport was the nation's largest air terminal and its second-busiest in 1996, handling 373,263 aircraft departures and serving 26.2 million passengers.

11 HISTORY

When the first Europeans arrived in the 16th century, the Native Americans in present-day Texas were still largely hunter-gatherers. Along the Gulf coast and overlapping into northeastern Mexico were the Coahuiltecan and Karankawa peoples. In central Texas lived the Tonkawa, who hunted buffalo and used dogs for hauling. They proved extremely susceptible to European diseases and evidently died out, whereas the Karankawa migrated to northern Mexico.

About two dozen tribes of Caddo in eastern and northeastern Texas were, at the time of European penetration, the most technologically advanced Native Americans living within the state's present borders. Having developed agriculture, the Caddo were relatively sedentary and village-oriented. Those belonging to the Hasinai Confederation called each other *tayshas*, a term that translates as "allies" or "friends." When the Hasinai told Spanish explorers that they were *tayshas*, the Spaniards wrote the word as *Tejas*, which in time became *Texas*.

In trans-Pecos Texas, to the west, lived a fourth tribal group, the Jumano, probably descendants of the Pueblo cultures. Some of the Jumano were nomadic hunters in the Davis and Chisos mountains, while others became farmers along the Rio Grande and the lower Rio Conchos.

Spanish Settlement

The first European to enter Texas was Spanish explorer Alonso Alvarez de Pineda, who sailed into the mouth of the Rio Grande in 1519. For more than 150 years, the Spanish had little interest in Texas, regarding it as too remote for successful settlement. However, their attitude toward the colonization of Texas was changed by fear of competition from the French with the establishment of Fort St. Louis by La Salle on the Gulf coast in 1685. Four years later, Captain Alonso de León, governor of Coahuila, sent out an expedition to expel the French and establish both a fort and a mission.

During the next several decades, a string of mission-forts were built across Texas. After fear of the French presence eased, Spain tended to neglect these establishments. But when the French entered Louisiana in force during the early 18th century, Spanish fears of French expansion were re-ignited. In 1718, the Spanish established a presence at the site of the present city of San Antonio. As a halfway post between Mexico and the Louisiana border, San Antonio grew to be Texas's most important city during the Spanish period.

Mexican State

Until the 19th century, the US showed little interest in Texas. But the purchase of Louisiana Territory from the French by the US government in 1803 made Texas a next-door neighbor. "Filibusters" (military adventurers) began to filter across the border into Spanish territory. In 1810–11, the Mexicans launched their revolution against Spain, and though only an outpost, Texas as a Spanish-Mexican colony was naturally involved, becoming a Mexican state in 1813.

The Spanish finally gave up on Mexico in 1821, leaving Texas as a Mexican province with a European population of about 7,000. A year earlier, Moses Austin of Missouri had received permission from Spanish authorities to introduce Anglo-American colonists into Texas, presumably as a barrier against aggression by the US. When Spanish rule ended, his son, Stephen F. Austin, secured permission from the new Mexican government to settle 300 families in the area between the lower Colorado and Brazos rivers. Other colonizers made similar arrangements to settle Anglo-Americans in the region. Texas thus began a pattern of growth through migration that has continued to the present day.

Most new settlers were non-Hispanics who often distrusted Mexico. They disliked Mexican culture and government; the Protestants among them disliked the dominance of the Roman Catholic Church. The incompetence of the Mexican government made the situation even worse. Troubled by a rising spirit of rebellion, the Mexican Congress enacted the Law of 1830, which forbade most immigration and imposed duties on all imports.

Texas Revolution

In the early 1830s, skirmishes began between Anglo-Texans and Mexicans. When Mexican President Antonio López de Santa Anna tried to enforce customs collections, colonists at Anahuae drove Mexican officials out of town. Santa Anna's answer was to place Texas under military jurisdiction. On 2 October 1835, Anglo-Texan civilians at Gonzalez defeated the forces of Colonel Domingo de Ugartechea in a battle that is generally considered to mark the start of the Texas Revolution.

Texas sent three envoys to Washington, D.C., to request aid from the US. Sam Houston, who six years earlier had resigned the governorship of Tennessee, was named commander in chief of the upstart Texas army. In February 1836, Santa Anna led an army across the Rio Grande. The Mexicans concentrated outside San Antonio at a mission-fort called the Alamo. There, 187 or so Texans, commanded by Colonel William Barret Travis, had taken shelter. The Mexicans besieged the Alamo until 6 March, when Santa Anna's forces, now numbering more than 4,000, stormed the fortress. When the battle ended, all the Alamo's defenders, including several native Mexicans, were dead. Among those killed were Travis and two Americans who became legends—James Bowie and Davy Crockett.

On 27 March 1836, three weeks after the Alamo fell, the Mexicans killed 342 Texans who had surrendered at Goliad, thinking they would be treated as prisoners of war. Coming on the heels of the Alamo tragedy, the "Goliad massacre" impelled Texans to seek total victory over Mexico. On 21 April, the Texans surprised the Mexicans during their siesta period at San Jacinto. Mexican losses were 630 killed, 280 wounded, and 730 taken prisoner, while the Texans had only 9 killed and 30 wounded. This decisive battle—fought to the cry of "Remember the Alamo, remember Goliad!"—freed Texas from Mexico once and for all.

The Republic of Texas and US Statehood

For ten years, Texas existed as an independent republic, recognized by the US and several European nations. Sam Houston, the victorious commander at San Jacinto, became the republic's first nationally elected president. Strife-torn and short of cash, Texas joined the Union on 29 December 1845. The US annexation of Texas was largely responsible for the Mexican War, which was ended on 2 February 1848 by the Treaty of Guadalupe Hidalgo, under which Mexico dropped its claim to the territory between the Rio Grande and the Nueces River.

With the coming of the Civil War, Texas followed its pro-slavery southern neighbors out of the Union into the Confederacy. The state, which saw little fighting, suffered from the war far less than most of the South. During Reconstruction, Texas was governed briefly by a military occupation force and then by a Republican regime.

While most southern states were economically devastated, the Texas economy flourished because of the rapid development of the cattle industry. The widespread use of barbed wire to fence cattle ranches in the 1880s ended the open range and encouraged scientific cattle-breeding. By 1900, Texas began to transform its predominantly agricultural economy into an industrial one.

Oil and Politics

This process was hastened by the discovery of the Spindletop oil field—the state's first gusher—near Beaumont in 1901, and by the subsequent development of the petroleum and petrochemical industries. World War I saw the emergence of Texas as a military training center. The rapid growth of the aircraft industry and other high-technology fields contributed to the continuing industrialization of Texas during and after World War II.

Texas politics remained solidly Democratic during most of the modern era, and the significant political conflict in the state was between the liberal and conservative wings of the Democratic Party. During the 1960s and 1970s, the Republican Party gathered strength in the state, electing John G. Tower as US senator in 1961 and William P. Clements, Jr., as governor in 1978—the first Republicans to hold those offices since Reconstruction. In general, the state's recent political leaders, Democrats was well as Republicans, have represented property interests and taken a conservative line.

On the national level, Texans have been influential since the 1930s, notably through such congressional leaders as US House Speaker Sam Rayburn and Senate Majority Leader Lyndon B. Johnson. Johnson, elected vice-president under John F. Kennedy, was riding in the motorcade when Kennedy was assassinated in Dallas on 22 November 1963. Johnson served

Texas Governors: 1846–2001

1846–1847	James Pinckney Henderson	Democrat		1911–1915	Oscar Branch Colquitt	Democrat
1847–1849	George Thomas Wood	Democrat		1915–1917	James Edward Ferguson	Democrat
1849–1853	Peter Hasbrough Bell	Democrat		1917–1921	William Pettus Hobby	Democrat
1853	James Wilson Henderson	Democrat		1921–1925	Patrick Morris Neff	Democrat
1853–1857	Elisha Marshall Pease	Democrat		1925–1927	Miriam Amanda Ferguson	Democrat
1857–1859	Hardin Richard Runnels	Democrat		1927–1931	Daniel J. Moody	Democrat
1859–1861	Samuel Houston	Democrat		1931–1933	Ross Shaw Sterling	Democrat
1861	Edward Clark	Democrat		1933–1935	Miriam Amanda Ferguson	Democrat
1861–1863	Francis Richard Lubbock	Democrat		1935–1939	James V. Allred	Democrat
1863–1865	Pendleton Murrah	Democrat		1939–1941	Wilbert Lee O'Daniel	Democrat
1865	Fletcher S. Stockdale	Democrat		1941–1947	Coke Robert Stevenson	Democrat
1865–1866	Andrew Jackson Hamilton	Indep-Dem		1947–1949	Beauford Halbert Jester	Democrat
1866–1867	James Webb Throckmorton	Conservative		1949–1957	Allan Shivers	Democrat
1867–1869	Elisha Marshall Pease	Democrat		1957–1963	Price Marion Daniel	Democrat
1870–1874	Edmund Jackson Davis	Rep-Prov		1963–1969	John Bowden Connally	Democrat
1874–1876	Richard Coke	Democrat		1969–1973	Preston Earnest Smith	Democrat
1876–1879	Richard Bennett Hubbard	Democrat		1973–1979	Dolph Briscoe, Jr.	Democrat
1879–1883	Oran Milo Roberts	Democrat		1979–1983	William Perry Clements, Jr.	Republican
1883–1887	John Ireland	Democrat		1983–1987	Mark White	Democrat
1887–1891	Lawrence Sullivan Ross	Democrat		1987–1991	William Perry Clements, Jr.	Republican
1891–1895	James Stephen Hogg	Democrat		1991–1995	Dorethy Ann Willis Richards	Democrat
1895–1899	Charles Allen Culberson	Democrat		1995–2000	George W. Bush	Republican
1899–1903	Joseph Draper Sayers	Democrat		2000–	Rick Perry	Republican
1903–1907	Samuel Willis Tucker Lanham	Democrat				
1907–1911	Thomas Mitchell Campbell	Democrat				

Independent Democrat – Indep-Dem
Republican Provisional – Rep-Prov

out the remainder of Kennedy's term, then was himself elected to the presidency by a landslide in 1964. Johnson retired to his LBJ ranch in 1969.

The most prominent Texan on the national scene since Johnson is Republican George Bush, who served as vice-president for eight years under Ronald Reagan before being elected to the presidency in 1988. Bush was defeated by Bill Clinton in his 1992 bid for reelection.

Oil and Economics

Texas benefited from a booming oil industry in the 1970s, but the boom collapsed in the early 1980s as overproduction caused world oil prices to drop. To make up the $100 million in revenues that the government estimated it lost for every $1

dollar decline in the price of a barrel of oil, the government in 1985 imposed or raised fees on everything from vanity license plates to day care centers. The state also took steps to encourage economic diversification by soliciting service, electronics, and high-technology companies to come to Texas.

In the late 1980s, a number of Texas's financial institutions collapsed, brought down by the slump in the oil industry and unsound real estate loans. Since then, oil prices have increased and stabilized. The high rate of migration into Texas which accompanied the oil boom had a profound effect on the state's population distribution. About 19% of the state's adults have come to Texas since 1974, giving it the second largest population of any state.

The state capitol building in Austin.

On 19 April 1993, a 51–day confrontation between the FBI and the Branch Davidian cult near Waco ended tragically when the groups compound burned to the ground, killing at least 72 people, some of them children. There is still controversy to this day on how the situation was handled by the government.

In November 2000, George W. Bush was elected the 43rd president of the United States. He was raised in Midland, Texas, where he was active in the oil business before becoming governor of the state in 1994. He is the son of former president George H. W. Bush.

12 STATE GOVERNMENT

The state legislature consists of a senate of 31 members elected to four-year terms, and a house of representatives of 150 members elected to two-year terms. The state's chief executives are the governor and lieutenant governor, separately elected to four-year terms. Other elected executives include the attorney general, comptroller, and treasurer. A uniquely important executive agency is the Texas Railroad Commission, established in 1891, which regulates the state's oil and gas production, coal and uranium mining, and trucking industry, in addition to the railroads.

To become law, a bill must be approved by a majority of members present and voting in each house, with a quorum of two-thirds of the membership present. The bill must then be signed by the governor or left unsigned for 10 days while the legislature is in session or 20 days after it has adjourned. A gubernatorial veto may be overridden by a two-thirds vote of members present in the house of the bill's origin, followed by either a vote of two-thirds of members present in the house of representatives or two-thirds of the entire membership of the senate.

13 POLITICAL PARTIES

The Democratic Party has dominated politics in Texas. William P. Clements, Jr.,

elected governor in 1978, was the first Republican since Reconstruction to hold that office. No Republican carried Texas in a presidential election until 1928, when Herbert Hoover defeated Democrat Al Smith, a Roman Catholic who was at a severe disadvantage in a largely Protestant state. Another Roman Catholic, Democratic presidential candidate John F. Kennedy, carried the state in 1960 largely because he had a Texan, Lyndon B. Johnson, on his ticket.

There is no voter registration by party in Texas. As of November 1993, the state had 8,439,874 registered voters. Republican and native son George Bush captured 56% of the vote in the 1988 presidential election and 41% in the 1992 election. In

Texas Presidential Vote by Political Parties, 1948–2000

YEAR	TEXAS WINNER	DEMOCRAT	REPUBLICAN	STATES' RIGHTS DEMOCRAT	PROGRESSIVE	PROHIBITION
1948	*Truman (D)	750,700	282,240	106,909	3,764	2,758
				CONSTITUTION		
1952	*Eisenhower (R)	969,227	1,102,818	1,563	—	1,983
1956	*Eisenhower (R)	859,958	1,080,619	14,591	—	—
1960	*Kennedy (D)	1,167,935	1,121,693	18,170	—	3,868
1964	*Johnson (D)	1,663,185	958,566	5,060	—	—
				AMERICAN IND.		
1968	Humphrey (D)	1,266,804	1,227,844	584,269	—	—
				AMERICAN	SOC. WORKERS	
1972	*Nixon (R)	1,154,289	2,298,896	6,039	8,664	—
1976	*Carter (D)	2,082,319	1,953,300	11,442	1,723	—
				LIBERTARIAN		
1980	*Reagan (R)	1,881,147	2,510,705	37,643	—	—
1984	*Reagan (R)	1,949,276	3,433,428	—	—	—
					NEW ALLIANCE	
1988	*Bush (R)	2,352,748	3,036,829	30,355	7,208	—
				POPULIST/AMERICA FIRST		IND. (Perot)
1992	Bush (R)	2,281,815	2,496,071	19,699	505	1,354,781
1996	Dole (R)	2,549,683	2,736,167	20,256	—	378,537
				LIBERTARIAN		REFORM
2000	*Bush (R)	2,433,746	3,799,639	23,160	137,994	12,394

* Won US presidential election.

2000, Texans gave another native son, Republican George W. Bush, 59% of the vote. Democratic candidate Al Gore received 38%. In the November 1994 elections, George W. Bush, Jr. upset Ann Richards to become governor. The young Bush won a resounding reelection in 1998. Republican Kay Bailey Hutchison was elected in 1993 to fill the seat vacated by Democratic Senator Lloyd Bentsen, who resigned to become Secretary of the Treasury in the Clinton Administration. In 1994 and 2000, Hutchison won reelection. In 2001, Democrats held 17 seats in the US House of Representatives and the Republicans held 13. That same year, Republicans held 16 state senate seats to the Democrats' 15. Democrats controlled the state house with 78 seats, while the Republicans held 72.

Third parties have generally played a minor role in Texas politics. In 1968, George Wallace of the American Independent Party won 19% of the Texas popular vote; and in 1992, native son Ross Perot ran independently and picked up 22% of the vote.

14 LOCAL GOVERNMENT

The Texas constitution grants considerable autonomy to local governments. As of 1997, Texas had 254 counties, a number that has remained constant since 1931. In 1997, there were 1,177 municipal governments. Each county is governed by a commissioner's court of five members. Other elected officials generally include a county clerk, attorney, and treasurer.

15 JUDICIAL SYSTEM

The Texas judiciary comprises the supreme court, the state court of criminal appeals, 14 courts of appeals, and more than 380 district courts. The highest court is the supreme court, consisting of a chief justice and eight associate justices. The court of criminal appeals, which has final jurisdiction in most criminal cases, consists of a presiding judge and eight associate judges. Justices of the courts of appeals sit in 14 judicial districts; each court has a chief justice and at least 2 associate justices. There are 386 district court judges. County, justice of the peace, and police courts handle local matters.

Overall, Texas had a 1998 crime rate of 5,112 per 100,000 population, higher than the national rate. The population of federal and state prisons was 146,180 in 1997. Texas criminal law allows for capital punishment, and as of December 1997, there were 438 inmates on death row. Texas leads the nation in the number of executions.

16 MIGRATION

The first great wave of white settlers, beginning in 1821, came from nearby southern states, particularly Tennessee, Alabama, Arkansas, and Mississippi. During the 1840s, a second wave of immigrants arrived directly from Germany, France, and eastern Europe. Many immigrants from Mexico came during 1890–1910. Particularly notable since 1900 has been the intrastate movement from rural areas to the cities. This trend was especially pronounced from the end of World War II, when about half the state's population was rural, to the late 1970s, when nearly four out of every five Texans made their homes in metropolitan areas.

A significant proportion of postwar immigrants were seasonal laborers from Mexico, remaining in the US either legally or illegally. During 1980–83, Texas had the highest net migration gain—922,000—in the nation. From 1985 to 1990, the net gain from migration was 36,700. During 1990–98, the net gain from interstate migration was 541,000, and 655,700 from international migration. In 1996, an estimated 11% of all Texans were foreign-born. Mexico was the country of origin for about two-thirds of the foreign-born population. Texas admitted 44,428 immigrants in 1998, 4th highest in the nation. The federal government estimated that Texas had an illegal immigrant population of 700,000 in 1996.

17 ECONOMY

Traditionally, the Texas economy has been dependent on the production of cotton, cattle, timber, and petroleum. But in the 1970s, as a result of rising world petroleum prices, oil and natural gas emerged as the state's most important resource. The decades since World War II have also witnessed a boom in the electronics, computer, transport equipment, aerospace, and communications industries, which has placed Texas second only to California in manufacturing among all the states of the Sunbelt region.

In 1982, however, Texas began to be affected by worldwide recession. In addition, lower energy demand, worldwide overproduction of oil, and the resulting fall in prices caused a steep decline in the state's petroleum industry. The rise and fall in the oil industry's fortunes affected other industries as well. By the late 1980s, many banks that had speculated in real estate earlier in the decade had too much debt and were declared insolvent.

In the wake of the oil-centered recession, Texas has begun attempts to diversify, successfully attracting high-technology industries. Electronics, telecommunications, food processing, services, and retail trade saw substantial growth in the late 1980s and helped Texas through the national recession of 1990. Its gross state product in 1997 was $602 billion.

18 INCOME

In 1998, per capita (per person) income reached $25,369, 28th among the states. Median family income in 1998 was $54,148. In 1998, 16.1% of all Texans were living below the federal poverty level. Famed for its cattle barons and oil millionaires, about 2.4% of state's households have incomes exceeding $125,000, ranking it 3rd in total personal income in 1998.

19 INDUSTRY

The value of all shipments by manufacturers in 1997 was over $302 billion. Three of the state's leading industrial products—refined petroleum, industrial organic chemicals, and oil-field machinery—all stem directly from the petrochemical sector. Major oil refineries are located at Houston and other Gulf ports.

Aircraft plants include those of North American Aviation and Chance-Vought at Grand Prairie, General Dynamics near Fort Worth, and Bell Aircraft's helicopter division at Hurst. In 1997, Texas was home to 36 Fortune 500 companies, including Exxon, which ranked as the third-largest industrial corporation.

20 LABOR

With a civilian labor force of 10.12 million in mid-1998, Texas ranked second among the 50 states. The statewide unemployment rate was 4.8%. The Bryan-College Station, Austin-San Marcos, and San Angelo metropolitan areas typically have lower unemployment rates than the state as a whole, while the El Paso, Laredo, Brownsville-Harlingen-San Benito and McAllen-Edinburg-Mission areas have higher unemployment rates.

Organized labor has never been able to establish a strong base in Texas. As of 1998, 5.9% of all state workers were members of labor unions.

21 AGRICULTURE

Texas ranked second among the 50 states in agricultural production in 1999, with farm marketing totaling over $13 billion. Texas leads the nation in output of cotton, grain sorghum, watermelons, cabbages, and spinach. It is a major producer of onions, cabbages, potatoes, and melons. About 130 million acres (52.6 million hectares) are devoted to farms and ranches, representing more than three-fourths of the state's total area.

After 1900, Texas farmers developed plentiful crops of wheat, corn, and other grains by irrigating dry land. They transformed the "great Sahara" of West Texas into one of the nation's foremost grain-growing regions. Texans also grow practically every vegetable suited to a temperate or semitropical climate. Since World War II, farms have become fewer and larger, more specialized in raising certain crops and meat animals, more expensive to operate, and far more productive.

Production of major crops in 1998 included 3.5million bales of Upland cotton (valued at $1.9 billion); 6.8 million tons of hay ($565 million); 185 million bushels of corn ($434 million); 105 million bushels of sorghum ($232 million); and 136 million bushels of wheat ($368 million).

22 DOMESTICATED ANIMALS

In 1999, Texas ranked first in livestock production, which contributed 64% of the state's total agricultural income. The state leads the US in output of cattle, goats, and sheep, and in the production of wool and mohair. In 1998, Texas ranked first in the number of cattle, at 14.1 million (14% of the US total). Texas had 640,000 hogs, 1.7 million sheep, 385,000 dairy cows, and 21.3 million chickens in 1996.

About 90% of the dairy industry is located in eastern Texas. In 1997, milk production was 5.7 billion pounds. Poultry production included 2.1 billion pounds of broilers, sixth highest among the states.

Breeding of palominos, Arabians, Appaloosas, thoroughbreds, and quarter

The Dallas skyline.

horses is a major industry in Texas. It is not unusual for residential subdivisions of metropolitan areas to include facilities for keeping and riding horses.

23 FISHING

Texas in 1998 recorded a commercial catch of 89.2 million pounds, valued at $183.3 million (fifth among the states). Shrimp accounts for about 81% of the total volume of the catch. Other commercial shellfish include blue crabs and oysters. Species of saltwater fish with the greatest commercial value are yellowfin tuna, red snapper, swordfish, and flounder.

The state issued nearly 1.45 million sport fishing licenses in 1998.

24 FORESTRY

Texas forestland covered 18 million acres in 1997, representing 2.5% of the US total. Most forested land, including practically all commercial timberland, is located in the Piney Woods region of east Texas. In 1997, Texas timberlands yielded a harvest of totalling $660 million, but that represents only a small fraction of the economic impact of the state's wood-based industry. In 1994, trees were planted on 92,208 acres (37,317 hectares) to help sustain the forest resource of the state.

Primary forest products manufactured in 1994 included 1.54 billion board feet (128 million cubic feet/3.6 million cubic meters) of lumber, 2.6 billion square feet (73 million cubic meters) of plywood and waferboard, and 5.5 million cords (700 million cubic feet/19.7 million cubic meters) of pulpwood. Texas wood-treating plants processed 24.5 million cubic feet of timber products in 1994. Major treated products included 233,512 utility poles, 2 million crossties, 144.7 million board feet (12 million cubic feet/0.3 million cubic meters) of lumber, and 241,216 fence posts.

The Texas Forest Service, a member of the Texas A&M (Agricultural and Mechanical) University System, manages several state and federal reforestation and forest stewardship incentives programs. There are four national forests in Texas—Angelina, Davy Crockett, Sabine, and Sam Houston—with a total area of 637,134 acres (257,848 hectares).

25 MINING

According to estimates, 1998 nonfuel mineral production in Texas was valued at $1.92 billion. Texas ranked fifth in overall mineral value. The most valuable mineral commodities are portland cement, construction sand and gravel, crushed stone, lime, and salt. Together, these minerals accounted for 83% of the total value. Texas ranked first in crushed stone and magnesium metal, and second in portland cement, construction sand and gravel, slate, and common clays.

26 ENERGY AND POWER

Texas is an energy-rich state. It is also the largest producer and exporter of oil and natural gas to other states, and it leads the US in electric power production.

As of 1999, Texas power plants had a combined output of 293.1 billion kilowatt hours. Some 45% of this electricity came from coal-fired power plants. Texas has four nuclear power plants.

Crude oil production in 1999 was 449.2 million barrels, including over 1 million barrels from offshore wells. In 1998, Texas produced 6.3 trillion cubic feet (180 billion cubic meters) of natural gas, representing 32% of total US production. As of 1999, proven natural gas reserves were estimated at 37.6 trillion cubic feet, 23% of the US total. Coal production totaled 52.6 million tons in 1998.

27 COMMERCE

Wholesale sales totaled $270 billion in 1997, third in the nation; retail sales were $130.7 billion (second after California). Foreign exports through Texas customs districts in 1998 totaled $79 billion. Texas ranked second among the 50 states in 1998 as a producer of goods for export.

28 PUBLIC FINANCE

The Texas budget operates on a "pay as you go" basis in that expenditures cannot exceed revenue during the budget cycle. The Governor has line-item veto authority over the budget and must sign the Appropriations Bill before it becomes law. As the state's economy has diversi-

The Governor's Mansion in Austin.

fied, the budget has shown greater stability. Total revenues for fiscal 1997 were $63.86 billion; expenditures were $48.89 billion. The state's outstanding debt as of 1997 totaled $12.46 billion, or $641 per capita (per person), the fourth lowest ratio of state public debt per person among the states.

29 TAXATION

Texas's total state tax collections for 2000/01 are estimated to be over $44 billion. Only South Dakota and New Hampshire have lower tax rates. The principal source of state tax revenue is the 6.25% sales and use tax. Other major sources of revenue are oil and natural-gas production taxes, motor fuel taxes, motor vehicle sales and rental tax, and cigarette and tobacco taxes. Other state levies include the corporation franchise tax, alcoholic beverage tax, public utility taxes, inheritance tax, and a tax on telephones.

Local property tax rates varied widely throughout the state. The city sales tax is a major source of revenue for the municipalities. In 1984, the legislature significantly increased taxes for the first time in 13 years. Federal income tax payments by Texans during 1996 exceeded $92 billion.

30 HEALTH

Many remote parts of Texas suffer from a general shortage of health care personnel.

Medical care ranges from adequate to excellent in the state's largest cities, but many small communities are without doctors (24 rural counties in 1996) and hospitals. Texas ranked below the national rate in deaths due to heart disease, cancer, cerebrovascular diseases, and suicide, but above average in deaths from accidents.

In 1998, Texas's 400 community hospitals had a total of 56,573 beds. The average hospital expense per inpatient day was $1,165 in 1998, or $6,045 for an average cost per stay. Texas had 39,556 nonfederal licensed physicians in 1996 and 101,900 nurses. The University of Texas Cancer Center at Houston is one of the nation's major facilities for cancer research. Houston is also noted as a center for cardiovascular surgery. On 3 May 1968, Houston surgeon Denton Cooley performed the first human heart transplant in the US.

31 HOUSING

The variety of Texas architectural styles reflects the diversity of the state's topography and climate. During the late 19th century, the familiar ranch house, constructed of stone and usually stuccoed or whitewashed, and with a shingle roof and a long porch, spread throughout the state. The modern ranch house in southwestern Texas shows a distinct Mexican-Spanish influence.

As of 1999, Texas had an estimated 7.8 million year-round housing units. In 1998, the state authorized construction of 156,700 new housing units valued at almost $13.7 billion. In 1998, the median

home value was $120,400, in Dallas. The median monthly costs for owners (with a mortgage) and renters in 1990 were $712 and $395, respectively.

32 EDUCATION

Texas ranks second only to California in number of public schools and in public school enrollment. Only California has a more extensive public college and university system. In 1998, 78.3% of the population 25 years old and over had completed at least four years of high school, and 23.3% had four or more years of college. Enrollment in Texas's public schools in 1997 totaled 3.89 million. Expenditures for public elementary and secondary schools amounted to $5,168 per student in 1995/96, 31st among the states.

Institutions of higher education in 1997 included 35 public senior colleges and universities, 50 public community college campuses, and 38 private institutions with a combined enrollment of 969,283. The leading public universities are Texas A&M (Agricultural and Mechanical) in College Station and the University of Texas in Austin. Each institution is now the center of its own university system, including campuses in several other cities. Other state-supported institutions are the University of Houston and Texas Tech (Lubbock).

The oldest private institution still active in the state is Baylor University (1845) at Waco. Other major private universities include Lamar (Beaumont), Rice (Houston), Southern Methodist (Dallas), and Texas Christian (Fort Worth). Well-

Photo credit: Courtesy of Austin Convention & Visitors Bureau.

Rowing on Town Lake in Austin.

known black-oriented institutions of higher learning include Texas Southern University in Houston.

33 ARTS

Texas has five major symphony orchestras—the Dallas Symphony, Houston Symphony, San Antonio Symphony, Austin Symphony, and Fort Worth Symphony—and 25 orchestras in other cities. The Houston Grand Opera performs at Jones Hall. Other opera companies perform regularly in Beaumont, Dallas, El Paso, Fort Worth, and San Antonio. All these cities also have resident dance companies, as do several other Texas cities.

34 LIBRARIES AND MUSEUMS

Public libraries in Texas, serving 246 counties in 1998, had a combined book stock of 49.7 million volumes and a circulation of 77.2 million volumes. The largest municipal library systems are those of Houston, Dallas, and San Antonio. The University of Texas at Austin, noted for outstanding collections in the humanities and in Latin American studies, had 7.2 million volumes in 1998. The Lyndon B. Johnson Presidential Library is also located in Austin, as are the state archives.

Among the state's 389 museums are Austin's Texas Memorial Museum; the

Dallas Museum of Fine Arts and the Dallas Museum of Art; and the Fort Worth Art Museums. Houston has the Museum of Fine Arts, Contemporary Arts Museum, and at least 30 galleries. National historic sites in Texas are Fort Davis, President Johnson's boyhood home in Blanco County, and the Alamo.

35 COMMUNICATIONS

In 1999, 92.4% of the occupied housing units in Texas had telephones. Texas had 817 radio stations (294 AM, 523 FM) in 2000, and 145 television stations. Twelve Texan television stations broadcast in Spanish. A total of 439,135 domain names were registered for the Internet in 2000.

36 PRESS

In 1998, Texas had 88 morning, evening, and all-day dailies and 85 Sunday papers. The newspapers with the largest daily circulations were the *Houston Chronicle* (555,763); the *Dallas Morning News* (479,863); and the *San Antonio Express News* (218,661). In 1997, there were 437 weekly newspapers.

37 TOURISM, TRAVEL, AND RECREATION

Outstanding attractions are found throughout the state. East Texas has one of the state's oldest cities, Nacogdoches, with the nation's oldest public thoroughfare and a reconstruction of the Old Stone Fort, a Spanish trading post dating from 1779. Tyler, which bills itself as the "rose capital of the world," features a 28-acre

(11-hectare) municipal rose garden. The Gulf Coast region of southeastern Texas offers the Lyndon B. Johnson Space Center, the Astrodome sports stadium and adjacent Astroworld amusement park, plus many museums, galleries, and shops. Also, Spindletop Park in Beaumont commemorates the state's first great oil gusher; and Galveston offers sandy beaches and deep-sea fishing.

The Hill Country of south-central Texas encompasses many tourist sites, including the state capitol in Austin and the Lyndon B. Johnson National Historic Site. South Texas has the state's most famous historic site—the Alamo, in San Antonio. The Great Plains region of the Texas panhandle offers Palo Duro Canyon—Texas's largest state park, covering 16,402 acres (6,638 hectares).

Texas' growing park system attracted 24.2 million visitors in 1995. In addition to Palo Duro Canyon, notable state parks include Big Creek, Brazos Island, Caddo Lake, and Dinosaur Valley. State historical parks include San Jacinto Battleground. Hunting and fishing are extremely popular in Texas; there were 1.5 million hunting licenses and 2.5 million fishing licenses issued in 1995.

38 SPORTS

Texas has nine major league professional sports teams: the Texas Rangers (Arlington) and Houston Astros of Major League Baseball; the Dallas Cowboys of the National Football League; the Dallas Stars of the National Hockey League; the Houston Rockets, San Antonio Spurs, and Dallas Mavericks of the National Basketball Association; the Houston Comets of the Women's National Basketball Association; and the Dallas Burn of Major League Soccer.

Quarter-horse racing is popular, and rodeo is a leading spectator sport. Pari-mutual betting was legalized in the early 1990s; by 1996, attendance at Thorough-bred horse races was 647,000, and 296,500 at dog races. Participant sports popular with Texans include hunting, fishing, horseback riding, boating, swimming, tennis, and golf. State professional and amateur golf tournaments are held annually, as are numerous rodeos.

39 FAMOUS TEXANS

Two native sons of Texas have served as president of the US. Dwight D. Eisenhower (1890–1969), the 34th president, was born in Denison. Lyndon Baines Johnson (1908–73), the 36th president, was the only lifelong resident of the state to serve in that office, serving first as vice-president under John F. Kennedy. Texas's other native vice-president was John Nance Garner (1868–1967), former speaker of the US House of Representatives. George Bush (b.Massachusetts, 1924) was elected president in 1988 on the Republican ticket and his son, George W. Bush (b.Connecticut, 1946), was elected president in 2000.

Tom C. Clark (1899–1977) served as an associate justice on the US Supreme Court from 1949 to 1967. Texas native Sandra Day O'Connor (b.1930) became the first female associate justice on the US Supreme Court.

Photo credit: EPD Photos/LBJ Library

Lyndon Baynes Johnson, 36th president of the United States, is shown here taking the oath of office on Air Force One after the assassination of John F. Kennedy.

The state's most famous legislative leader was Sam Rayburn (1882–1961), who served the longest tenure in the nation's history as Speaker of the US House of Representatives. Barbara C. Jordan (1936–96) was a forceful member of the House Judiciary Committee during its impeachment deliberations in 1974.

Famous figures in early Texas history include Moses Austin (b.Connecticut, 1761–1821) and his son, Stephen F. Austin (b.Virginia, 1793–1836), often called the "father of Texas." Samuel "Sam" Houston (b.Virginia, 1793–1863), adopted as a youth by the Cherokee, won enduring fame as commander in chief of the Texas revolutionary army and president of the Texas Republic.

Texas military heroes include Audie Murphy (1924–71), the most decorated soldier of World War II (and later a film actor), and Admiral of the Fleet Chester W. Nimitz (1885–1966). Figures of history and legend include James Bowie (b.Kentucky, 1796?–1836), popularly credited with the invention of the bowie knife, and frontiersman David "Davy" Crockett (b.Tennessee, 1786–1836), both of whom lost their lives at the Alamo.

Howard Hughes (1905–76), an industrialist, aviation pioneer, film producer, and casino owner, became a fabulously wealthy recluse in his later years. H. Ross Perot (b.1930) became a billionaire as a computer software developer and was an independent presidential candidate in 1992 and 1996. Dan Rather (b.1931) is known nationwide as a television reporter and anchorman.

Among Texas-born musicians, Scott Joplin (1868–1917) and Blind Lemon Jefferson (1897–1930) were famous ragtime and blues musicians, respectively. Buddy Holly (Charles Holley, 1936–59) was an early rock and roll singer. Musicians Trini Lopez (b.1937) and Johnny Rodriguez (b.1951) have earned popular followings based on their Mexican-American backgrounds. Willie Nelson (b.1933) and Waylon Jennings (b.1937) are prominent country musicians.

The imposing list of Texas athletes is headed by Mildred "Babe" Didrikson Zaharias (1913–56), who gained fame as an All-American basketball player in 1930, won two gold medals in track and field in the 1932 Olympics, and was the leading woman golfer during the 1940s and early 1950s. Another Texan, John Arthur "Jack" Johnson (1878–1946), was boxing's first black heavyweight champion.

Among other Texas sports greats are baseball Hall of Famers Tris Speaker (1888–1958), Rogers Hornsby (1896–1963), Ernie Banks (b.1931), and Joe Morgan (b.1943); golfers Ben Hogan (1912–97), Byron Nelson (b.1912), and Lee Trevino (b.1939); auto-racing driver A(nthony) J(oseph) Foyt (b.1935); and jockey William Lee "Willie" Shoemaker (b.1931). Nolan Ryan, pitching giant, was born 31 January 1947 in Refugio.

40 BIBLIOGRAPHY

Aylesworth, Thomas G. *The Southwest: Colorado, New Mexico, Texas*. New York: Chelsea House, 1996.

Bredeson, Carmen. *Texas*. New York: Benchmark Books, 1997.

Hanson-Harding, Alexandra. *Texas*. New York: Children's Press, 2001.

McComb, David G. *Texas, an Illustrated History*. New York: Oxford University Press, 1995.

Richardson, Rupert N., et al. *Texas: The Lone Star State*. 4th ed. Englewood Cliffs, N.J.: Prentice-Hall, 1981.

Turner, Robyn. *Texas Traditions: the Culture of the Lone Star State*. Boston: Little, Brown, 1996.

Welsbacher, Anne. *Texas*. Minneapolis: ABDO & Daughters, 1998.

Web sites

Lone Star Junction. A Texas History Resource. [Online] Available http://www.lsjunction.com Accessed May 31, 2001.

State of Texas. State of Texas Government Information: All About Texas for Texans, Future Texans, and Visitors. [Online] Available http://www.texas.gov/ Accessed May 31, 2001.

TravelTex. TEXAS: It's Like a Whole Other Country. [Online] Available http://www.traveltex.com Accessed May 31, 2001.

UTAH

State of Utah

ORIGIN OF STATE NAME: Named for the Ute Indians.

NICKNAME: The Beehive State.

CAPITAL: Salt Lake City.

ENTERED UNION: 4 January 1896 (45th).

SONG: "Utah, We Love Thee."

MOTTO: Industry.

COAT OF ARMS: In the center, a shield, flanked by American flags, shows a beehive with the state motto and six arrows above, sego lilies on either side, and the numerals "1847" (the year the Mormons settled in Utah) below. Perched atop the shield is an American eagle.

FLAG: Inside a thin gold circle, the coat of arms and the year of statehood are centered on a blue field, fringed with gold.

OFFICIAL SEAL: The coat of arms with the words "The Great Seal of the State of Utah 1896" surrounding it.

ANIMAL: Elk.

BIRD: Sea gull.

FISH: Bonneville cutthroat trout.

FLOWER: Sego lily.

TREE: Blue spruce.

GEM: Topaz.

EMBLEM: Beehive.

TIME: 5 AM MST = noon GMT.

1 LOCATION AND SIZE

Located in the Rocky Mountain region of the western US, Utah ranks 11th in size among the 50 states. The state's area totals 84,899 square miles (219,899 square kilometers). Utah extends 275 miles (443 kilometers) east-west and 345 miles (555 kilometers) north-south. The total boundary length is 1,226 miles (1,973 kilometers).

2 TOPOGRAPHY

The eastern and southern two-thirds of Utah belong to the Colorado Plateau. The Rocky Mountains are represented by the Bear River, Wasatch, and Uinta ranges in the north and northeast. The state's highest point is Kings Peak at an altitude of 13,528 feet (4,123 meters).

The arid, sparsely populated Great Basin dominates the western third of the state. To the north are the Great Salt Lake and the Great Salt Lake Desert (containing the Bonneville Salt Flats). Lake Powell is formed by the Glen Canyon Dam on the Colorado River. Other important rivers include the Green, the Sevier, and the Bear.

3 CLIMATE

The climate of Utah is generally semiarid to arid. At Salt Lake City, the temperature ranges from 28°F (–2°C) in January to 77°F (25°C) in July. The record high temperature, 117°F (47°C), was set in 1985; the record low temperature, set the same year, was –69°F (–56°C). The average precipitation varies from less than 5 inches (12.7 centimeters) in the west to over 40 inches (102 centimeters) in the mountains.

4 PLANTS AND ANIMALS

Botanists have recognized more than 4,000 floral species in Utah's six major life zones. Common trees and shrubs include four species of pine and three of juniper, as well as the Utah oak, Joshua tree, and blue spruce (the state tree). The sego lily is the state flower. Mule deer are the most common of Utah's large mammals. Other mammals include pronghorn antelope, lynx, and grizzly and black bears. Among native bird species are the great horned owl and plain titmouse. Among Utah's 28 endangered animal species are the bald eagle and Utah prairie dog.

5 ENVIRONMENTAL PROTECTION

Air pollution is a serious problem along the Wasatch Front where 70% of the state's population resides. High levels of ozone and carbon monoxide affect communities in Salt Lake, Weber, and Utah counties. Another environmental problem is the pollution of Great Salt Lake by industrial waste. As of 1998, Utah had 16 hazardous waste sites. The State has 30 municipal

Utah Population Profile

Total population in 2000:	2,233,169
Population change, 1990–2000:	29.6%
Hispanic or Latino†:	9.0%
Population by race	
One race:	97.9%
White:	89.2%
Black or African American:	0.8%
American Indian/Alaska Native:	1.3%
Asian:	1.7%
Native Hawaiian/Pacific Islander:	0.7%
Some other race:	4.2%
Two or more races:	2.1%

Population by Age Group

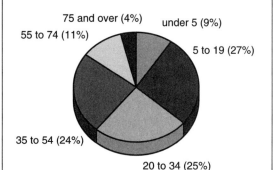

75 and over (4%)
under 5 (9%)
55 to 74 (11%)
5 to 19 (27%)
35 to 54 (24%)
20 to 34 (25%)

Top Cities by Population

City	Population	% change 1990–2000
Salt Lake City	181,743	13.6
West Valley City	108,896	25.2
Provo	105,166	21.1
Sandy	88,418	17.8
Orem	84,324	24.8
Ogden	77,226	20.8
West Jordan	68,336	59.3
Layton	58,474	39.9
Taylorsville	57,439	NA
St. George	49,663	74.2

Notes: †A person of Hispanic or Latino origin may be of any race. NA indicates that data are not available.
Sources: U.S. Census Bureau. Public Information Office. *Demographic Profiles.* [Online] Available http://www.census.gov/Press-Release/www/2001/demoprofile.html. Accessed June 1, 2001. U.S. Census Bureau. *Census 2000: Redistricting Data.* Press release issued by the Redistricting Data Office. Washington, D.C., March, 2001.

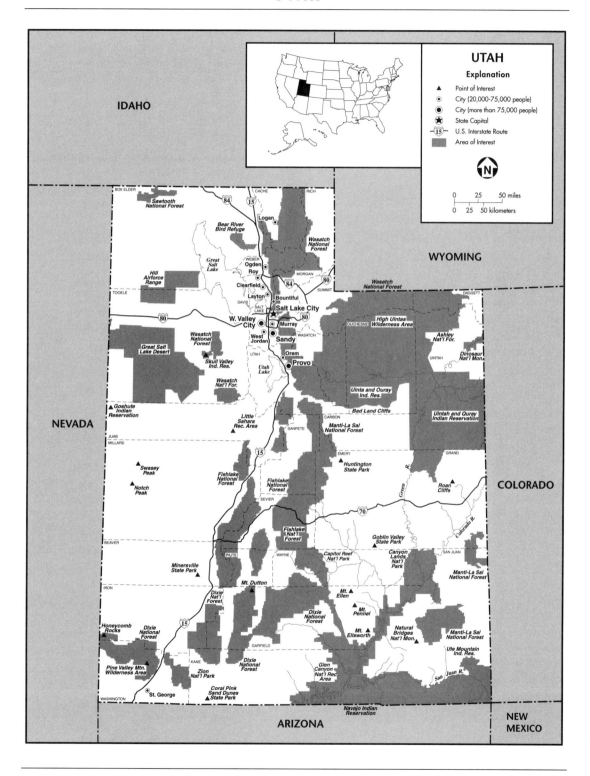

Photo credit: Jack K. Blonk.

Zion National Park.

landfills and 5 curbside recycling programs. Utah has one municipal incinerator.

[6] POPULATION

At the 2000 census, Utah had a population of 2,233,169, surpassing Nevada to rank 34th in the US. A population of 2.41 million is projected for 2005. Utah's population density was 27.2 persons per square mile (10.5 persons per square kilometer) in 2000. Salt Lake City is Utah's most populous city, with a 2000 population of 181,743. Approximately 59% of state residents live in its metropolitan region. Other major cities and their 2000 populations included West Valley City, 108,896; Provo,

105,166; Sandy, 88,418; and Orem, 84,324. Utah has the country's youngest population. The median age is only 27.1 years of age, considerably younger than the national average of 35.3. About 36% of the country is 19 years of age and younger.

[7] ETHNIC GROUPS

Hispanic Americans, who may be of any race, constitute the largest ethnic minority in Utah, with an estimated 1997 population of 133,400. About 50,900 Asian-Pacific peoples (primarily Japanese, Chinese and Vietnamese) lived in Utah in 1997, accounting for 2.5% of the popula-

Utah Population by Race

Census 2000 was the first national census in which the instructions to respondents said, "Mark one or more races." This table shows the number of people who are of one, two, or three or more races. For those claiming two races, the number of people belonging to the various categories is listed. The U.S. government conducts a census of the population every ten years.

	Number	Percent
Total population	2,233,169	100.0
One race	2,185,974	97.9
Two races	44,560	2.0
White *and* Black or African American	4,188	0.2
White *and* American Indian/Alaska Native	7,917	0.4
White *and* Asian	7,550	0.3
White *and* Native Hawaiian/Pacific Islander	3,316	0.1
White *and* some other race	15,994	0.7
Black or African American *and* American Indian/Alaska Native	388	—
Black or African American *and* Asian	293	—
Black or African American *and* Native Hawaiian/Pacific Islander	154	—
Black or African American *and* some other race	821	—
American Indian/Alaska Native *and* Asian	210	—
American Indian/Alaska Native *and* Native Hawaiian/Pacific Islander	179	—
American Indian/Alaska Native *and* some other race	962	—
Asian *and* Native Hawaiian/Pacific Islander	790	—
Asian *and* some other race	1,206	0.1
Native Hawaiian/Pacific Islander *and* some other race	592	—
Three or more races	2,635	0.1

Source: U.S. Census Bureau. *Census 2000: Redistricting Data*. Press release issued by the Redistricting Data Office. Washington, D.C., March, 2001. A dash (—) indicates that the percent is less than 0.1.

tion. Native Americans were estimated at 29,100 in 1997 (1.4%). Utah also had an estimated 17,500 black Americans in 1997 (0.9%).

8 LANGUAGES

Utah English is primarily a merger of Northern and Midland dialects carried west by the Mormons, whose original New York dialect later incorporated features from southern Ohio and central Illinois. In 1990, 92.2% of all state residents five years of age or older spoke only English at home. Other languages spoken at home, and the number of people who spoke them, included Spanish, 51,945; and German, 11,233.

9 RELIGIONS

The dominant religious group in Utah is the Church of Jesus Christ of Latter-day Saints, popularly known as the Mormons. The church was founded by Joseph Smith, Jr., in 1830, the same year he published the *Book of Mormon*, the group's sacred text. The Latter-day Saints had 1,236,242 members in Utah in 1990. Other leading Christian denominations (and their 1990 memberships) include Presbyterians (6,658), Episcopalians (5,436), and various Baptist

Photo credit: EPD Photos.

A statue of Brigham Young stands near the Temple of the Church of Jesus Christ of Latter-day Saints in downtown Salt Lake City.

groups. In 1990 there were 66,316 Roman Catholics and an estimated 2,950 Jews.

10 TRANSPORTATION

Utah, where the golden spike was driven in 1869 to mark the completion of the first transcontinental railroad, had 2,247 rail miles (3,615 kilometers) of track in 1998. Utah in 1997 had 42,970 miles (69,139 kilometers) of public roads and streets. There were 1.52 million registered motor

vehicles. By far the busiest airfield of the 88 total was Salt Lake City International Airport, handling 100,029 departures in 1996 and boarding 9.46 million passengers.

11 HISTORY

Utah's historic Native American groups are primarily Shoshonean: the Ute branch in the eastern two-thirds of the state, the Goshute of the western desert, and the Southern Paiute of southwestern Utah. The Athapaskan-speaking Navaho of southeastern Utah migrated from western Canada, arriving not long before the Spaniards. White settlement from 1847 led to wars between whites and Native Americans in 1853–54 and 1865–68, with many Native Americans finally removed to reservations.

Mexicans and Spaniards entered Utah in 1765. In July 1776, a party led by two Franciscan priests, Francisco Atanasio Domínguez and Silvestre Vélez de Escalanta, explored the region. Trade between Santa Fe, the capital of the Spanish province of New Mexico, and the tribes of Utah was fairly well established by the early 1800s. Until 1848, the 1,200-miles (1,900-kilometers) Spanish Trail, the longest segment of which lies in Utah, was the main route through the Southwest.

When Joseph Smith, Jr., founder of the Church of Jesus Christ of Latter-day Saints (Mormons), was lynched in 1844, Brigham Young and other Mormon leaders decided to move west. By April 1847, a pioneer company of Mormons was on its way to Utah. The church organization served as the first government.

Deseret

After the Treaty of Guadalupe-Hidalgo (1848) gave the US title to much of the Southwest, the Mormons established the provisional state of Deseret. Congress refused to admit Deseret to the Union, choosing instead to create the Utah Territory, which encompassed, in addition to present-day Utah, most of Nevada and parts of Wyoming and Colorado. By the 1860s, Utah was assigned its present boundaries.

The territorial period lasted for 46 years, marked by immigration, growth, and conflict. Mormon militia clashed with federal troops in the so-called Utah War of 1857–58, which left Mormon leaders hostile to federal authorities. Almost 98% of Utah's total population was Mormon until after 1870, and the Mormon way of life dominated politics, economics, and social and cultural activities. As church president, Brigham Young remained the principal figure in the territory until his death in 1877.

In 1863, with the discovery of silver-bearing ore in Bingham Canyon, a boom in precious metals began, and those connected with mining—mostly non-Mormons—began to exert influence in the territory. Several factors made the non-Mormon minority fearful of Mormon domination. These included the lack of free public schools, new immigration by Mormon converts, the mingling of church and state, and—most notably—the Mormon practice of polygamy (marrying multiple wives). This practice was finally renounced by the Mormons in 1890.

Photo credit: Jack K. Blonk.

Prehistoric drawings on Newspaper Rock.

Statehood

A constitutional convention was held in 1895, and statehood became a reality on 4 January 1896. The early 20th century saw further growth of the mineral industry. Gradually, modern cities emerged, along with power plants, interurban railroads, and highways. By 1920, nearly half the population lived along the Wasatch Front. The influx of various ethnic groups diversified the state's social and cultural life, and the proportion of Mormons in the total population declined to about 68% by 1920.

Utah businesses enjoyed the postwar prosperity of the 1920s. On the other hand, mining and agriculture were depressed throughout the 1920s and 1930s, decades marked by increased union activity, particularly in the coal and copper industries. The depression of the 1930s hit Utah especially hard. Severe droughts hurt farmers in 1931 and 1934, and high freight rates limited the expansion of manufacturing. With the coming of World War II, increased demand for food revived Utah's agriculture, and important military installations and war-related industries brought new jobs to the state.

In the years since World War II, the state's population has more than doubled. Politics generally reflect prevailing Mormon attitudes and tend to be conservative. The state successfully opposed plans for storing nerve-gas bombs in Utah and for the location in the western desert of an MX missile system.

Utah had one of the nation's fastest growing economies in the 1990s, and one of the lowest rates of unemployment. A major issue at the end of the 20th century is the protection for the environment versus residential and commercial development.

12 STATE GOVERNMENT

The state legislature consists of a 29-member senate and a 75-seat house of representatives. Senators serve for four years, representatives for two. The chief executive officers, all elected for four-year terms, include the governor, lieutenant governor, attorney general, treasurer, and auditor. Gubernatorial vetoes may be overridden by two-thirds of the elected members of each house of the legislature.

Utah Governors: 1896–2001

1896–1905	Heber Manning Wells	Republican
1905–1909	John Christopher Cutler	Republican
1909–1917	William Spry	Republican
1917–1921	Simon Bamberger	Democrat
1921–1925	Charles Rendell Mabey	Republican
1925–1933	George Henry Dern	Democrat
1933–1941	Henry Hooper Blood	Democrat
1941–1949	Herbert Brown Maw	Democrat
1949–1957	Joseph Bracken Lee	Republican
1957–1965	George Dewey Clyde	Republican
1965–1977	Calvin Lewellyn Rampton	Democrat
1977–1985	Scott Milne Matheson	Democrat
1985–1993	Norman Howard Bangerter	Republican
1993–	Michael Okerlund Leavitt	Republican

13 POLITICAL PARTIES

In November 2000, Utah residents cast 67% of their presidential votes for Republican George W. Bush and 26% for Democrat Al Gore. There were 1,115,821 registered voters in 1998. Orrin Hatch was reelected to a fifth term in the US Senate in 2000. As of the 2000 election, the US House delegation consisted of two Republicans and one Democrat. The state house had 51 Republicans and 24 Democrats, while the state senate had 20 Republicans and 9 Democrats.

Utah Presidential Vote by Major Political Parties, 1948–2000

YEAR	UTAH WINNER	DEMOCRAT	REPUBLICAN
1948	*Truman (D)	149,151	124,402
1952	*Eisenhower (R)	135,364	194,190
1956	*Eisenhower (R)	118,364	215,631
1960	Nixon (R)	169,248	205,361
1964	*Johnson (D)	219,628	181,785
1968	*Nixon (R)	156,665	238,728
1972	*Nixon (R)	126,284	323,643
1976	Ford (R)	182,110	337,908
1980	*Reagan (R)	124,266	439,687
1984	*Reagan (R)	155,369	469,105
1988	*Bush (R)	207,343	428,442
1992**	Bush (R)	183,429	322,632
1996**	Dole (R)	221,633	361,911
2000	*Bush (R)	203,053	515,096

* Won US presidential election.
**Independent candidate Ross Perot received 203,400 votes in 1992 and 66,461 votes in 1996.

Downtown Salt Lake City.

14 LOCAL GOVERNMENT

Utah has 29 counties, governed by elected commissioners. Other elected county officials include clerk-auditor, sheriff, assessor, recorder, treasurer, county attorney, and surveyor. There were 230 municipal governments in 1997.

15 JUDICIAL SYSTEM

Utah's highest court is the supreme court, consisting of a chief justice and four other justices. There are 35 district court judges. In 1984, to ease the supreme court's caseload, Utahns approved a constitutional amendment allowing the legislature to create an intermediate court. In 1998, the FBI reported a crime-index total of 5,506 crimes per 100,000 inhabitants. Prisoners under jurisdiction of state and federal correctional facilities numbered 4,469 in 1999. In 1977, Utah became the first state in over a decade to carry out a death sentence (by firing squad) of prisoner, Gary Gilmore.

16 MIGRATION

After the initial exodus of Latter-day Saints from the eastern US to Utah, Mormon missionaries attracted other immigrants to the state, and some 90,000 foreign converts arrived between 1850 and 1905. Utah had a net gain from migration of 176,000 between 1940 and 1985. From 1985 to 1990, there was a net loss from migration of 10,500. During 1990–98, the population increased 22%, making it the 4th fastest growing state in the US.

17 ECONOMY

Trade replaced government as the leading employer in Utah in 1980. With more than 70% of Utah lands under US control and some 31,000 civilian workers on federal payrolls—and others employed by defense industries or the military—the federal presence in Utah is a major economic force in the state. Utah suffered disproportionately from cuts in the federal military budget in the late 1980s and early 1990s.

18 INCOME

Total personal income was $46.7 billion in 1998 (35th among the 50 states). Per capita (per person) income in 1998 averaged $22,240 (41st). In 1998, 8.5% of all state residents were living below the federal poverty level.

19 INDUSTRY

Utah's diversified manufacturing is concentrated in Salt Lake City, Weber, Utah, and Cache counties. Total employment in major industries was 824,120 at the end of 1997. The total estimated value of shipments by manufacturers in 1997 was almost $24 billion. The main industry groups by payroll were services, retail trade, transportation and utilities, wholesale trade, and construction. Among the state's largest manufacturing employers are Thiokol Corporation (aerospace equipment) and WordPerfect Corporation (software).

20 LABOR

In mid-1998, Utah's civilian labor force amounted to 1.06 million, with an unemployment rate of 3.8%. The union movement has weakened since the 1980s, when mechanization eliminated thousands of mining and manufacturing jobs. In 1998, 6.8% of Utah's workers belonged to labor unions.

21 AGRICULTURE

Utah ranked 36th in the US in value of farm marketing in 1999, with $954 million. Crops accounted for $241 million; livestock and livestock products for $713 million. The chief crops in 1998 were hay, 2.8 million tons; wheat, 8.8 million bushels; and tart cherries, 33 million pounds.

22 DOMESTICATED ANIMALS

Livestock and livestock products account for over three-fourths of Utah's agricultural income. In 1999 there were 890,000 cattle on Utah farms and ranches. There were 380,000 hogs and pigs in 1998. Dairy farms had 91,000 milk cows in 1997, producing 1.5 billion pounds (667 million kilograms) of milk.

23 FISHING

Fishing in Utah is for recreation only. Fish farms distribute trout for restoration or commercialization purposes.

Photo credit: Jack K. Blonk.

Harvest in Loa.

24 FORESTRY

Utah had 15.7 million acres (6.35 million hectares) of forestland in 1997. By 1999, 8.1 million acres (3.3 million hectares) were in the state's nine national forests. Only 4.7 million acres (1.2 million hectares) were classified as commercial timberland.

25 MINING

The total value of nonfuel mineral production in Utah was approximately $1.83 billion in 1998, with metals accounting for 80%. In 1998, Utah was second in the nation in the output of copper and potash, and third in mercury. It was the only US source of mined beryllium—the largest operating beryllium mine in the world is in Juab County.

26 ENERGY AND POWER

During 1999, electric utilities in the state produced 35.2 billion kilowatt hours of power. Some 96% of this was derived from coal-fired power plants. Utah has no nuclear power plants. Crude oil production was 19.3 million barrels in 1997, and natural gas production totaled 257 billion cubic feet (7.2 billion cubic meters). The state's reserves of bituminous coal were estimated at nearly 433 million tons in 1998, the entire production coming from underground mines.

27 COMMERCE

Wholesale sales totaled $23 billion in 1997; retail sales were $20 billion in the same year–all heavily concentrated in the Salt Lake City-Ogden area. Foreign exports of Utah's goods totaled $3 billion in 1998.

28 PUBLIC FINANCE

The annual budget is prepared by the State Budget Office and submitted by the governor to the legislature for amendment and approval. The state revenues for fiscal year 1997 were $7.72 billion; expenditures were $6.82 billion. The state's outstanding debt totaled $2.45 billion as of 1997, or $1,190 per capita (per person).

29 TAXATION

The main source of state revenue is a 4.875% general sales and gross receipts tax. Utah also taxes personal and corporate income. Taxes are levied on motor fuels, alcoholic beverages, tobacco products, and other items. Property taxes are the main source of local revenue. Utah's state tax collections in 1997/98 totaled $3.4 billion, or $1,647 per person (36th among the states). Utah's total federal income tax burden was $6.9 billion in 1995, while federal funding totaled $8.5 billion.

30 HEALTH

In 1997, Utah's birth rate of 21.3 per 1,000 population was the highest in the country, and the death rate of 554.6 per 100,000 population. Death rates per 100,000 population for heart disease, cancer, cerebrovascular disease, and accidents were lower than US averages, while the suicide rate was above the national norm. In 1998, there were 41 hospitals in the state, with 4,010 beds. The average hospital expense per inpatient day was $1,223 in 1998. Utah had the lowest proportion of adult smokers in the US in 1998.

31 HOUSING

In 1999, there were an estimated 731,000 housing units in Utah. An additional 20,900 units were authorized for construction in 1998 with a total value of $2.2 billion. The median monthly costs for owners (with a mortgage) and renters in 1990 were $667 and $369, respectively. In 1990, the median home value was $68,900.

32 EDUCATION

Utahns are among the nation's leaders in educational attainments. In 1998, Utah had the second-highest proportion of adult high school graduates—89.3%. Nearly 27.6% had four years or more of college. In 1997, Utah public schools had an enrollment of 482,957. Expenditures on public elementary and secondary education averaged $3,670 per pupil (51st in the nation) in 1995/96.

Enrollment at Utah's higher educational institutions totaled 157,891 in 1997. Major public institutions include the University of Utah (Salt Lake City), Utah State University (Logan), and Weber State College (Ogden). Brigham Young University (Provo), affiliated with the Latter-day Saints, is the main private institution.

33 ARTS

Music has a central role in Utah's cultural life. The Utah Symphony (Salt Lake City) has become one of the nation's leading orchestras. The Mormon Tabernacle Choir has won world renown, and Ballet West is ranked among the nation's leading dance companies. The Utah Opera Company was founded in 1976. Art museums and galleries include Utah State University's Nora Eccles Harrison Museum in Logan and the LDS Church Museum of Art and History in Salt Lake City. As of 1999, Utah had 450 arts associations and 60 local arts groups.

34 LIBRARIES AND MUSEUMS

In 1998, Utah had 69 public libraries with a circulation of 19.4 million. In 1996, the combined book stock of public libraries was 5.94 million. The leading academic libraries are the University of Utah (Salt Lake City) and Brigham Young University (Provo). Utah, in 2000, has 60 museums, notably the Utah Museum of Natural History and Utah Museum of Fine Arts in Salt Lake City, the Hill Aerospace Museum near Ogden, and the Museum of Peoples and Cultures at Provo.

35 COMMUNICATIONS

In 1999, 95.6% of Utah's occupied houses had telephones. A total of 99 radio stations broadcast in Utah in 2000; 39 were AM stations, and 60 were FM. There were 19 television stations in the same year. A total of 64,217 domain names were registered on the Internet in 2000.

36 PRESS

Utah in 1998 had six daily newspapers and six Sunday papers. Leading daily newspapers with their 1998 daily circulation are the *Salt Lake City Tribune* (129,612); the *Deseret News* (61,074); and the *Ogden Standard-Examiner* (60,996).

37 TOURISM, TRAVEL, AND RECREATION

Temple Square and Pioneer Trail State Park are among the leading attractions of Salt Lake City. At the Bonneville Salt Flats, experimental automobiles have set world land-speed records. Under federal jurisdiction are 13 national parks, Glen Canyon National Recreation Area; 7 national monuments; and 1 national historical site, Golden Spike. Mountain and rock climbing, skiing, fishing, and hunting are major recreations. Utah's 35 state parks had over 7 million visitors in 1995. Park City was the site of the 2002 Winter Olympics.

38 SPORTS

Utah has two major league professional sports teams, the Utah Jazz of the National Basketball Association and the Utah Starzz of the Women's National Basketball Association. Basketball is also popular at the college level. Various skiing events are held at Utah's world class resort in Park City.

39 FAMOUS UTAHNS

George Sutherland (b.England, 1862–1942) served as an associate justice of the US Supreme Court (1922–38). Other important federal officeholders from Utah include Ezra Taft Benson (b.Idaho, 1899–1994), President Dwight Eisenhower's secretary of agriculture and leader of the Mormon church from 1985 until his death. Jacob "Jake" Garn (b.1932), first elected to the US Senate in 1974, was launched into space aboard the space shuttle in 1985.

The dominant figure in Utah history is undoubtedly Brigham Young (b.Vermont, 1801–77), leader of the Mormons for more than 30 years. Utah's most important scientist is John A. Widtsoe (b.Norway, 1872–1952), whose pioneering research in dryland farming revolutionized agricultural practices. Frank Zamboni (1901–88) invented the ice-resurfacing machine that bears his name.

Utah's artists and writers include sculptor Mahonri M. Young (1877–1957); painter Henry L. A. Culmer (b.England, 1854–1914); author-critic Bernard A. DeVoto (1897–1955); and novelist Edward Abbey (b.1927). Donald "Donny" Osmond (b.1957) and his sister Marie (b.1959) are Utah's best-known popular singers, and comedienne Roseanne (b.1952) is also a native. Maurice Abravanel (Greece, 1903–93) conducted the Utah Symphony for many years. Sports figures of note are former world middleweight boxing champion Gene Fullmer (b.1931); Merlin Olsen (b.1940), a tackle on the Los Angeles Rams who went on to become an actor; and Steve Young (b.1961), a quarterback on the San Francisco 49ers.

40 BIBLIOGRAPHY

Alexander, Thomas. *Mormons and Gentiles: A History of Salt Lake City*. Boulder, Colo.: Pruett Publishing, 1984.

Aylesworth, Thomas G. *The West: Arizona, Nevada, Utah*. New York: Chelsea House Publishers, 1992.

Ellsworth, Samuel G. *Utah's Heritage*. Salt Lake City: Peregrine Smith, 1984.

Feeney, Kathy. *Utah Facts and Symbols*. Mankato, Minn.: Bridgestone Books, 2000.

Fradin, Dennis B. *Utah*. Chicago: Childrens Press, 1993.

Joseph, Paul. *Utah*. Edina, Minn.: Abdo & Daughters, 1998.

Kent, Deborah. *Utah*. New York: Children's Press, 2000.

Stefoff, Rebecca. *Utah*. New York: Benchmark Books, 2001.

Web sites

State of Utah. Welcome to the State of Utah. [Online] Available http://www.utah.gov/ Accessed May 31, 2001.

Utah Travel Council. Utah! Travel and Adventure Online. [Online] Available http://www.utah.com Accessed May 31, 2001.

VERMONT

ORIGIN OF STATE NAME: Derived from the French words *vert* (green) and *mont* (mountain).

NICKNAME: The Green Mountain State.

CAPITAL: Montpelier.

ENTERED UNION: 4 March 1791 (14th).

SONG: "These Green Mountains"

MOTTO: Freedom and Unity.

COAT OF ARMS: Rural Vermont is represented by a pine tree in the center, three sheaves of grain on the left, and a cow on the right, with a background of fields and mountains. A deer crests the shield. Below are crossed pine branches and the state name and motto.

FLAG: The coat of arms on a field of dark blue.

OFFICIAL SEAL: Bisecting Vermont's golden seal is a row of wooded hills above the state name. The upper half has a spearhead, pine tree, cow, and two sheaves of wheat, while two more sheaves and the state motto fill the lower half.

ANIMAL: Morgan horse.

BIRD: Hermit thrush.

FISH: Brook trout (cold water); walleye pike (warm water).

FLOWER: Red clover.

TREE: Sugar maple.

INSECT: Honeybee.

BEVERAGE: Milk.

TIME: 7 AM EST = noon GMT.

1 LOCATION AND SIZE

Situated in the northeastern US, Vermont is the second largest of the six New England states, and ranks 43d in size among the 50 states. Vermont's total area is 9,614 square miles (24,900 square kilometers). Its maximum east-west extension is 97 miles (156 kilometers); its maximum north-south extension is 158 miles (254 kilometers). Vermont's total boundary length is 561 miles (903 kilometers). The state's territory includes several islands and the lower part of a peninsula jutting south into Lake Champlain.

2 TOPOGRAPHY

The Green Mountains are Vermont's most prominent physical feature, including Mt. Mansfield, at 4,393 feet (1,339 meters), the state's highest point. A much lower range, the Taconic Mountains, straddles the New York–Vermont border. To their north are the Valley of Vermont and the Champlain Valley. The hills and valleys of the Vermont piedmont lie east of the Green Mountains, and the Northeast Highlands are near the New Hampshire border. The Connecticut River forms the border between Vermont and New Hampshire. Vermont's major inland rivers are the Missisquoi, Lamoille, and Winooski. The state includes parts of Lake Champlain and Lake Memphremagog.

3 CLIMATE

Burlington's mean temperature ranges from 17°F (–8°C) in January to 70°F (21°C) in July. Winters are generally colder and summer nights cooler in the Green Mountains. The record high temperature for the state is 105°F (41°C), registered in 1911; the record low, –50°F (–46°C), occurred in 1933. Vermont's average annual precipitation is 40 inches (102 centimeters). Annual snowfall ranges from 55 inches (140 centimeters) in the lowlands to 100 inches (254 centimeters) in the mountain areas.

4 PLANTS AND ANIMALS

Common trees of Vermont include the commercially important sugar maple (the state tree), ash, and the poplar. Other native plants include 15 types of conifer and 130 grasses. Native mammals include coyote, red fox, and snowshoe hare. Characteristic birds include the raven and Canada jay. Among the five endangered animal species in Vermont are the Indiana bat and bald eagle.

Vermont Population Profile

Total population in 2000:	608,827
Population change, 1990–2000:	8.2%
Hispanic or Latino†:	0.9%
Population by race	
One race:	98.8%
White:	96.8%
Black or African American:	0.5%
American Indian/Alaska Native:	0.4%
Asian:	0.9%
Native Hawaiian/Pacific Islander:	—
Some other race:	0.2%
Two or more races:	1.2%

Population by Age Group

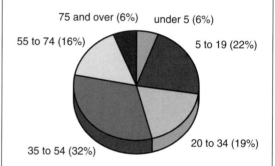

75 and over (6%) under 5 (6%)
55 to 74 (16%)
5 to 19 (22%)
35 to 54 (32%)
20 to 34 (19%)

Top Cities by Population

City	Population	% change 1990–2000
Burlington	38,889	–0.6
Essex	18,626	12.9
Rutland	17,292	–5.1
Colchester	16,986	15.3
South Burlington	15,814	23.5
Bennington	15,737	–4.3
Brattleboro	12,005	–1.9
Hartford	10,367	10.2
Milton	9,479	12.8
Barre	9,291	–2.0

Notes: †A person of Hispanic or Latino origin may be of any race. NA indicates that data are not available.
Sources: U.S. Census Bureau. Public Information Office. *Demographic Profiles.* [Online] Available http://www.census.gov/Press-Release/www/2001/demoprofile.html. Accessed June 1, 2001. U.S. Census Bureau. *Census 2000: Redistricting Data.* Press release issued by the Redistricting Data Office. Washington, D.C., March, 2001.

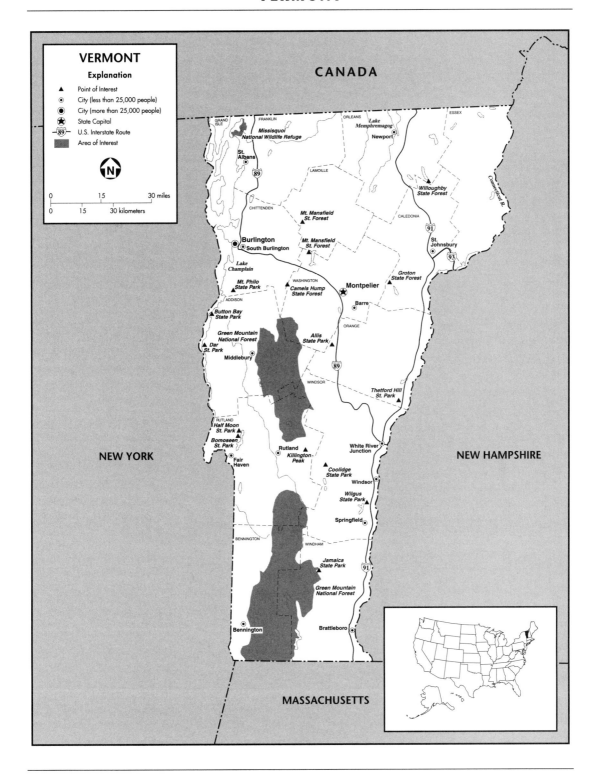

5 ENVIRONMENTAL PROTECTION

All natural resource regulation, planning, and operation are coordinated by the Agency of Environmental Conservation. Legislation enacted in 1972 bans the use of throwaway beverage containers in Vermont, and billboards are also banned. In the 1980s and early 1990s, the effects of acid rain became a source of concern. The state had nine hazardous waste sites as of 1998.

6 POPULATION

Vermont fell behind Alaska, North Dakota, and South Dakota to rank 49th among the 50 states in population, with a 2000 census total of 608,827 (less then the size of Memphis, Tennessee). In 1990, Vermont's population was 68% rural, the highest percentage of all states. Burlington had 38,889 residents in 2000. Other cities with their 2000 populations were Essex, 18,626; Rutland, 17,292; and Colchester, 16,986. South Burlington, with a population of 15,814 the same year, grew by nearly 24% between 1990 and 2000 alone. About 28% of the population is 19 years of age and younger.

7 ETHNIC GROUPS

According to a 1997 federal estimate, Vermont's proportion of white residents—98.4%—was the highest of any state. Over 33,000 residents reported French Canadian ancestry in 1990. There were approximately 4,900 Asians and Pacific Islanders, 3,100 blacks, and about 1,500 Native Americans in 1997. An estimated 0.9% of residents had Hispanic origins in 1997.

8 LANGUAGES

Vermont English, although typical of the Northern dialect, differs from that of New Hampshire in several respects. In 1990, 521,521 Vermonters—94.2% of the population—spoke only English at home. Other languages spoken at home, and number of speakers, included French, 17,171; and Spanish, 3,196.

9 RELIGIONS

The largest single religious organization in Vermont is the Roman Catholic Church, with 143,938 members in 1990. Congregationalists (whose church is now known as the United Church of Christ) had 24,461 known members in 1990. Other Protestant groups include the United Methodists, 24,678; American Baptists, 8,788; and Episcopalians, 9,628. In the same year, the state had 2,855 Mormons. In 1994, Vermont had a Jewish population of 6,000.

10 TRANSPORTATION

In 1998 there were 639 rail miles (1,028 kilometers) of track in Vermont, none of it Class I line. Eleven railroads together transported 9.4 million tons of freight that year. There were 14,240 miles (22,912 kilometers) of streets, roads, and highways in 1997, and a total of 495,716 motor vehicles were registered. Burlington International Airport, the state's major air terminal, had 6,886 aircraft departures in 1996.

Vermont Population by Race

Census 2000 was the first national census in which the instructions to respondents said, "Mark one or more races." This table shows the number of people who are of one, two, or three or more races. For those claiming two races, the number of people belonging to the various categories is listed. The U.S. government conducts a census of the population every ten years.

	Number	Percent
Total population	608,827	100.0
One race	601,492	98.8
Two races	6,938	1.1
White *and* Black or African American	922	0.2
White *and* American Indian/Alaska Native	3,484	0.6
White *and* Asian	1,061	0.2
White *and* Native Hawaiian/Pacific Islander	75	—
White *and* some other race	943	0.2
Black or African American *and* American Indian/Alaska Native	97	—
Black or African American *and* Asian	38	—
Black or African American *and* Native Hawaiian/Pacific Islander	8	—
Black or African American *and* some other race	69	—
American Indian/Alaska Native *and* Asian	21	—
American Indian/Alaska Native *and* Native Hawaiian/Pacific Islander	2	—
American Indian/Alaska Native *and* some other race	55	—
Asian *and* Native Hawaiian/Pacific Islander	29	—
Asian *and* some other race	126	—
Native Hawaiian/Pacific Islander *and* some other race	8	—
Three or more races	397	0.1

Source: U.S. Census Bureau. *Census 2000: Redistricting Data.* Press release issued by the Redistricting Data Office. Washington, D.C., March, 2001. A dash (—) indicates that the percent is less than 0.1.

11 HISTORY

Algonkian-speaking Abnaki settled along Lake Champlain and in the Connecticut Valley, and Mahican settled in the southern counties of what is now Vermont between 1200 and 1790. However, the region has shown signs of continuous habitation for the last 10,000 years. In 1609, Samuel de Champlain became the first European explorer of Vermont. From the mid-17th to the mid-18th centuries, there was regular traffic through the state and attempts at settlement by the French. Fort Dummer, built in 1724 near present-day Brattleboro, was the first permanent settlement.

Governor Benning Wentworth of New Hampshire, claiming that his colony extended as far west as did Massachusetts and Connecticut, had granted 131 town charters in the territory by 1764. In that year, the crown declared that New York's northeastern boundary was the Connecticut River. Owners of New Hampshire titles, fearful of losing their land, prevented New York from enforcing its jurisdiction. The Green Mountain Boys, organized by Ethan Allen in 1770–71, scared off the defenseless settlers under the New York title and scorned the New York courts.

Shortly after the outbreak of the Revo-

Vermont Governors: 1778–2001

1778–1789	Thomas Chittenden	—
1789–1790	Moses Robinson	Dem-Rep
1790–1797	Thomas Chittenden	—
1797	Paul Brigham	Dem-Rep
1797–1807	Isaac Tichenor	Federalist
1807–1808	Israel Smith	Dem-Rep
1808–1809	Isaac Tichenor	Federalist
1809–1913	Jonas Galusha	Dem-Rep
1813–1815	Martin Chittenden	Federalist
1815–1820	Jonas Galusha	Dem-Rep
1820–1823	Richard Skinner	Dem-Rep
1823–1826	Cornelius P. Van Ness	Dem-Rep
1826–1828	Ezra Butler	Dem-Rep
1828–1831	Samuel Chandler Crafts	Nat-Rep
1831–1835	William Adams Palmer	Anti–Mason Dem
1835–1841	Silas Hemenway Jennison	Whig
1841–1843	Charles Paine	Whig
1843–1844	John Mattocks	Whig
1844–1846	William Slade	Whig
1846–1848	Horace Eaton	Whig
1848–1850	Carlos Coolidge	Whig
1850–1852	Charles Kilborn Williams	Whig
1852–1853	Erastus Fairbanks	Whig
1853–1854	John Staniford Robinson	Democrat
1854–1856	Stephen Royce	Whig, Republican
1856–1858	Ryland Fletcher	Know Nothing
1858–1860	Hiland Hall	Republican
1860–1861	Erastus Fairbanks	Whig
1861–1863	Frederick Holbrook	Whig Republican
1863–1865	John Gregory Smith	Republican
1865–1867	Paul Dillingham, Jr.	Republican
1867–1869	John Boardman Page	Republican
1869–1870	Peter Thacher Washburn	Republican
1870	George Whitman Hendee	Republican
1870–1872	John Wolcott Stewart	Republican
1872–1874	Julius Converse	Republican
1874–1876	Asahel Peck	Republican
1876–1878	Horace Fairbanks	Republican
1878–1880	Redfield Proctor, Sr.	Republican
1880–1882	Roswell Farnham	Republican
1882–1884	John Lester Barstow	Republican
1884–1886	Samuel Everett Pingree	Republican
1886–1888	Ebenezer Jolls Ormsbee	Republican
1888–1890	William Paul Dillingham	Republican
1890–1892	Carroll Smalley Page	Republican
1892–1894	Levi Knight Fuller	Republican
1894–1896	Urban Andrain Woodbury	Republican
1896–1898	Josiah Grout	Republican
1898–1900	Edward Curtis Smith	Republican
1900–1902	William Wallace Stickney	Republican
1902–1904	John Griffith McCullough	Republican
1904–1906	Charles James Bell	Republican
1906–1908	Fletcher Dutton Proctor	Republican
1908–1910	George Herbert Prouty	Republican
1910–1912	John Abner Mead	Republican
1912–1915	Allen Miller Fletcher	Republican
1915–1917	Charles Winslow Gates	Republican
1917–1919	Horace French Graham	Republican
1919–1921	Percival Wood Clement	Republican
1921–1923	James Hartness	Republican
1923–1925	Redfield Proctor, Jr.	Republican
1925–1927	Frankin Swift Billings	Republican
1927–1931	John Eliakim Weeks	Republican
1931–1935	Stanley Calef Wilson	Republican
1935–1937	Charles Manley Smith	Republican
1937–1941	George David Aiken	Republican
1941–1945	William Henry Wills	Republican
1945–1947	Mortimer Robinson Proctor	Republican
1947–1950	Ernest William Gibson, Jr.	Republican
1950–1951	Harold John Arthur	Republican
1951–1955	Lee Earl Emerson	Republican
1955–1959	Joseph Blaine Johnson	Republican
1959–1961	Robert Theodore Stafford	Republican
1961–1963	Frank Ray Keyser, Jr.	Republican
1963–1969	Philip Henderson Hoff	Democrat
1969–1973	Deane Chandler Davis	Republican
1973–1977	Thomas Paul Salmon	Democrat
1977–1985	Richard Arkwright Snelling	Republican
1985–1991	Madeleine May Kunin	Democrat
1991	Richard Arkwright Snelling	Republican
1991–	Howard Dean, MD	Democrat

Anti–Mason Democrat – Anti–Mason Dem
Democratic Republican – Dem-Rep
National Republican – Nat-Rep

lutionary War, Ethan Allen's Green Mountain Boys helped capture Fort Ticonderoga. There were several British raids on Vermont towns during the war. After the Revolution, most Vermonters wanted to join the US, but members of the dominant Allen faction refused in order to protect their large landholdings. Vermont declared itself an independent republic with the name "New Connecticut." Following the political defeat of Allen and his followers in 1789, Vermont sought statehood and was admitted to the Union on 4 March 1791.

Granite quarry near Barre. Mineral production is one of Vermont's leading industries.

State Development

Second-generation Vermonters developed towns and villages with water-powered mills, charcoal-fired furnaces, general stores, newspapers, craft shops, churches, and schools. In the War of 1812, Vermont soldiers fought in the Battle of Plattsburgh, New York. The Mexican War (1846–48) was unpopular in the state, but Vermont, which had strongly opposed slavery, was an enthusiastic supporter of the Union during the Civil War.

The opening of the Champlain-Hudson Canal in 1823, and the building of the early railroad lines in 1846–53, made Vermont more vulnerable to competition from the West, destroying many small farms and businesses. However, immigration by the Irish and by French Canadians stabilized the population, and the expansion of light industry bolstered the economy.

During the 20th century and especially after World War II, manufacturing prospered in valley villages, and Vermont's picturesque landscape began to attract city buyers of second homes. New highways made the cities and rural areas more accessible, and Vermont absorbed an influx of young professionals from New York and Massachusetts. Longtime Vermonters, accustomed to their state's natural beauty, were confronted in the 1980s with the question of how much development was necessary for the state's economic health.

12 STATE GOVERNMENT

The general assembly consists of a 150-member house of representatives and a 30-member senate. State elective officials include the governor, lieutenant governor (elected separately), treasurer, and secretary of state. All bills require a majority vote in each house for passage. Bills can be vetoed by the governor, and vetoes can be overridden by a two-thirds vote of each legislative house.

13 POLITICAL PARTIES

The Republican Party gained control of Vermont state offices in 1856 and kept it for more than 100 years. No Democrat was elected governor from 1853 until 1962.

In 1998, there were 402,603 registered voters. Democrat Howard Dean was elected governor in 1992, and was reelected twice, in 1996 and 2000. That same year, Democrats controlled the state senate, with 16 seats out of 30. In the state house of representatives, the Democrats held 83 seats; the Republicans had 62; Independents had 1; and Progressive Coalition members held 4. Democratic US senator, Patrick Leahy, was elected to his fifth term in 1998. In 2001, Senator James Jeffords, after winning re-election in 2000 as a Republican, became an Independent. His move stunned the nation and shifted control of the evenly divided Senate to the Democrats. Vermont's delegation to the House of Representatives consists of one Independent, Bernard Sanders.

Vermont has often shown its independence in national political elections. In 2000, the state gave 51% of the vote to Democratic nominee Al Gore and 41% to Republican George W. Bush.

Vermont Presidential Vote by Major Political Parties, 1948–2000

YEAR	VERMONT WINNER	DEMOCRAT	REPUBLICAN
1948	Dewey (R)	45,557	75,926
1952	*Eisenhower (R)	43,299	109,717
1956	*Eisenhower (R)	42,540	110,390
1960	Nixon (R)	69,186	98,131
1964	*Johnson (D)	108,127	54,942
1968	*Nixon (R)	70,255	85,142
1972	*Nixon (R)	68,174	117,149
1976	Ford (R)	77,798	100,387
1980	*Reagan (R)	81,891	94,598
1984	*Reagan (R)	95,730	135,865
1988	*Bush (R)	115,775	124,331
1992**	*Clinton (D)	133,592	88,122
1996**	*Clinton (D)	137,984	80,532
2000	Gore (D)	149,022	119,775

* Won US presidential election.
** Independent candidate Ross Perot received 65,991 votes in 1992 and 31,024 votes in 1996.

14 LOCAL GOVERNMENT

As of 1997, there were 14 counties, 49 municipal governments, and 236 townships in Vermont. County officers, operating out of shire towns (county seats), include the probate courts judge, county clerk, state's attorney, and treasurer. All cities have mayor-council systems. Towns are governed by selectmen; larger towns also have town managers.

15 JUDICIAL SYSTEM

Vermont's highest court is the supreme court, which consists of a chief justice and four associate justices. Other courts include the superior and district courts. There are also 28 assistant judges and 19 probate court judges. Crime rates in nearly

Photo credit: Jim McElholm.

The Bennington Monument commemorates the Revolutionary War battle that led to British General Burgoyne's defeat.

every category are far below the national average. The 1998 crime rate for the nation was 3,139 crimes per 100,000 inhabitants; Vermont has no death penalty.

16 MIGRATION

From 1985 to 1990, Vermont had a net gain from migration of nearly 21,400. During 1990–98, the net gain from interstate migration was 5,000, and 4,000 from abroad. At 32.1%, Vermont's urban population in 1990 was the lowest among the states.

17 ECONOMY

After World War II, agriculture was replaced by manufacturing and tourism as the backbone of the economy. Durable goods manufacturing (primarily electronics and machine parts), construction, wholesale and retail trade, and other service industries showed the largest growth in employment during the 1990s. Vermont's 1997 gross state product, at $15 billion, was the smallest in the US.

18 INCOME

Vermont ranked 33d in per capita (per person) income with $24,602 in 1998, and total personal income was $14.5 billion that year. About 10.6% of all Vermonters were living below the federal poverty level in 1998.

19 INDUSTRY

The value of shipments of manufactured goods was $8 billion in 1997—a figure important to the state's economy, though very small by national standards. Leading industry groups were electrical and electronic equipment, food products, printing and publishing, paper and allied products, fabricated metal products, and industrial machinery and equipment. Scales, machine tools, and electronic components are important manufactured items.

20 LABOR

According to the US Department of Labor, 333,300 Vermonters were in the labor force in mid-1998. The unemployment rate then was 3.4%. Some 9.4% of all workers were members of labor unions in Vermont in 1998.

21 AGRICULTURE

Although Vermont is one of the nation's most rural states, its agricultural income was only $542 million in 1999, 43d among the 50 states. More than 80% of that came from livestock and livestock products, especially dairy products. The leading crops were corn for silage, 1.8 million tons; hay, 504,000 tons; and apples, 34.5 million pounds.

22 DOMESTICATED ANIMALS

Today the merino sheep and the Morgan horse (a breed developed in Vermont) have been for the most part replaced by dairy cattle. Vermont leads New England in milk production. Dairy products accounted for 70% of agricultural receipts in 1995.

23 FISHING

Sport-fishers can find ample species of trout, perch, walleye pike, bass, and pickerel in Vermont's waters, many of which are stocked by the Department of Fish and Game. There is little commercial fishing.

24 FORESTRY

The Green Mountain State is covered by 4.6 million acres (1.8 million hectares) of forestland—77% of the state's total land area. Shipments of logs in 1997 was $468 million; 25% of all manufacturing establishments depend on the lumber industry. Vermont is the nation's leading producer of maple syrup; the 1994 output was 435,000 gallons.

25 MINING

The value of nonfuel mineral production in Vermont in 1998 was estimated to be $96 million. Nationally, the state ranked third among nine states that produced talc. Granite is quarried near Barre, and slate is found in the southwest. The West Rutland-Proctor area has the world's largest marble reserve, the Danby quarry.

26 ENERGY AND POWER

Because of the state's lack of fossil fuel resources, utility bills are higher in Vermont than most states. In 1998 Vermont generated 4.4 billion kilowatt hours of power, 76% of which was produced by the state's lone nuclear plant at Vernon.

27 COMMERCE

Wholesale sales totaled $4.5 billion in 1997; retail sales were $6 billion (48th in the nation). Foreign exports of Vermont manufacturers were estimated at $3.7 billion for 1998.

28 PUBLIC FINANCE

The total revenues for 1997 were $2.37 billion and expenditures were $2.12 billion. The total debt outstanding as of 1997 was $2.03 billion, or $3,459 per capita (per person).

29 TAXATION

Vermont ranked 29th in the US in state taxes per person in 1997, at $1,527. Total state tax receipts that year were $899 million. Sales taxes accounted for about 46% of state tax receipts; individual income taxes, 36%. The state imposes personal and corporate income taxes, sales and use taxes, a franchise tax, and an inheritance tax. Taxes are also levied on beverages, electrical energy, insurance, meals and rooms, old-age assistance, real estate transfers, and tobacco products, among other items. In 1995, Vermonters paid $1.7 billion in federal income taxes.

30 HEALTH

Heart disease was the leading cause of death in 1998. The death rate from HIV–related disease was one on the lowest in the country. There were 14 hospitals operating in 1998. In 1998, the average hospital expenses per inpatient day were $754, or $56,139 for an average cost per stay. Some 9.9% of all state residents did not have health insurance in 1998.

31 HOUSING

As rustic farmhouses gradually disappear, modern units (many of them vacation homes for Vermonters and out-of-staters) are being built to replace them. In 1999, there were an estimated 289,000 housing units in Vermont. The median monthly cost for an owner with a mortgage in 1990 was $719; renters had a median monthly cost of $446.

32 EDUCATION

As of 1998, some 86.7% of Vermonters above the age of 25 were high school graduates, and 27.1% had completed at least four years of postsecondary study. During the 1997 school year, 105,984 students were enrolled in Vermont's public schools.

Vermont's back roads.

Expenditures on public elementary and secondary education for 1996 averaged $6,505 per pupil (11th in the nation). The total 1997 enrollment in the state's two-, four-year, and private colleges was 36,482. The state operates the University of Vermont (Burlington), as well as the three state colleges, at Castleton, Johnson, and Lyndonville. Notable private institutions include Bennington College, Middlebury College, St. Michael's College (Winooski), and Norwich University (Northfield), the oldest private military college in the US.

33 ARTS

The Vermont State Crafts Centers at Frog Hollow (Middlebury) and Windsor dis-

play the works of Vermont artisans. The Vermont Symphony Orchestra, in Burlington, makes extensive statewide tours. Marlboro College is the home of the summer Marlboro Music Festival, founded by pianist Rudolf Serkin. Among the summer theaters in the state are those at Dorset and Weston, and the University of Vermont Shakespeare Festival. The Middlebury College Bread Loaf Writers' Conference meets each August in Ripton. In 1999, the state had 100 arts associations and 5 local arts groups.

34 LIBRARIES AND MUSEUMS

During 1998, the state's public libraries held 2.54 million volumes and had a combined circulation of 3.6 million. The largest academic library was at the University of Vermont (Burlington), with a book stock of over 1 million. Vermont has 89 museums and 65 historic sites. Among them are the Bennington Museum, with its collection of Early American glass, pottery, furniture, and Grandma Moses paintings, and the Art Gallery–St. Johnsbury Athenaeum, featuring 19th-century American artists.

35 COMMUNICATIONS

In 1999, 95.3% of Vermont's occupied households had telephones. There were 20 AM and 52 FM radio stations and 8 television stations in operation in 2000.

36 PRESS

In 1998 there were eight daily papers, and three Sunday papers. The leading daily was the *Burlington Free Press* (53,256 mornings; 68,841 Sundays).

37 TOURISM, TRAVEL, AND RECREATION

With the building of the first ski slopes in the 1930s and the development of modern highways, tourism became a major industry in Vermont. In the winter, the state's ski areas offer some of the finest skiing in the East.

38 SPORTS

Vermont has no major league professional sports teams. Skiing is, perhaps, the most popular participation sport and Vermont ski areas have hosted national and international ski competitions in both Alpine and Nordic events.

Photo credit: EPD Photos

Entertainer Rudy Vallee was born Hubert Prior Vallee in Island Pond, Vermont on July 21, 1901. One of America's first crooner-sensations, he hosted a popular radio show called the Fleischmann Hour *during the Depression in the 1930s. Vallee used the show to introduce many people who went on to stardom including entertainers like Bob Hope, Milton Berle, George Burns, and Gracie Allen.*

39 FAMOUS VERMONTERS

Two US presidents, both of whom assumed office on the death of their predecessors, were born in Vermont. Chester Alan Arthur (1829–86) became the 21st president after James A. Garfield's assassination in 1881 and finished Garfield's term. Calvin Coolidge (1872–1933), 28th president, became president on the death of Warren G. Harding in 1923 and was elected to a full term in 1924.

Important state leaders were Ethan Allen (1738–89), a frontier folk hero and leader of the Green Mountain Boys; and Ira Allen (1751–1814), the brother of Ethan, who led the fight for statehood.

Vermont's many entrepreneurs and inventors include plow and tractor manufacturer John Deere (1804–86); and Elisha G. Otis (1811–61), inventor of a steam elevator.

Robert Frost (b.California, 1874–1963) maintained a summer home near Ripton, where he helped found Middlebury College's Bread Loaf Writers' Conference. In 1992, Louise Gluck (b.1943) became the first Vermont woman to win a Pulitzer Prize for poetry.

40 BIBLIOGRAPHY

Aylesworth, Thomas G. *Northern New England: Maine, New Hampshire, Vermont.* New York: Chelsea House, 1996.

Elish, Dan. *Vermont.* New York: Benchmark Books, 1997.

Feeney, Kathy. *Vermont Facts and Symbols.* Mankato, Minn.: Hilltop Books, 2001.

Heinrichs, Ann. *Vermont.* New York: Children's Press, 2001.

Kummer, Patricia K. *Vermont.* Mankato, Minn.: Capstone, 1999.

Thompson, Kathleen. *Vermont.* Austin: Raintree Steck-Vaughn, 1996.

Web sites

State of Vermont. Welcome to the State of Vermont, "The Green Mountain State." [Online] Available http://www.state.vt.us/ Accessed May 31, 2001.

Vermont Department of Tourism and Marketing. Vermont Traveler's Guide. [Online] Available http://www.1-800-vermont.com/ Accessed May 31, 2001.

VIRGINIA

Commonwealth of Virginia

ORIGIN OF STATE NAME: Named for Queen Elizabeth I of England, the "Virgin Queen."

NICKNAME: The Old Dominion.

CAPITAL: Richmond.

ENTERED UNION: 25 June 1788 (10th).

SONG EMERITUS: "Carry Me Back to Old Virginia" was formally retired from use in 1997 but has not yet been replaced.

MOTTO: *Sic semper tyrannis* (Thus ever to tyrants).

FLAG: On a blue field, the state seal is centered on a white circle.

OFFICIAL SEAL: Obverse: the Roman goddess Virtus, dressed as an Amazon and holding a sheathed sword in one hand and a spear in the other, stands over the body of Tyranny, who is pictured with a broken chain in his hand and a fallen crown nearby. The state motto appears below, the word "Virginia" above, and a border of Virginia creeper encircles the whole. Reverse: the Roman goddesses of Liberty, Eternity, and Fruitfulness, with the word "Perseverando" (by persevering) above.

BIRD: Cardinal.

FLOWER: Dogwood.

TREE: Dogwood.

DOG: Foxhound.

SHELL: Oyster.

BEVERAGE: Milk.

TIME: 7 AM EST = noon GMT.

1 LOCATION AND SIZE

Situated on the eastern seaboard of the US, Virginia is the fourth largest of the South Atlantic states and ranks 36th in size among the 50 states. The total area of Virginia is 40,598 square miles (105,149 square kilometers). Virginia extends approximately 462 miles (743 kilometers) east-west; the maximum north-south extension is about 200 miles (320 kilometers). The boundaries of Virginia total 1,356 miles (2,182 kilometers). Virginia's offshore islands in the Atlantic include Chincoteague, Wallops, Cedar, Parramore, Hog Cobb, and Smith.

2 TOPOGRAPHY

Virginia consists of three principal areas: the Atlantic Coastal Plain, or Tidewater; the Piedmont Plateau, in the central section; and the Blue Ridge and Allegheny Mountains of the Appalachian chain, in the west and northwest. The latter reach a maximum elevation of 5,729 feet (1,746 meters) at Mt. Rogers, the state's highest point.

The state's four main rivers are the Potomac, Rappahannock, York, and James. Smith Mountain Lake—at 31 square miles (80 square kilometers)—is the largest lake wholly within the state. The John H. Kerr Reservoir, covering 76 square miles (197 square kilometers), straddles the Virginia–North Carolina line. Across the Chesapeake Bay is Virginia's low-lying Eastern Shore, the southern tip of the Delmarva Peninsula.

3 CLIMATE

A mild, humid coastal climate is characteristic of Virginia. Temperatures become increasingly cooler with the rising altitudes as one moves westward. The normal daily mean temperature at Richmond ranges from 37°F (3°C) in January to 78°F (26°C) in July. The record high, 110°F (43°C), was registered in 1954; the record low, –30°F (–34°C), was set in 1985. Precipitation at Richmond averages 44 inches (112 centimeters) a year.

4 PLANTS AND ANIMALS

Native to Virginia are 12 varieties of oak, 5 of pine, and 2 each of walnut, locust, gum, and poplar. Pines predominate in the coastal areas, with numerous hardwoods on slopes and ridges inland. Characteristic wildflowers include trailing arbutus and mountain laurel.

Among native mammals are white-tailed (Virginia) deer, elk, black bear, and bobcat. Principal game birds include the ruffed grouse (commonly called pheasant in Virginia), wild turkey, and bobwhite quail. Tidal waters abound with gray and

Virginia Population Profile

Total population in 2000:	7,078,515
Population change, 1990–2000:	14.4%
Hispanic or Latino†:	4.7%
Population by race	
One race:	98.0%
White:	72.3%
Black or African American:	19.6%
American Indian/Alaska Native:	0.3%
Asian:	3.7%
Native Hawaiian/Pacific Islander:	0.1%
Some other race:	2.0%
Two or more races:	2.0%

Population by Age Group

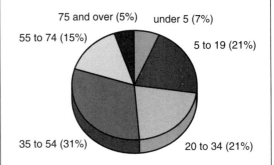

75 and over (5%)   under 5 (7%)
55 to 74 (15%)
5 to 19 (21%)
35 to 54 (31%)
20 to 34 (21%)

Top Cities by Population

City	Population	% change 1990–2000
Virginia Beach	425,257	8.2
Norfolk	234,403	–10.3
Chesapeake	199,184	31.1
Richmond	197,790	–2.6
Newport News	180,150	5.9
Hampton	146,437	9.5
Alexandria	128,283	15.4
Portsmouth	100,565	–3.2
Roanoke	94,911	–1.5
Lynchburg	65,269	–1.2

Notes: †A person of Hispanic or Latino origin may be of any race. NA indicates that data are not available.
Sources: U.S. Census Bureau. Public Information Office. *Demographic Profiles.* [Online] Available http://www.census.gov/PressRelease/www/2001/demoprofile.html. Accessed June 1, 2001. U.S. Census Bureau. *Census 2000: Redistricting Data.* Press release issued by the Redistricting Data Office. Washington, D.C., March, 2001.

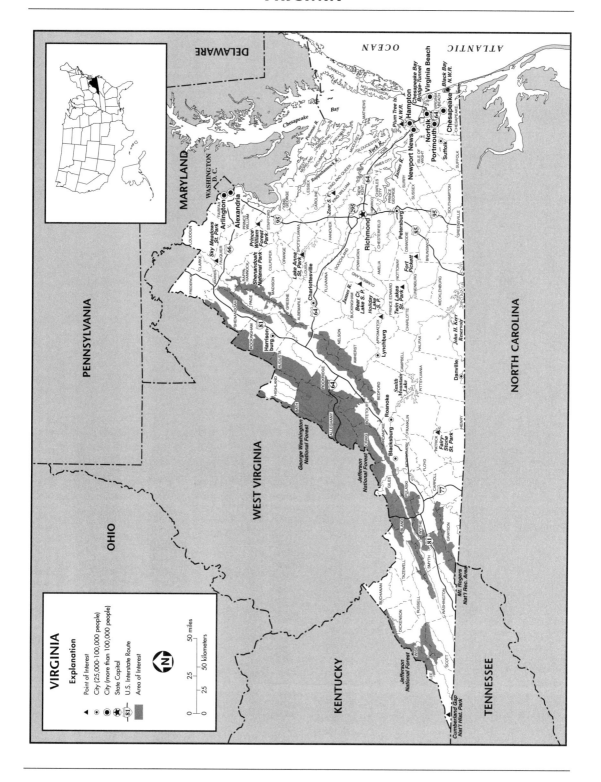

spotted trout, and flounder; bass, bream, and bluegill live in freshwater ponds and streams. Native reptiles include such poisonous snakes as the northern copperhead and eastern cottonmouth. There are 40 endangered/threatened species in Virginia including Delmarva fox squirrel and southern bald eagle.

5 ENVIRONMENTAL PROTECTION

The Department of Environmental Quality is responsible for coordinating the state's environmental protection programs as well as administering federal environmental programs. The State Air Pollution Control Board monitors air quality throughout the state and enforces federal emissions standards. The State Water Control Board has developed programs and regulations to conserve water resources and has instituted water pollution controls and groundwater management plans.

The state has implemented programs to improve the air quality in the northern Virginia (suburban Washington D.C.), Richmond, and Hampton Roads regions. The pollution of Chesapeake Bay is another problem, but restoration efforts continue. Virginia had 27 hazardous waste sites as of 1998.

6 POPULATION

Virginia ranked 12th among the 50 states at the 2000 census with a population of nearly 7.1 million. The population density in 2000 was 178.8 persons per square mile (69 persons per square kilometer). In

Photo credit: Virginia Division of Tourism.

Highland County.

1990, 72.5% of all Virginians lived in metropolitan areas. The largest city in 2000 was Virginia Beach, with 425,257 residents (38th in the US). Norfolk is the second largest with 234,403 residents. Other cities and their 2000 populations were, Chesapeake, 199,184; Richmond (the capital), 197,790; Newport News, 180,150; Hampton, 146,437; and Alexandria, 128,283. Approximately 28% of the population is 19 years of age and younger. One-fifth are 55 years or older.

7 ETHNIC GROUPS

In 1997, Virginia's white population was estimated at 5.14 million, or 73.2% of the

Virginia Population by Race

Census 2000 was the first national census in which the instructions to respondents said, "Mark one or more races." This table shows the number of people who are of one, two, or three or more races. For those claiming two races, the number of people belonging to the various categories is listed. The U.S. government conducts a census of the population every ten years.

	Number	Percent
Total population	7,078,515	100.0
One race	6,935,446	98.0
Two races	133,369	1.9
White *and* Black or African American	24,537	0.3
White *and* American Indian/Alaska Native	17,671	0.2
White *and* Asian	27,827	0.4
White *and* Native Hawaiian/Pacific Islander	1,547	—
White *and* some other race	33,137	0.5
Black or African American *and* American Indian/Alaska Native	6,261	0.1
Black or African American *and* Asian	3,790	0.1
Black or African American *and* Native Hawaiian/Pacific Islander	629	—
Black or African American *and* some other race	8,628	0.1
American Indian/Alaska Native *and* Asian	936	—
American Indian/Alaska Native *and* Native Hawaiian/Pacific Islander	62	—
American Indian/Alaska Native *and* some other race	950	—
Asian *and* Native Hawaiian/Pacific Islander	1,783	—
Asian *and* some other race	5,237	0.1
Native Hawaiian/Pacific Islander *and* some other race	374	—
Three or more races	9,700	0.1

Source: U.S. Census Bureau. *Census 2000: Redistricting Data.* Press release issued by the Redistricting Data Office. Washington, D.C., March, 2001. A dash (—) indicates that the percent is less than 0.1.

state's population. Blacks were estimated at 1.34 million, or 20% of the total population. Virginia had 238,900 Hispanic residents in 1997, chiefly Salvadorans and Mexicans. The 1997 estimate also included some 232,900 Asians and Pacific Islanders (3.5%), primarily Filipinos, Koreans, Chinese, Vietnamese, Asian Indians, and Japanese. The Native American population was only 18,300 during the same year (0.3%). An estimated 5.8% of the population was foreign-born in 1996. Salvadorans accounted for 9.7% of the foreign-born; Vietnamese, 6.2%; Koreans, 5.6%.

8 LANGUAGES

Although the expanding suburban area south of the District of Columbia has many different dialects, the rest of the state has retained its essentially Southern speech features. Regional contrasts distinguish the South Midland of the Appalachians from the Southern of the piedmont and Tidewater. In 1990, Virginia residents five years of age and over who spoke only English at home numbered 5,327,898, or 92.7% of the total. Other languages spoken at home, and the number of people who spoke them, included Spanish, 152,663; French, 40,353; German, 32,069; and Korean, 25,736.

9 RELIGIONS

Protestant denominations combined had the greatest number of known members in 1990, when the leading groups were the Southern Baptist Convention, with 742,860 members; United Methodist Church, 490,789; Episcopal Church, 129,070; and Presbyterian Church, 138,554. As of 1990, there were 384,285 Roman Catholics in Virginia, and the Jewish population was estimated at 69,000 in 1994.

10 TRANSPORTATION

Virginia has one of the nation's most extensive highway systems, one of the leading port systems—Hampton Roads, and two of the nation's busiest air terminals. In 1998, 11 railroads operated on 3,202 route miles (5,152 kilometers) of track.

As of 1997, Virginia had 69,632 miles (112,038 kilometers) of public roads and 5.58 million registered vehicles. The 18-mile (29-kilometer) Chesapeake Bay Bridge–Tunnel, completed in 1964, connects the Eastern Shore with the southeastern mainland. Popular scenic highways include the Blue Ridge Parkway, Colonial National Historical Parkway, and George Washington Memorial Parkway. Virginia's District of Columbia suburbs are linked to the nation's capital by the Washington Metropolitan Area Transit Authority's bus and rail systems.

Coastal and ocean shipping are vital to Virginia's commerce. The Port of Hampton Roads consists of marine terminals in Chesapeake, Newport News, Norfolk, and Portsmouth. In 1996, the ports at Norfolk Harbor and Newport News handled 49.2 million and 24.8 million tons of freight, respectively, ranking 14th and 28th nationally. Each year some 6 million passengers board at Dulles International Airport, northwest of Arlington. Over 7 million also board at Washington National Airport, at Arlington, a major center for domestic flights.

11 HISTORY

At the time of English contact, early in the 17th century, Tidewater Virginia was occupied principally by Algonkian-speakers, planters as well as hunters and fishers. The piedmont area was the home of the Manahoac, Monacan, and Tutelo, all of Siouan stock. Cherokee lived in Virginia's far southwestern triangle.

The first permanent English settlement in America was established at Jamestown on 13 May 1607 in the new land named Virginia in honor of Elizabeth I, the "Virgin Queen." The successful settlement was sponsored by the London Company, chartered by King James I in 1606. The charter defined Virginia as all of the North American coast between 30° and 45°N, and extending inland for 50 miles (80 kilometers). Virginia at one time stretched from southern Maine to California and encompassed all or part of 42 of the present 50 states, as well as Bermuda and part of the Canadian province of Ontario.

The energy, resourcefulness, and military skill of Captain John Smith saved the colony from both starvation and destruction by Native Americans. He was taken prisoner by Powhatan, his chief adversary, but was able to work out a fragile peace later cemented by the marriage in 1614 of the chief's favorite daughter, Pocahontas, to John Rolfe, a Jamestown settler. In 1619, the first representative assembly in the New World convened in Jamestown, as self-government through locally elected representatives became a reality in America and an important precedent for the English colonies.

Despite serious setbacks because of Indian massacres in 1622 and 1644, the colony's population expanded rapidly along the James, York, Rappahannock, and Potomac rivers, and along the Eastern Shore. The 17th century closed on a note of material and cultural progress, as the College of William and Mary, the second institution of higher learning in America, was chartered in 1693. Middle Plantation (renamed Williamsburg in 1722), the site of the college, became the seat of government when the capital was moved from Jamestown in 1699.

Photo credit: Buddy Mays.

St. John's Church, site of Patrick Henry's famous "Give me liberty or give me death" speech.

18th Century

In the decades that followed, eastern Virginians moving into the Valley of Virginia were joined by Scot-Irish and Germans moving southward from Maryland and Pennsylvania. Virginians caught up in western settlement lost much of their awe of the mother country during the French and Indian War (1756–63). Virginia, acting independently and with other colonies, repeatedly challenged agents of the Crown. In 1765, the House of Burgesses adopted five resolutions opposing the Stamp Act, through which the English Parliament had sought to tax the colonists for their own defense. In 1769, Virginia initiated a boycott of British goods in answer to the taxation provisions of the hated Townshend Acts.

Virginia joined the other colonies at the First Continental Congress, which met in Philadelphia in 1774 and elected Virginia's Peyton Randolph president. One native son, Richard Henry Lee, introduced the resolution for independence at the Continental Congress of 1776. Another, Thomas Jefferson, wrote the Declaration of Independence. In the same year, Virginians proclaimed their government a commonwealth and adopted a constitution and declaration of rights, which became the

Photo credit: Metro Richmond Convention & Visitors Bureau.

Hollywood Cemetery in Richmond, the burial place of Presidents Monroe and Tyler, Confederate President Davis, and 18,000 confederate soldiers who died in the Civil War.

basis for the Bill of Rights in the US Constitution.

Virginians were equally active in the Revolutionary War. George Washington was commander in chief of the Continental Army, and the greatest American naval hero was a Scottish-born Virginian, John Paul Jones. Virginia itself was a major battlefield, and it was on Virginia soil, at Yorktown on 19 October 1781, that British General Charles Cornwallis surrendered to Washington, effectively ending the war.

During the early federal period, Virginia's leadership was as notable as it had been during the American Revolution.

James Madison is honored as the "father of the Constitution," and Washington, who was president of the constitutional convention, became the first US president in 1789. Indeed, Virginians occupied the presidency for all but four of the nation's first 28 years.

19th Century

During the first half of the 19th century, Virginians became increasingly concerned with the problem of slavery. Nat Turner's slave revolt—which took the lives of at least 55 white men, women, and children in Southampton County in 1831—increased white fears of black emancipation. Nevertheless, legislation to end sla-

Virginia Governors: 1776–2001

1776–1779	Patrick Henry	
1779–1781	Thomas Jefferson	
1781	William Fleming	
1781	Thomas Nelson	
1781–1784	Benjamin Harrison	
1784–1786	Patrick Henry	
1786–1788	Edmund Randolph	
1788–1791	Beverley Randolph	—
1791–1794	Henry Lee	Federalist
1794–1796	Robert Brooke	Dem-Rep
1796–1799	James Wood	Federalist
1799–1802	James Monroe	Dem-Rep
1802–1805	John Page	Dem-Rep
1805–1808	William Henry Cabell	Dem-Rep
1808–1811	John Tyler, Sr.	Dem-Rep
1811	James Monroe	Dem-Rep
1811	George William Smith	Dem-Rep
1811–1812	Peyton Randolph	Dem-Rep
1812–1814	James Barbour	AD/S.R.P.
1814–1816	Wilson Cary Nicholas	Republican
1816–1819	James Patton Preston	Dem-Rep
1819–1822	Thomas Mann Randolph	Republican
1822–1825	James Pleasants	Republican
1825–1827	John Tyler, Jr.	Dem-Rep
1827–1830	William Branch Giles	Republican
1830–1834	John Floyd	Democrat
1834–1836	Littleton Waller Tazewell	Democrat
1836–1837	Wyndham Robertson	S.R. Dem
1837–1840	David Campbell	States Whigs
1840–1841	Thomas Walker Gilmer	State Rights Whigs
1841	John Mercer Patton	State Rights Whigs
1841–1842	John Rutherford	State Rights Whigs
1842–1843	John Munford Gregory	States Whigs
1843–1846	James McDowell	Democrat
1846–1849	William Smith	Confed-Dem
1849–1852	John Buchanan Floyd	Democrat
1852–1856	Joseph Johnson	Democrat
1856–1860	Henry Alexander Wise	Democrat
1860–1864	John Letcher	Democrat
1864–1865	William Smith	Confed-Dem
1865–1868	Francis Harrison Pierpoint	Unionist
1867–1869	Gen. J. M. Schofield	Military
1868–1869	Henry Horatio Wells	Dem-Prov
1869–1870	Gen. E. R. S. Canby	Military
1869–1870	Gilbert Carlton Walker	Dem-Prov
1870–1874	Gilbert Carlton Walker	Democrat
1874–1878	James Lawson Kemper	Democrat
1878–1882	Frederick William Hilliday	Democrat
1882–1886	William Ewan Cameron	Readjuster
1886–1890	Fitzhugh Lee	Democrat
1890–1894	Philip Watkins McKinney	Democrat
1894–1898	Charles Triplett O'Ferrall	Democrat
1989–1902	James Hoge Tyler	Democrat
1902–1906	Andrew Jackson Montague	Democrat
1906–1910	Claude Augustus Swanson	Democrat
1910–1914	William Hodges Mann	Democrat
1914–1918	Henry Carter Stuart	Democrat
1918–1922	Westmoreland Davis	Democrat
1922–1926	Elbert Lee Trinkle	Democrat
1926–1930	Harry Flood Byrd	Democrat
1930–1934	John Garland Pollard	Democrat
1934–1938	George Campbell Peery	Democrat
1938–1942	James Hubert Price	Democrat
1942–1946	Colgate Whitehead Darden, Jr.	Democrat
1946–1950	William Munford Tuck	Democrat
1950–1954	John Stewart Battle	Democrat
1954–1958	Thomas Bahnson Stanley	Democrat
1958–1962	James Lindsay Almond, Jr.	Democrat
1962–1966	Albertis Sydney Harrison, Jr.	Democrat
1966–1970	Mills Edwin Godwin, Jr.	Democrat
1970–1974	Abner Linwood Holton, Jr.	Republican
1974–1978	Mills Edwin Godwin, Jr.	Republican
1978–1982	John Nichols Dalton	Republican
1982–1986	Charles Spittal Robb	Democrat
1986–1990	Gerald L. Baliles	Democrat
1990–1994	Lawrence Douglas Wilder	Democrat
1994–1998	George Felix Allen	Republican
1998–	James S. Gilmore, III	Republican

Anti–Democrat/State Rights Party – AD/S.R.P.
Confederate Democrat – Confed-Dem
Democrat Provisional – Dem-Prov
Democratic Republican – Dem-Rep
State Rights Democrat – S.R. Dem

very in Virginia failed adoption by only seven votes the following year.

The first half of the 19th century saw the state become a leading center of scientific, artistic, and educational advancement. But this era ended with the coming of the Civil War, a conflict about which many Virginians had grave misgivings. A statewide convention, assembled in Richmond in April 1861, adopted an ordinance of secession only after President Abraham Lincoln sought to send troops across Virginia to punish the states that had already seceded and called upon the commonwealth to furnish soldiers for that task. Shortly afterward, Richmond, the capital of Virginia since 1780, became the capital of the Confederacy.

Robert E. Lee, offered field command of the Union armies, instead resigned his US commission in order to serve his native state as commander of the Army of Northern Virginia and eventually as chief of the Confederate armies. Virginia became the principal battlefield of the Civil War, the scene of brilliant victories won by General Lee's army at Bull Run, Fredericksburg, and Chancellorsville. But the overwhelming numbers and industrial and naval might of the Union compelled Lee's surrender at Appomattox on 9 April 1865.

The war cost Virginia one-third of its territory when West Virginia was admitted to the Union as a separate state on 20 June 1863. Richmond was left in ruins, and agriculture and industry throughout the commonwealth were destroyed. In 1867, Virginia was placed under US military rule. After adopting a constitution providing for universal manhood suffrage, Virginia was readmitted to the Union on 26 January 1870.

After a postwar period of unprecedented racial emancipation, Virginia once again moved toward segregation and discrimination as the 19th century neared an end. In 1902, the Virginia constitutional convention enacted a literacy test and poll tax that effectively reduced the black vote to negligible size.

20th Century

Two decades later, Harry F. Byrd, a liberal Democrat, defeated G. Walter Mapp in the election of 1925. Immediately after taking office, Byrd launched the state on an era of reform. In a whirlwind 60 days, the general assembly revised balloting procedures and adopted measures to lure industry to Virginia. The Anti-Lynch Act of 1927 made anyone present at the scene of a lynching who did not intervene guilty of murder. There has not been a lynching in Virginia since its passage.

Following the depression of the 1930s, Virginia became one of the most prosperous states of the Southeast. It profited partly from national defense contracts and military and naval expansion, but also from increased manufacturing and from what became one of the nation's leading tourist industries. Few states made so great a contribution as Virginia to the US effort in World War II. More than 300,000 Virginians served in the armed forces; 9,000 lost their lives and 10 were awarded the Medal of Honor.

The postwar period brought many changes in the commonwealth's public life. During the first administration of Governor Mills E. Godwin, Jr. (1966–70), the state enacted a sales tax, expanded funding for four-year colleges, and instituted a system of low-tuition community colleges.

In 1970, A. Linwood Holton, Jr., became the first Republican governor of Virginia since 1874. Pledging to "make today's Virginia a model in race relations," Holton increased black representation in government. By the mid-1970s, public school integration in Virginia had been achieved to a degree not yet accomplished in many northern states.

The northeast and Virginia Beach/Norfolk area of Virginia boomed in the early 1980s, spurred by an expansion of federal jobs and a national military build-up. In the late 1980s, however, Virginia was hit by a recession. Douglas Wilder, the first black governor in the nation and a moderate Democrat, responded to a significant shortfall in state revenues by refusing to raise taxes and by insisting on maintaining a $200 million reserve fund. Instead, Wilder reduced the budgets and staff of state services and of the state's college and university system.

Wilder, limited by law to one term in office, was succeeded in 1993 by conservative Republican Richard Allen, who ended 12 years of Democratic rule. He was succeeded in 1998 by another Republican, James S. Gilmore, III.

12 STATE GOVERNMENT

The general assembly consists of a 40-member senate, elected to four-year terms, and a 100-member house of delegates, serving for two years. The governor, lieutenant governor, and attorney general, all serving only one four-year term, are the only officials elected statewide. Most state officials are appointed by the governor but must be confirmed by both houses of the legislature. Bills become law when signed by the governor or left unsigned for seven days while

Virginia Presidential Vote by Political Parties, 1948–2000

YEAR	VIRGINIA WINNER	DEMOCRAT	REPUBLICAN	STATES' RIGHTS DEMOCRAT	SOCIALIST	SOCIALIST LABOR
1948	*Truman (D)	200,786	172,070	43,393	726	234
1952	*Eisenhower (R)	268,677	349,037	—	504	1,160
				CONSTITUTION		
1956	*Eisenhower (R)	267,760	386,459	42,964	444	351
				VA. CONSERVATIVE		
1960	Nixon (R)	362,327	404,521	4,204	—	397
1964	*Johnson (D)	558,038	481,334	—	—	2,895
				AMERICAN IND.	PEACE & FREEDOM	
1968	*Nixon (R)	442,387	590,319	320,272	1,680	4,671
				AMERICAN		
1972	*Nixon (R)	438,887	988,493	19,721	—	9,918
					US LABOR	SOC. WORKERS
1976	Ford (R)	813,896	836,554	16,686	7,508	17,802
					CITIZENS	
1980	*Reagan (R)	752,174	989,609	—	**14,024	1,986
1984	*Reagan (R)	796,250	1,337,078	—	—	—
				NEW ALLIANCE		
1988	*Bush (R)	859,799	1,309,162	14,312	—	—
					IND. (Perot)	IND. (LaRouche)
1992	Bush (R)	1,038,650	1,150,517	3,192	348,639	11,937
1996	Dole (R)	1,091,060	1,138,350	—	159,861	—
				PROGRESSIVE (Nader)	LIBERTARIAN	REFORM
2000	*Bush (R)	1,217,290	1,437,490	59,398	15,198	5,455

* Won US presidential election.
** Candidates of the nationwide Citizens and Socialist Workers parties were listed as independents on the Virginia ballot; another independent, John Anderson, won 95,418 votes.

The state capitol in Richmond, designed by Thomas Jefferson, is home to the oldest legislative body in the Western Hemisphere.

the legislature is in session. A bill dies if left unsigned for 30 days after the legislature has adjourned. A two-thirds majority in each house is needed to override a gubernatorial veto.

13 POLITICAL PARTIES

The modern Democratic Party traces its origins to the original Republican Party (usually referred to as the Democratic-Republican Party, or the Jeffersonian Democrats), led by two native sons of Virginia, Thomas Jefferson and James Madison. From the end of Reconstruction through the 1960s, conservative Democrats dominated state politics, with few exceptions. During the 1970s, Virginians,

still staunchly conservative, turned increasingly to the Republican Party, whose presidential nominees carried the state in every election from 1952 through 1984, except for 1964.

Democrat L. Douglas Wilder was elected governor in 1989, and became the first black governor in United States history. Two Republicans, George Allen and James S. Gilmore, III, succeeded him in 1993 and 1997 respectively. Former Democratic governor Charles S. Robb won election to the US Senate in 1988 and reelection in 1994, and John Warner, a Republican, was elected to a fourth term in the Senate in 1996. Former Republican governor George Allen was elected to the

US Senate in 2000. In 2001, Virginia's delegation to the US House of Representatives consisted of four Democrats, six Republicans, and one Independent.

As of 2001, the state's legislature was controlled by the Republicans with 22 seats. The Democrats held 18. In the house, Democrats held 52 seats to the Republicans' 47, with one Independent.

14 LOCAL GOVERNMENT

As of 1997, Virginia had 95 counties, and 231 municipal governments. In all, there were 483 local government units. Currently, 41 cities elect their own officials, levy their own taxes, and are unencumbered by any county obligations. The 189 incorporated towns remain part of the counties. In general, counties are governed by elected boards of supervisors, with a county administrator or executive handling day-to-day affairs. Incorporated towns have elected mayors and councils.

15 JUDICIAL SYSTEM

The highest judicial body in the commonwealth is the supreme court, consisting of a chief justice and six other justices. The court of appeals has ten judges. The state has 31 circuit courts. District courts hear all misdemeanors, including civil cases involving $1,000 or less. They also hold preliminary hearings concerning felony cases. Each of the 31 judicial districts has a juvenile and a domestic relations court. The state's crime rate per 100,000 population was 3,968.3 in 1996. Virginia's state and federal prisons had 29,761 inmates in 1999.

16 MIGRATION

Since 1900, the dominant migratory trend has been intrastate, from farm to city. Urbanization has been most noticeable, since World War II, in the Richmond and Hampton Roads areas. At the same time, the movement of middle-income Virginians to the suburbs and increasing concentrations of blacks in the central cities have been evident in Virginia as in other states. Between 1940 and 1970, Virginia enjoyed a net gain from migration of 325,000. During 1985–90, the net gain was 377,000 (fourth highest among the states for that period). From 1990 to 1998, Virginia had a net gain of 68,000 from interstate migration and 131,500 from international migration. In 1998, 15,686 foreign immigrants were legally admitted into Virginia, ninth highest total in the US. The federal government estimated that the state had an illegal immigrant population of 55,000 in 1996.

17 ECONOMY

Services, trade, and government are important economic areas. Because of Virginia's extensive military installations and the large number of Virginia residents working for the federal government in the Washington, D.C., metropolitan area, the federal government plays a larger role in the Virginia economy than in any other state except Hawaii. In 1994, federal civilian employment reached 178,000, and military personnel stationed in Virginia totaled 170,000.

The industries that experienced the most growth in the 1980s and early 1990s were printing, transportation equipment, and electronic and other electrical equipment. Virginia has a high concentration of high-technology industry, with 158,000 people employed in 3,600 companies. The two largest high-technology fields are computer and data processing services and electronic equipment.

18 INCOME

Virginia's per capita (per person) income in 1998 averaged $28,063, 16th among the 50 states. Total personal disposable income was $190.5 billion in 1998. In the same year, 11.3% of all state residents were below the federal poverty level.

19 INDUSTRY

In general, manufacturing has shown more consistent growth in Virginia than at the national level. Manufacturing employment increased 10.2% between 1970 and 1993, compared with an 8.3% decline in manufacturing employment on the national level in the same period. In 1997, the value of shipments by manufacturers was about $87 billion. The leading sectors were services industries; manufacturing; retail and wholesale trade; and finance, insurance, and real estate.

Richmond is a principal industrial area for tobacco processing, paper and printing, clothing, and food products. Nearby Hopewell is a center of the chemical industry. Newport News, Hampton, and Norfolk are sites for shipbuilding and the manufacture of other transportation equipment. In the western part of the state, Lynchburg is a center for electrical machinery, metals, clothing, and printing; and Roanoke for food, clothing, and tex-tiles. In the south, Martinsville has furniture and textile-manufacturing plants.

20 LABOR

In mid-1998, Virginia's civilian labor force was 3.38 million persons. The state had an unemployment rate of 2.9% in the same period. Some 6.8% of all workers were union members in 1998.

21 AGRICULTURE

Virginia, ranking 29th among the 50 states in 1999 with farm marketing of more than $2.2 billion, is an important producer of tobacco, soybeans, peanuts, cotton, potatoes, and peaches. There were an estimated 49,000 farms in 1999.

The Tidewater (coastal plain) is still a major farming region, as it has been since the early 17th century. Corn, wheat, tobacco, peanuts, and truck crops are all grown there, and potatoes are cultivated on the Eastern Shore. The piedmont is known for its apples and other fruits, while the Shenandoah Valley is one of the nation's main apple-growing regions.

In 1998, Virginia ranked 6th among the states in peanuts and apples, and 4th in tobacco. Production of major crops in 1995 included tobacco, 9.8 million pounds, value unknown; hay, 2.5 billion tons, valued at $217 million; corn for grain, 25 million bushels, valued at $55.4 million; soybeans, 11 million bushels, worth $62.9 million; wheat, 11 million bushels, valued at $26.4 million; and peanuts, 210 million pounds, worth $52 million.

Photo credit: Virginia Division of Tourism.

Richmond, and the riverboat Annabel Lee on the James River.

22 DOMESTICATED ANIMALS

Cattle-raising, poultry-farming, and dairying, which together account for 60% of all cash receipts from farm marketing, play an important role in Virginia agriculture. In 1999, there were 1.7 million head of cattle, 128,000 milk cows, 390,000 hogs, and 6.2 million lbs of sheep. In 1995, broilers accounted for 18% of agricultural receipts; cattle products, 12%; dairy products, 12%; and turkeys, 9%.

23 FISHING

The relative importance of Chesapeake Bay and Atlantic fisheries to Virginia's economy has lessened in recent decades, although the state continues to place high in national rankings. In 1998, Virginia's commercial fish landings ranked third by volume, totaling 591.9 million pounds and worth $112.7 million. The bulk of the catch consists of shellfish such as crabs, scallops, and clams, and finfish such as flounder and menhaden.

Both saltwater and freshwater fish are avidly sought by sport-fishers. In 1998, the state issued 632,179 fishing licenses. Some 734,000 recreational fishers went marine fishing in coastal Atlantic waters during 1997. A threat to Virginia fisheries has been the chemical and oil pollution of Chesapeake Bay and its tributaries.

[24] FORESTRY

Virginia has 16 million acres (6.9 million hectares) of forestland, representing more than 63% of the state's land area. Practically every county has some commercial forestland and supports a wood products industry. Shipments of lumber and wood products were valued at $2.9 billion in 1995. State-funded tree nurseries produce 60-70 million seedlings annually. For recreational purposes, there were 2.6 million acres of forested public lands in 1997.

[25] MINING

Virginia remained one of the nation's most diverse producers of industrial minerals, including crushed stone, sand and gravel, shale, lime, feldspar, gypsum, and vermiculite. Virginia is the only state to mine kyanite. The value of nonfuel mineral production in Virginia in 1998 was about $679 million. Crushed stone was the leading mineral commodity produced in Virginia, accounting for 65% of the total value.

[26] ENERGY AND POWER

In 1998, Virginia's electricity production totaled 63.8 billion kilowatt hours. Coal-fired steam units accounted for 49% of electric power production that year. The state had two nuclear power plants as of 2000.

Although Virginia has no petroleum deposits, it does have a major oil refinery at Yorktown that uses imported petroleum. The state is supplied with natural gas by three major interstate pipeline companies. As a result of rising oil prices during the 1970s, the state's utilities have converted many oil-fired electric plants to coal. Virginia's 173 coal mines, all in the Appalachian Mountain area, produced 33.7 million tons of coal in 1996.

[27] COMMERCE

Wholesale sales totaled $65 billion in 1997; retail sales were $65 billion. Virginia, a major container shipping center, handled import and export cargo worth nearly $23 billion combined in 1995, almost all through the Hampton Roads estuary. Exports of goods originating within Virginia totaled $12.5 billion in 1998.

[28] PUBLIC FINANCE

As of 1997, debts incurred by the state totaled $9.94 billion, or about $1,476 per person. Revenues for 1997 were $24.32 billion, and expenditures were $19.27 billion.

[29] TAXATION

Virginians bear a lighter tax burden than residents of most states. In 1998, for example, the state tax burden was $1,552 per capita (per person), 42d among the 50 states.

As of 1997, the state taxed personal income at 2% to 5.75% and corporate income at 6%. Other taxes included a sales and use tax (3.5%), gasoline tax (17.5¢ per gallon), and cigarette tax (2.5¢ per pack). Also taxed by the state are motor vehicles, watercraft, alcoholic beverages, railroad property, timber, motor fuel, estates and wills, and insurance transactions. The real estate tax and utility taxes are levied by counties and independent cities. Virginians paid $25 billion in income taxes to the federal government in 1995.

30 HEALTH

Virginia's death rates in 1996 for the leading causes of death—heart disease, cancer, and stroke—were below the national norms. In 1998, Virginia's 93 community hospitals had 17,890 beds. The average hospital expense in 1998 amounted to $5,656 for an average cost of stay. Virginia had at least 14% of its residents who were uninsured in 1998.

31 HOUSING

In 1999, Virginia had an estimated 2.8 million housing units. That year, the state authorized the construction of 50,200 privately owned units, valued at about $4.7 billion. In 1990, the median monthly cost for owners with a mortgage throughout Virginia was $831; renters had a median cost of $495.

32 EDUCATION

About 82.6% of all state residents 25 years of age or older were high school graduates in 1998, and more than 30.3% had at least four years of college. Under a Literacy Passport program adopted in 1990, students must pass writing tests in reading, writing, and math in order to enter high school. During the 1997 school year, Virginia had public schools with 1.11 million pupils. Expenditures on public elementary and secondary schools averaged $5,655 per pupil (23d in the nation) in 1995/96.

Virginia has had a distinguished record in higher education since the College of William and Mary was founded at Williamsburg in 1693. Thomas Jefferson established the University of Virginia at Charlottesville in 1819. In 1997, colleges and universities in the state enrolled a total of 364,904 students.

Public state-supported institutions include Virginia Polytechnic Institute and State University, in Blacksburg; Virginia Commonwealth University, at Richmond; and George Mason University, near Fairfax. Well-known private institutions include the Hampton Institute; University of Richmond; Sweet Briar College; and Washington and Lee University (Lexington).

33 ARTS

Richmond and Norfolk are the principal centers for both the creative and the performing arts in Virginia. In Richmond, the Landmark Theatre (formerly called "the Mosque") is the long-time venue of concerts by internationally famous orchestras and soloists, and for musical events. The 500-seat Virginia Museum Theater presents professionally acted plays. The Barksdale Theater and its repertory company present serious plays. In Norfolk, the performing arts are featured in the Scope auditorium, Chrysler Hall, and the Wells Theater, which houses the Virginia Stage Company repertory theater. The Virginia Opera Association, centered in Norfolk, is internationally recognized.

Wolf Trap Farm Park for the Performing Arts, west of Arlington, provides theatrical, operatic, and symphonic performances featuring internationally celebrated perform-

The main rotunda at the University of Virginia was designed by Thomas Jefferson.

ers. William and Mary's Phi Beta Kappa Hall in Williamsburg is the site of the annual Virginia Shakespeare Festival. Abingdon is the home of the Barter Theater, a repertory company that has performed widely in the United States and abroad.

34 LIBRARIES AND MUSEUMS

A total of 108 county, city, town, and regional library systems served the population in 1998. Their combined book stock reached 17 million volumes, and their combined circulation was 41.7 million. The Library of Virginia in Richmond and the libraries of the University of Virginia (Charlottesville) and the College of Will-

iam and Mary (Williamsburg) have the personal papers of such notables as George Washington, Thomas Jefferson, James Madison, Robert E. Lee, and William Faulkner.

There were 260 museums in 1997. In Richmond, the Virginia Museum of Fine Arts has a collection that ranges from ancient Egyptian artifacts to mobile jewelry by Salvador Dali. The Science Museum of Virginia has a 280-seat planetarium that features a simulated excursion to outer space. Perhaps the most extensive "museum" in the US is Williamsburg's mile-long Duke of Gloucester Street, with such remarkable restorations as the Christopher Wren Building of the College of William and Mary, Bruton Parish Church, the Governor's Palace, and the colonial capital.

More historic sites are maintained as museums in Virginia than in any other state. These include George Washington's home at Mount Vernon (near Alexandria) and Thomas Jefferson's residence at Monticello (near Charlottesville).

35 COMMUNICATIONS

According to the Federal Communications Commission, in 1999, 93.2% of Virginia's occupied housing units had telephones. In 2000, broadcasters operated 145 AM radio stations and 182 FM stations. In the same year, Virginia had 39 television stations. A total of 187,445 Internet domain names were registered in 2000.

36 PRESS

In 1998, Virginia had 20 morning dailies, 9 evening, and 17 Sunday papers. Leading Virginia newspapers with their 1998 daily circulations include the *Richmond Times-Dispatch* (207,175); *the Norfolk Virginian-Pilot* (197,773); and the *Newport News Daily Press* (97,245).

37 TOURISM, TRAVEL, AND RECREATION

Attractions in the coastal region alone include the Jamestown and Yorktown historic sites, the Williamsburg restoration, and the homes of George Washington and Robert E. Lee. Also featured are the National Aeronautics and Space Administration's Langley Research Center and the resort pleasures of Virginia Beach.

The interior offers numerous Civil War Sites, including Appomattox; Thomas Jefferson's Monticello; Booker T. Washington's birthplace near Smith Mountain Lake; and the historic cities of Richmond, Petersburg, and Fredericksburg. In the west, the Blue Ridge Parkway and Shenandoah National Park, traversed by the breathtaking Skyline Drive, are favorite tourist destinations, as are Cumberland Gap and, in the Lexington area, the home of Confederate General Thomas "Stonewall" Jackson.

The state's many recreation areas include state parks, national forests, a major national park, scenic parkways, and thousands of miles of hiking trails and shoreline. Part of the famous Appalachian Trail winds through Virginia's Blue Ridge and Appalachian mountains.

38 SPORTS

Although Virginia has no major league professional sports team, it does support two class AAA baseball teams: the Richmond Braves, and the Norfolk and Portsmouth Tidewater Tides. In collegiate sports, the University of Virginia belongs to the Atlantic Coast Conference while Virginia Military Institute competes in the Southern Conference. Participant sports popular with Virginians include tennis, golf, swimming, skiing, boating, and water skiing. The state has at least 180 public and private golf courses.

39 FAMOUS VIRGINIANS

Virginia is the birthplace of eight US presidents. The first president of the US, George Washington (1732–99), was

The Edgar Allen Poe Museum in Richmond.

unanimously elected president in 1789 and served two four-year terms, declining a third. Thomas Jefferson (1743–1826), the nation's third president, after serving as vice-president under John Adams, was elected president of the US in 1800 and was reelected in 1804.

James Madison (1751–1836) was secretary of state during Jefferson's two terms and then occupied the presidency from 1809 to 1817. Madison was succeeded as president in 1817 by James Monroe (1758–1831), who was reelected to a second term starting in 1821 and is best known for the Monroe Doctrine, which has been a part of US policy since his administration. William

Henry Harrison (1773–1841) became the ninth president in 1841 but died of pneumonia one month after his inauguration. Harrison was succeeded by his vice-president, John Tyler (1790–1862), a native and resident of Virginia.

Another native Virginian, Zachary Taylor (1784–1850), renowned chiefly as a military leader, became the 12th US president in 1849 but died midway through his term. The eighth Virginia-born president, (Thomas) Woodrow Wilson (1856–1924), became the 28th president of the US in 1913 after serving as governor of New Jersey. John Marshall (1755–1835) was the third confirmed chief justice of the US and is generally regarded by historians as the first great American jurist. Five other Virginians have served as associate justices, including Lewis Powell (1908-98). Distinguished Virginians who have served in the cabinet include Carter Glass (1858–1946), secretary of the treasury, creator of the Federal Reserve System, and US senator for 26 years.

Other prominent US senators from Virginia include Richard Henry Lee (1732–94), former president of the Continental Congress; James M. Mason (b.District of Columbia, 1798–1871), who later was the Confederacy's commissioner to the United Kingdom and France; Harry F. Byrd (1887–1966), governor of Virginia from 1926 to 1930 and US senator from 1933 to 1965; and Harry F. Byrd, Jr. (b.1914), senator from 1965 to 1982. Some native-born Virginians have become famous as leaders in other nations. Joseph Jenkins Roberts (1809–76) was the first president of the Republic of Liberia; and Nancy Langhorne Astor (1879–1964) was the first woman to serve in the British House of Commons.

Captain John Smith (b.England, 1580?–1631) was the founder of Virginia and its first colonial governor. Virginia signers of the Declaration of Independence, besides Thomas Jefferson and Richard Henry Lee, included Benjamin Harrison (1726?–1791), father of President William Henry Harrison. Virginia furnished both the first president of the Continental Congress, Peyton Randolph (1721–75), and the last, Cyrus Griffin (1748–1810).

Notable Virginia governors include Patrick Henry (1736–99), the first governor of the commonwealth, though best remembered as a Revolutionary orator. Chief among Virginia's great military and naval leaders, besides George Washington and Zachary Taylor, are John Paul Jones (b.Scotland, 1747–92); Robert E. Lee (1807–70), the Confederate commander who earlier served in the Mexican War; James Ewell Brown "Jeb" Stuart (1833–64), commander of Confederate cavalry during the Civil War; and George C. Marshall (b.Pennsylvania, 1880–1959). Virginians' names are also written high in the history of exploration. Daniel Boone (b.Pennsylvania, 1734–1820) pioneered in Kentucky and Missouri. Meriwether Lewis (1774–1809) and William Clark (1770–1838), both native Virginians, led the most famous expedition in US history. Richard E. Byrd (1888–1957) was both an explorer of Antarctica and a pioneer aviator.

Woodrow Wilson and George C. Marshall both received the Nobel Peace Prize, in 1919 and 1953, respectively. Distinguished Virginia-born scientists and inventors include Matthew Fontaine Maury (1806–73), founder of the science of oceanography; Cyrus H. McCormick (1809–84), who perfected the mechanical reaper; and Dr. Walter Reed (1851–1902), who proved that yellow fever was transmitted by a mosquito. Booker T. Washington (1856–1915) was the nation's foremost black educator.

William Byrd II (1674–1744) is widely acknowledged to have been the most graceful writer in English America in his day, while Thomas Jefferson was a leading author of the Revolutionary period. Edgar Allen Poe (b.Massachusetts, 1809–49) was one of America's great poets and short-story writers. Notable 20th-century novelists include Willa Cather (1873–1947), Ellen Glasgow (1874–1945), and James Branch Cabell (1879–1958). Willard Huntington Wright (1888–1939), better known as S. S. Van Dine, wrote many detective thrillers. Twice winner of the Pulitzer Prize for biography, and often regarded as the greatest American master of that genre, was Douglas Southall Freeman (1886–1953). Some contemporary Virginia authors are novelist William Styron (b.1925) and journalist Tom Wolfe (Thomas Kennerly Wolfe, Jr., b. 1931). Celebrated Virginia artists include sculptor Moses Ezekiel (1844–1917) and painters George Caleb Bingham (1811–79) and Jerome Myers (1867–1940). A protégé of Thomas Jefferson's, Robert Mills (b.South Carolina, 1781–1855), designed the Washington Monument.

The roster of Virginians prominent in the entertainment world includes Bill "Bojangles" Robinson (1878–1949), Joseph Cotten (1905–94), George C. Scott (1927-99), Shirley MacLaine (b.1934), and her brother Warren Beatty (b.1938). Virginia's most eminent contemporary composer is Thea Musgrave (b.Scotland, 1928). Popular musical stars include Kathryn Elizabeth "Kate" Smith (1907–86), Pearl Bailey (1918–90), Ella Fitzgerald (1918–96), Roy Clark (b.1933), and Wayne Newton (b.1942).

Virginia's sports champions include golfers Sam Snead (b.1912) and Chandler Harper (b.1914); tennis star Arthur Ashe (1943–93); football players Bill Dudley (b.1921) and Francis "Fran" Tarkenton (b.1940); and baseball pitcher Eppa Rixey (1891–1963). At age 15, Olympic swimming champion Melissa Belote (b.1957) won three gold medals. Helen Chenery "Penny" Tweedy (b.1922) is a famous breeder and racer of horses, from whose stables have come Secretariat and other champions. Equestrienne Jean McLean Davis (b.1929) won 65 world championships.

40 BIBLIOGRAPHY

Ashe, Dora J., comp. *Four Hundred Years of Virginia, 1584–1984: An Anthology.* Lanham, Md.: University Press of America, 1985.

Aylesworth, Thomas G. *Atlantic: District of Columbia, Virginia, West Virginia.* New York: Chelsea House, 1996.

Barrett, Tracy. *Virginia.* New York: Benchmark Books, 1997.

DeAngelis, Gina. *Virginia.* New York: Children's Press, 2001.

Joseph, Paul. *Virginia.* Minneapolis: Abdo & Daughters, 1998.

Mapp, Alf J., Jr. *The Virginia Experiment: The Old Dominion's Role in the Making of America, 1607–1781.* 2d ed. La Salle, Ill.: Open Court, 1975.

Morgan, Edmund S. *American Slavery, American Freedom: The Ordeal of Colonial Virginia.* New York: Norton, 1975.

Thompson, Kathleen. *Virginia.* Austin: Raintree Steck-Vaughn, 1996.

Web sites

Commonwealth of Virginia. Virginia Facts and Figures. [Online] Available http://www.state.va.us/ Accessed May 31, 2001.

Virginia Legislature. Kid's Korner. [Online] Available http://legis.state.va.us/vaonline/v.htm Accessed May 31, 2001.

WASHINGTON

State of Washington

ORIGIN OF STATE NAME: Named for George Washington.
NICKNAME: The Evergreen State.
CAPITAL: Olympia.
ENTERED UNION: 11 November 1889 (42d).
SONG: "Washington, My Home."
DANCE: Square dance.
MOTTO: Alki (By and by).
FLAG: The state seal centered on a dark green field.
OFFICIAL SEAL: Portrait of George Washington surrounded by the words "The Seal of the State of Washington 1889."
BIRD: Willow goldfinch.
FISH: Steelhead trout.
FLOWER: Western rhododendron.
TREE: Western hemlock.
GEM: Petrified wood.
TIME: 4 AM PST = noon GMT.

1 LOCATION AND SIZE

Located on the Pacific coast of the northwestern US, Washington ranks 20th in size among the 50 states. The total area of Washington is 68,138 square miles (176,477 square kilometers). The state extends about 360 miles (580 kilometers) east-west and 240 miles (390 kilometers) north-south. The state's boundary length totals 1,099 miles (1,769 kilometers). Major islands of the San Juan group include Orcas, San Juan, and Lopez; Whidbey is a large island in the upper Puget Sound.

2 TOPOGRAPHY

Much of Washington is mountainous. Along the Pacific coast are the Coast Ranges extending northward from Oregon and California. This chain forms two groups: the Olympic Mountains in the northwest and the Willapa Hills in the southwest. About 100 miles (160 kilometers) inward from the Pacific coast is the Cascade Range, extending northward from the Sierra Nevada in California. This chain includes Mount Rainier, which at 14,410 feet (4,392 meters) is the highest peak in the state. Between the Coast and Cascade ranges lies the Western Corridor—where most of Washington's major cities are concentrated. Of all the state's other major regions, only the Columbia River basin region of south-central Washington is generally flat.

The Cascade volcanoes were mostly dormant for over 100 years. Early in 1980, however, Mount St. Helens began to show ominous signs of activity. On 18 May, the volcano exploded, and the areas immediately surrounding Mount St. Helens were deluged with ash and mudflows. The eruption left 57 people dead or missing, and eruptions of lesser severity followed the main outburst. East of the Cascade Range, much of Washington is a plateau underlain by ancient lava flows. In the northeast are the Okanogan Highlands; in the southeast are the Blue Mountains and the Palouse Hills.

Among Washington's numerous rivers, the longest and most powerful is the Columbia, which forms part of the border with Oregon and then flows for more than 1,200 miles (1,900 kilometers) across the heart of the state. Washington's other major river is the Snake. The state has numerous lakes, of which the largest is the artificial Roosevelt Lake, covering 123 square miles (319 square kilometers). One of the largest and most famous dams in the US is Grand Coulee on the upper Columbia River.

3 CLIMATE

The Cascade Mountains divide Washington climatically. Despite its northerly location, western Washington is as mild as the middle and southeastern Atlantic coast; it is also one of the rainiest regions in the world. Eastern Washington, on the other hand, has a much more continental climate, characterized by cold winters, hot summers, and sparse rainfall.

Average January temperatures in western Washington range from 20°F (–7°C) to 48°F (9°C); July temperatures range from 44°F (7°C) to 80°F (27°C). In the east the temperature ranges are much more extreme. In January, ranges are from 8°F

Washington Population Profile

Total population in 2000:	5,894,121
Population change, 1990–2000:	21.1%
Hispanic or Latino†:	7.5%
Population by race	
One race:	96.4%
White:	81.8%
Black or African American:	3.2%
American Indian/Alaska Native:	1.6%
Asian:	5.5%
Native Hawaiian/Pacific Islander:	0.4%
Some other race:	3.9%
Two or more races:	3.6%

Population by Age Group

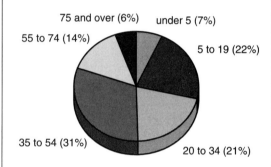

75 and over (6%)   under 5 (7%)
55 to 74 (14%)
5 to 19 (22%)
35 to 54 (31%)
20 to 34 (21%)

Top Cities by Population

City	Population	% change 1990–2000
Seattle	563,374	9.1
Spokane	195,629	10.4
Tacoma	193,556	9.6
Vancouver	143,560	209.5
Bellevue	109,569	26.1
Everett	91,488	30.8
Federal Way	83,259	NA
Kent	79,524	109.5
Yakima	71,845	31.0
Bellingham	67,171	28.7

Notes: †A person of Hispanic or Latino origin may be of any race. NA indicates that data are not available.
Sources: U.S. Census Bureau. Public Information Office. *Demographic Profiles.* [Online] Available http://www.census.gov/Press-Release/www/2001/demoprofile.html. Accessed June 1, 2001. U.S. Census Bureau. *Census 2000: Redistricting Data.* Press release issued by the Redistricting Data Office. Washington, D.C., March, 2001.

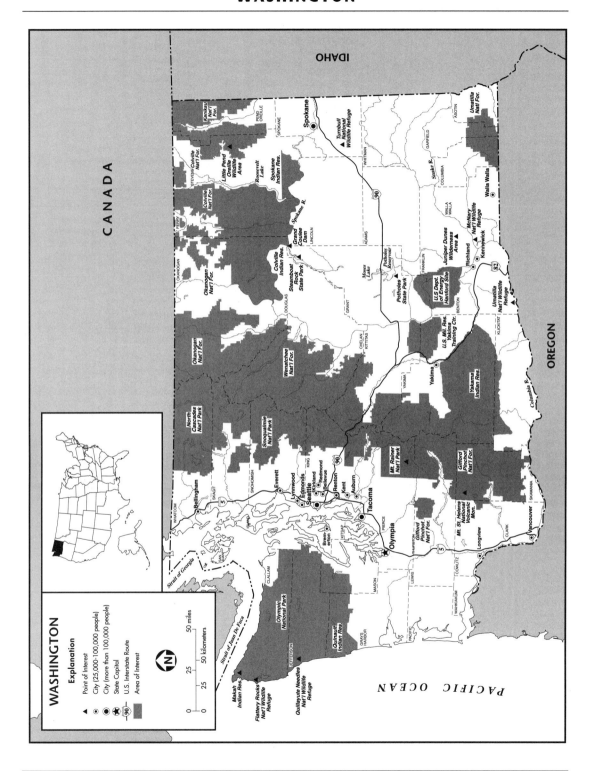

Mount Shuksan.

(–13°C) to 40°F (4°C); and in July, from 48°F (9°C) to 92°F (33°C). The lowest temperature ever recorded in the state is –48°F (–44°C), in 1968. The highest, in 1961, was 118°F (48°C).

The average annual precipitation in Seattle is 37 inches (94 centimeters), falling most heavily from October through March. Spokane receives only 17 inches (43 centimeters). Olympic Rainforest, in Olympic National Park, has an annual rainfall of over 145 inches (368 centimeters). Snowfall in Seattle averages 11.4 inches (29 centimeters) annually. In Spokane, the average is 49.4 inches (125.5 centimeters).

4 PLANTS AND ANIMALS

More than 1,300 plant species have been identified in Washington. Sand strawberries and beach peas are found among the dunes; fennel and spurry grow in salt marshes; greasewood and sagebrush predominate in the desert regions of the Columbia Plateau. Conifers include Sitka spruce, Douglas fir, and western hemlock. Big-leaf maple, red alder, and western yew are among the common deciduous trees. Wildflowers include the deerhead orchid and wake-robin. The western rhododendron is the state flower.

Forest and mountain regions support Columbia black-tailed and mule deer, elk, and black bear. Other native mammals are the Canadian lynx, red fox, and red western bobcat. Smaller mammals—raccoon, muskrat, and porcupine—are plentiful. Game birds include the ruffed grouse and ring-necked pheasant. The bald eagle is more numerous in Washington than in any other state except Alaska. Various salmon species thrive in coastal waters and along the Columbia River, and the hair seal and sea lion inhabit Puget Sound.

Animals driven away from the slopes of Mount St. Helens by the volcanic eruption in 1980 have largely returned. Endangered wildlife in the state includes the northern Aleutian Canada goose, Columbian white-tailed deer, and woodland caribou.

5 ENVIRONMENTAL PROTECTION

The mission of the Department of Ecology is to protect, preserve, and enhance Washington's environment and promote the

Washington Population by Race

Census 2000 was the first national census in which the instructions to respondents said, "Mark one or more races." This table shows the number of people who are of one, two, or three or more races. For those claiming two races, the number of people belonging to the various categories is listed. The U.S. government conducts a census of the population every ten years.

	Number	Percent
Total population	5,894,121	100.0
One race	5,680,602	96.4
Two races	196,689	3.3
White *and* Black or African American	26,234	0.4
White *and* American Indian/Alaska Native	47,795	0.8
White *and* Asian	45,963	0.8
White *and* Native Hawaiian/Pacific Islander	6,170	0.1
White *and* some other race	39,593	0.7
Black or African American *and* American Indian/Alaska Native	3,790	0.1
Black or African American *and* Asian	3,789	0.1
Black or African American *and* Native Hawaiian/Pacific Islander	631	—
Black or African American *and* some other race	5,157	0.1
American Indian/Alaska Native *and* Asian	2,204	—
American Indian/Alaska Native *and* Native Hawaiian/Pacific Islander	500	—
American Indian/Alaska Native *and* some other race	2,158	—
Asian *and* Native Hawaiian/Pacific Islander	5,559	0.1
Asian *and* some other race	6,360	0.1
Native Hawaiian/Pacific Islander *and* some other race	786	—
Three or more races	16,830	0.3

Source: U.S. Census Bureau. *Census 2000: Redistricting Data.* Press release issued by the Redistricting Data Office. Washington, D.C., March, 2001. A dash (—) indicates that the percent is less than 0.1.

wise management of air, land, and water for the benefit of current and future generations. Principal air pollutants in the state are particulate emissions, sulfur dioxides, carbon monoxide, hydrocarbons, lead, and dioxides of nitrogen.

Following reports of leakage from the Hanford Reservation (US Department of Energy Hanford Site), the nation's largest nuclear waste disposal site, a measure tightening controls on nuclear waste storage was approved by the voters in November 1980. Restoration is well underway or completed at a majority of the most polluted waste sites. Washington has the highest overall recycling rate of any state in the United States; more than 39% of the state's total solid waste was recycled in 1995, compared with 23% in 1987. There were 47 hazardous waste sites in 1998, seventh highest in the US.

6 POPULATION

Washington surpassed Tennessee and Missouri to be ranked the nation's 15th most populous state at the 2000 census, with over 5.89 million residents. Washington's estimated population density in 2000 was 88.6 persons per square mile (34.2 persons per square kilometer), just over the national average. The population projection for 2005 was 6.26 million.

Most Washingtonians live in the Western Corridor, between the Coast and Cascade ranges. The leading city in the Western Corridor is Seattle, with a 2000 population of 563,374 (almost identical in population to El Paso, Texas). The city of Seattle was the nation's 24th-largest in 2000. Other leading cities and their 2000 populations are Spokane, 195,629; Tacoma, 193,556; Vancouver, 143,560; and Bellevue, 109,569. The state's median age of 35.3 is identical to the national average. About 29% of Washingtonians are 19 years of age and younger.

7 ETHNIC GROUPS

According to a 1997 federal estimate, Washington had a white population of over 5 million, or 83.8% of the state total. According to the same estimate, Asians and Pacific Islanders numbered 311,300. This represented 5.5% of the total, giving Washington the third highest proportion of Asians (after Hawaii and California). The leading Asian-Pacific Islander groups are Filipino, Japanese, Chinese, Korean, and Vietnamese. Immigration from Southeast Asia was significant during the late 1970s and early 1980s. Hispanic Americans (includes all races), were estimated at 339,600 in 1997. The number of black Americans was estimated at 196,000 in 1997 (3.5%). There were an estimated 100,300 Native Americans, Eskimos, and Aleuts living in Washington in 1997, fifth highest in the nation.

8 LANGUAGES

Northern and Midland dialects dominate. Midland is strongest in eastern Washington and the Bellingham area, with Northern elsewhere. In 1990, English was the language spoken at home by 91% of Washington residents five years old and older. Other languages and the number of people speaking them were Spanish, 143,647; German, 39,011; and Chinese, 26,378.

9 RELIGIONS

First settled by Protestant missionaries, Washington remains a predominantly Protestant state. As of 1990, there were 1,052,281 known members of Protestant groups. The leading denominations were the Church of Jesus Christ of Latter-day Saints (Mormon), 150,634; United Methodist, 89,499; Evangelical Lutheran Church in America, 132,528; and Presbyterian, 72,273. In 1990, there were 526,546 Roman Catholics and an estimated 34,000 Jews in 1994.

10 TRANSPORTATION

As of 1998, Washington had 3,538 rail miles (5,693 kilometers) of railroad track. Washington ranks first in the volume of farm products arriving by rail into the state. Washington had 79,586 miles (128,054 kilometers) of public highways, roads, and streets in 1997. In that year, the state had 4.7 million registered motor vehicles, including 2.69 million automobiles.

Washington's principal ports include Seattle, Tacoma, and Anacortes, all in the Puget Sound area; plus Longview, Kalama, and Vancouver, along the Columbia River. State-operated ferry systems transported 13.6 million passengers and 10.6 million

Photo credit: © G. Braasch/Woodfin Camp.

Crains at the port of Seattle with the downtown skyline in the background.

vehicles across Puget Sound in the mid-1990s. Seattle-Tacoma (SEATAC) International Airport, by far the busiest airport, handled 11.5 million arriving and departing passengers and 159,162 tons of air freight in 1996.

11 HISTORY

The Cascade mountains prevented most communication between Native Americans of the coast and those of the eastern plateau, and their cultures evolved differently. The coastal tribes used timber to construct dugout canoes, wooden dwell-ings, and some stationary wooden furniture. They emphasized rank based on wealth, and warfare between villages was fairly common. The plateau (or "horse") tribes, on the other hand, paid little attention to class distinctions; their social organization was simpler and intertribal warfare less frequent. After the horse reached Washington around 1730, the plateau tribes became largely nomadic, traveling long distances in search of food.

The first Europeans known to have sailed along the Washington coast were Spaniards, who explored the coastline to the southern tip of Alaska in 1774 and 1775. English captain James Cook arrived in the Pacific Northwest in 1778 while searching for a northwest passage across America. Cook was the first of numerous British explorers and traders to be attracted by the valuable fur of the sea otter, and the maritime fur trade began to prosper.

American interest in the area increased after Meriwether Lewis and William Clark's expedition to inspect the Louisiana Purchase. They first sighted the Pacific Ocean in 1805 from the north bank of the Columbia River. As reports of the trip became known, a host of British and American fur traders followed portions of their route to the Pacific coast, and the formation of missionary settlements encouraged other Americans to journey to the Pacific Northwest.

Statehood

As early as 1843, an American provisional government had been established in the region. Three years later, a US-Canada boundary along the 49th parallel was established by agreement with the British. Oregon Territory, including the present state of Washington, was organized in 1848. In 1853, the land north of the Columbia River gained separate territorial status as Washington (which included part of present-day Idaho).

Although a series of treaties with the tribes of the Northwest had established a system of reservations, bloody uprisings by the Yakima, Nisqualli, and Cayuse were not suppressed until the late 1850s.

On the economic front, discoveries of gold in the Walla Walla area, in British Columbia, and in Idaho brought prosperity to the entire region. The completion in 1883 of the Northern Pacific Railroad line from the eastern US to Puget Sound encouraged immigration, and Washington's population swelled to 357,232 by 1890.

Cattle- and sheep-raising, farming, and lumbering were all established by the time Washington became the 42d state in 1889. In 1909, Seattle staged the Alaska-Yukon-Pacific Exposition, celebrating the Alaska gold rush and Seattle's new position as a major seaport. World War I brought the state several major new military installations, and the Puget Sound area thrived as a shipbuilding center. The war years also saw the emergence of radical labor activities, especially in the shipbuilding and logging industries.

1930s–1990s

Washington's economy was in dire straits during the Great Depression of the 1930s, when the market for forest products and field crops tumbled. The New Deal era brought numerous federally funded public works projects, notably the Bonneville and Grand Coulee dams on the Columbia River. They provided hydroelectric power for industry and water for the irrigation of desert lands. During World War II, Boeing led the way in establishing the aerospace industry as Washington's primary employer. Also during the war, the federal government built the Hanford Reservation nuclear research center. This was one of the major contractors in the construction of the first atomic bomb and later became a pioneer producer of atomic-powered electricity.

The 1960s and 1970s witnessed the growth of increasing public concern for protection of the state's unique natural heritage. An unforeseen environmental hazard emerged in May 1980 with the eruption of Mount St. Helens and the resultant widespread destruction.

Washington experienced a deep recession in 1979. The logging and lumber industries, competing with mills in the Southeast and in Canada, were particularly hard hit. Nuclear waste also became an issue with the publication in 1985 of a study claiming that plutonium produced at the Hanford Reservation bomb fuel

facility had leaked into the nearby Columbia River.

12 STATE GOVERNMENT

The legislative branch consists of a senate of 49 members elected to four-year terms, and a house of representatives with 98 members serving for two years. Executives elected statewide include the governor and lieutenant governor (who run separately), secretary of state, treasurer, attorney general, auditor, insurance commissioner, commissioner of public lands, and superintendent of public instruction.

A bill must first be passed by a majority of the elected members of each house. It then can be signed by the governor, or left

Washington Presidential Vote by Political Parties, 1948–2000

YEAR	WASHINGTON WINNER	DEMOCRAT	REPUBLICAN	PROGRESSIVE	SOCIALIST	PROHIBITION	SOCIALIST LABOR
1948	*Truman (D)	476,165	386,315	31,692	3,534	6,117	1,113
1952	*Eisenhower (R)	492,845	599,107	2,460	—	—	633
1956	*Eisenhower (R)	523,002	620,430	—	—	—	7,457
1960	Nixon (R)	599,298	629,273	—	—	—	10,895
1964	*Johnson (D)	779,699	470,366	—	—	—	7,772
				PEACE & FREEDOM		AMERICAN IND.	
1968	Humphrey (D)	616,037	588,510	1,669	—	96,900	491
				PEOPLE'S	LIBERTARIAN		
1972	*Nixon (R)	568,334	837,135	2,644	1,537	—	1,102
1976	Ford (R)	717,323	777,732	1,124	5,042	8,585	—
				CITIZENS			SOC. WORKERS
1980	*Reagan (R)	650,193	865,244	9,403	29,213	—	1,137
1984	*Reagan (R)	807,352	1,051,670	1,891	8,844	—	—
				NEW ALLIANCE		WORKER'S WORLD	
1988	Dukakis (D)	933,516	903,835	3,520	17,240	1,440	1,290
				IND. (Perot)		TAXPAYERS	NATURAL LAW
1992	*Clinton (D)	993,037	731,234	541,780	7,533	2,354	2,456
						IND. (Nader)	
1996	*Clinton (D)	1,123,323	840,712	201,003	12,522	60,322	—
						LIBERTARIAN	
2000	Gore (D)	1,247,652	1,108,864	103,002	660	13,135	304

* Won US presidential election.

unsigned for 5 days while the legislature is in session or 20 days after it has adjourned. A two-thirds vote of members present in each house is sufficient to override a gubernatorial veto.

Washington Governors: 1889–2001

1889–1893	Elisha Peyre Ferry	Republican
1893–1896	John Hart McGraw	Republican
1896–1901	John Rankin Rogers	Popular Democrat
1901–1905	Henry McBride	Republican
1905–1909	Albert Edward Mead	Republican
1909	Samuel Goodlove Cosgrove	Republican
1909–1913	Marion E. Hay	Republican
1913–1919	Earnest Lister	Democrat
1919–1925	Louis Folwell Hart	Republican
1925–1933	Roland Hill Hartley	Republican
1933–1941	Clarence Daniel Martin	Democrat
1941–1945	Arthur Bernard Langlie	Republican
1845–1953	Monrad Charles Wallgren	Democrat
1953–1957	Arthur Bernard Langlie	Republican
1957–1965	Albert Dean Rosellini	Democrat
1965–1977	Daniel Jackson Evans	Republican
1977–1981	Dixty Lee Ray	Democrat
1981–1985	John D. Spellman	Republican
1985–1993	Booth Gardner	Democrat
1993–1997	Michael Edward Lowry	Democrat
1997–	Gary Locke	Democrat

13 POLITICAL PARTIES

In recent decades, Washington has tended to favor Republicans in presidential elections, but Democrats have done well in other contests. Democrat Gary Locke was elected governor in 1996 and reelected in 2000. In November 1994, Slade Gorton, a Republican, was re-elected to a third term in the senate, but was defeated in 2000 by Democrat Maria Cantwell. Washington's other senator, Democrat Patty Murray, was reelected in 1998.

In the elections of 1994, Speaker of the US House of Representatives, Thomas S. Foley, lost his seat, the first time since 1860 that a sitting Speaker had lost. As of 2001, however, the Democrats had regrouped and held six of the state's nine US House seats.

As of 2001, there were 25 Democrats and 24 Republicans serving in the state senate, and 49 Democrats and 49 Republicans in the state house. Democratic candidate Al Gore won 50% of the vote in the 2000 presidential election and Republican nominee George W. Bush received 45%.

14 LOCAL GOVERNMENT

As of 1997, Washington had 39 counties, 276 municipal governments, and 296 school districts. Counties may establish their own institutions of government by charter; otherwise, the chief governing body is an elected board of three commissioners. Cities and towns are governed under the mayor-council or council-manager systems.

15 JUDICIAL SYSTEM

The state's highest court, the supreme court, consists of nine justices. Appeals of lower court decisions are normally heard in the court of appeals. The superior courts are the state trial courts. The crime index in 1998 was 5,867.4 reported offenses per 100,000 inhabitants. Prisoners in state or federal correctional facilities numbered 14,539 in 1999. This state imposes the death penalty.

16 MIGRATION

In recent decades, Washington has benefited from a second migratory wave even more massive than its first one in the late 19th century. From 1985 to 1990, the net migration gain was 317,832 (sixth among the states), and from 1990 to 1998 the net

Photo credit: Darrell Templeton.

Washington farmlands and, in the distance, Mount St. Helens.

domestic migration gain was about 373,900 (sixth highest). Many of those new residents were drawn from other states by Washington's defense- and trade-related industries. In addition, many immigrants from Southeast Asia arrived during the late 1970s. An estimated 7.1% of Washington's residents were foreign-born in 1996. As of 1990, 48.2% of state residents had been born in Washington.

17 ECONOMY

The mainstays of Washington's economy are services, financial institutions, manufacturing (especially aerospace equipment, shipbuilding, food processing, and wood products), agriculture, and tourism. The aerospace industry is the state's single lead-ing industry, although its impact is decreasing, especially with the move of the Boeing Aerospace, Inc. headquarters in 2001 to Chicago. Foreign trade, especially with Canada and Japan, was an important growth area during the 1970s and early 1980s. The eruption of Mount St. Helens in 1980 had a negative impact on the forestry industry (already clouded by a slow-down in housing construction) as well as on crop-growing and the tourist trade.

18 INCOME

With an income per capita (per person) of $28,719 in 1998, Washington ranked 13th among the 50 states. Total personal income was $163.3 billion in 1998. Some

Seattle skyline and the Space Needle.

10% of state residents were listed below the federal poverty level as of 1998.

[19] INDUSTRY

Aerospace/transportation equipment is the largest industry in Washington state, employing more than 80,000 people. Boeing's airplane sales make that company one of the top US exporters. This situation will likely change once the move of its corporate headquarters to Chicago is completed in 2001.

The 1980s were Washington's busiest years in terms of technology company start-ups, with software and computer-related businesses accounting for most of the activity. Many of Washington's high-technology companies are world leaders, such as Microsoft.

Food processing is one of Washington's largest manufacturing industries. In addition, Washington has a large concentration of biotechnology companies. More than two-thirds develop products for human health care. Others develop products and processes for agriculture, food processing, forestry, veterinary medicine, marine industries, and environmental management.

[20] LABOR

In mid-1998, Washington's civilian labor force numbered 3.04 million, of whom 4.8% were unemployed. Washington—

with its tradition of radical labor activities in mines and logging camps earlier in the century—has one of the most organized labor forces in the US. In 1998, 21% of all workers belonged to unions (5th among the states).

21 AGRICULTURE

Orchard and field crops dominate Washington's agricultural economy, which yielded $4.9 billion in farm marketing in 1999, 13th among the 50 states. Fruits and vegetables are raised in the humid and in the irrigated areas of the state, while wheat and other grains grow in the drier central and eastern regions.

Washington is the nation's leading producer of apples: the estimated 1998 apple crop, representing 55% of the US total, was 6 million tons. Among leading varieties, delicious apples ranked first, followed by golden delicious and winesap. Washington ranks first in the production of hops, red raspberries, pears, and cherries, and second in grapes and apricots. Other crop figures for 1998 included wheat, 154.7 million bushels; barley, 33.8 million bushels; and corn for grain, 19 million bushels.

22 DOMESTICATED ANIMALS

Livestock and livestock products accounted for 31% of Washington's agricultural income in 1995. In 1999, farms and ranches had 1.15 million cattle, 37,000 hogs, and 5.15 million pounds of sheep. In 1997, Washington dairy farmers had 264,000 milk cows that produced 5.3 billion pounds (2.4 billion kilograms) of milk. Poultry farmers produced 194 million pounds (88 million kilograms) of broilers in 1997, valued at $75 million, as well as 1.4 billion eggs, worth $75 million.

23 FISHING

In 1998, Washington's production of fish for consumption reached 419 million pounds (190 million kilograms), valued at $123 million. Washington's oyster landings in 1998 amounted to 83% of the Pacific region's total. There were 1,656 commercial fishing vessels in 1997; Westport, Bellingham, and Seattle are the leading commercial fishing ports. In 1997, on average, 4,927 workers were employed in the state's 198 fish processing plants. Washington issued 681,656 sport fishing licenses in 1998.

24 FORESTRY

Washington's forests cover 21.9 million acres (8.9 million hectares), and are an important commercial and recreational resource. The largest forests are Wenatchee, Snoqualmie, and Okanogan. Forest production is Washington's second-largest manufacturing industry. In 1995, the industry employed more than 56,400 people and generated $12.7 billion in revenue.

Lumber and plywood, logs for export, various chip products, pulp logs, and shakes and shingles are the leading forest commodities. The giant of Washington's forest industry is Weyerhaeuser, with headquarters in Tacoma. Federal, state, and private nurseries in Washington planted more than 148,000 acres (59,900 hectares) in 1996.

25 MINING

The estimated value of nonfuel mineral production for Washington in 1998 was $583 million. Gold and magnesium metal represented one-third of the total value. Construction sand and gravel, portland cement, and crushed stone accounted for most of the remaining value.

26 ENERGY AND POWER

In 1998, Washington power plants generated 97.1 billion kilowatt hours of electricity. About 82% of that electricity came from hydroelectric facilities, which are mostly public owned and operated. The state had one nuclear power plant as of 1996. The Hanford Reservation was the site of the first US nuclear energy plant. The state's lone major fossil fuel resource is coal. The state has been a pioneer in developing alternate sources of energy, saving significant amounts since 1983.

27 COMMERCE

Wholesale sales totaled $79 billion in 1997; retail sales were over $40 billion. The Seattle-Tacoma-Bremerton area accounted for 65% of retail sales. In 1998, exports of goods originating from the state had a value of $38 billion, third in the US.

28 PUBLIC FINANCE

The total revenues for 1997 were $26.84 billion, and the expenditures were $22.2 billion. The outstanding debt as of 1997 was $9.49 billion, or $1,692 per capita (per person).

29 TAXATION

Taxes, licenses, permits, and fees account for about three-fifths of Washington state government revenues. Washington has no individual or corporate income tax. As of 1996, the state levied a general sales tax of 6.5%, as well as taxes on gasoline, cigarettes, liquor sales, inheritances, most service activities, motor vehicles, and other items. The state property tax is dedicated to the public schools. In 1995, Washington paid more than $23 billion in taxes to the federal government and received $28.8 billion in federal funding.

30 HEALTH

Washington's death rate, 750.6 per 100,000 population, was well below the national rate of 864.7 in 1998. The death rates from heart disease and cancer were also lower than their respective national rates. As of 1998, there were 86 general hospitals, with 10,739 beds. The average hospital cost per inpatient day was $1,368 in 1998, or $6,625 for an average cost per stay. In 1999, at least 12.3% of the state's residents were uninsured.

31 HOUSING

In 1999, there were almost 2.4 million housing units in Washington. That year, 45,700 new privately owned housing units were authorized for construction, worth over $4.7 billion. In 1990, the median monthly cost for an owner-occupied housing unit (with mortgage) was $738; median rent was $445.

Photo credit: © G. Braasch/Woodfin Camp.

Grand Coulee Dam provides hydroelectric power for the citizens of Washington.

32 EDUCATION

Washingtonians rank exceptionally high by most educational standards. As of 1998, 92% of all Washingtonians 25 years of age or older were high school graduates, and 28.1% had four or more years of college. As of 1997, there were 991,235 pupils in Washington's public schools. Expenditures on education averaged $6,126 per pupil in 1999/2000.

As of 1999, Washington had 32 colleges and universities (8 public, 24 private) and 32 community colleges. The largest institution is the University of Washington (Seattle), enrolling 33,719 students in 1994. Other public institutions include Washington State University (Pullman), Central Washington University (Ellensburg), and Evergreen State College (Olympia). Private institutions include Gonzaga University (Spokane); Pacific Lutheran University (Tacoma); Seattle University, 4,844; and University of Puget Sound (Tacoma). Community colleges enrolled 159,249 students in 1994/95.

33 ARTS

The focus of professional performance activities in Washington is Seattle Center, home of the Seattle Symphony, Pacific Northwest Ballet Company, and Seattle Repertory Theater. The Seattle Opera Association, which also performs there throughout the year, is one of the nation's leading opera companies. Tacoma and Spokane have notable local orchestras.

Among Washington's many museums, universities, and other organizations exhibiting works of art on a permanent or periodic basis are the Seattle Art Museum, with its Modern Art Pavilion, and the Henry Art Gallery of the University of Washington at Seattle.

34 LIBRARIES AND MUSEUMS

In 1998, Washington's system of public libraries held more than 19.3 million volumes and had a combined circulation of nearly 54 million. Of Washington's 39 counties, 29 were served by the state's 21 county and multicounty libraries. The leading public library system is the Seattle Public Library, with 25 branches and 1.9 million volumes in 1998. The principal academic libraries are at the University of Washington (Seattle) and Washington State University (Pullman). Olympia is the home of the Washington State Library.

The state has 160 museums and historic sites. The Washington State Historical Society Museum (Tacoma) features Native American and other pioneer artifacts. Mount Rainer National Park displays zoological, botanical, geological, and historical collections.

35 COMMUNICATIONS

As of 1999, 95.9% of Washington's households had telephones. During 2000, Washington had 262 radio stations, of which 103 were AM and 159 were FM. There were 43 television stations. The total domain names registered in 2000 was 206,961.

36 PRESS

In 1998, Washington had 13 morning newspapers, 11 evening dailies, and 16 Sunday papers. Leading newspapers with their 1998 daily circulations are the *Seattle Times* (227,715); the *Seattle Post-Intelligencer* (196,271); and the *Tacoma News Tribune Ledger* (129,247).

37 TOURISM, TRAVEL, AND RECREATION

Seattle Center—featuring the 605-foot (184-meter) Space Needle tower, Opera House, and Pacific Science Center—helps make Washington's largest city one of the most exciting on the West Coast. Nevertheless, scenic beauty and opportunities for outdoor recreation are Washington's principal attractions for tourists from out of state.

Mount Rainier National Park, covering 235,404 acres (95,265 hectares) encompasses the state's highest peak. Glaciers, lakes, and mountain peaks are featured at North Cascades National Park, while Olympic National Park is famous as the site of Mount Olympus and the Olympic Rainforest. Washington also offers two national historic parks, two national historic sites (Fort Vancouver and the Whitman Mission), and three national recreation areas (Coulee Dam, Lake Chelan, and Ross Lake). Hunting is a highly popular pastime.

Tourism is the fourth-largest industry in Washington state after aerospace/transportation equipment, agriculture, and timber. Washington has been consistently ranked among the nation's top ten tourist destination states.

38 SPORTS

Washington is home to four major league professional sports teams, all of which play in Seattle: the Mariners, of Major League Baseball; the Seahawks, of the National Football League; the Storm, of the Women's National Basketball Association; and the Supersonics, of the National Basketball Association. In collegiate sports, the Huskies represent the University of Washington in football. Skiing, boating, and hiking are popular participant sports.

39 FAMOUS WASHINGTONIANS

Washington's most distinguished public figure was US Supreme Court Justice William O. Douglas (b.Minnesota, 1898–1980), whose 37-year tenure on the Court was an all-time high. Other federal office-holders from Washington include Lewis B. Schwellenbach (b.Wisconsin, 1894–1948), secretary of labor under Harry S Truman; and Brockman Adams (b.Georgia, 1927), secretary of transportation under Jimmy Carter. Serving in the US Senate from 1945 to 1981, Warren G. Magnuson (b.Minnesota, 1905-89) chaired the powerful Appropriations Committee. A fellow Democrat, Henry M. "Scoop" Jackson (1912–83,) was influential on the Armed Services Committee and ran unsuccessfully for his party's presidential nomination in 1976. Thomas Stephen Foley (b.1929)

Photo credit: EPD Photos

Gary Locke (1950–)was elected Washington's 21st governor on November 5, 1996, making him the first Chinese-American governor in U.S. history.

was Speaker of the House from 1987 until his defeat in the 1994 elections.

Dixy Lee Ray (1914–93), governor from 1977 to 1981, was the only woman governor in the state's history. Bertha Knight Landes (b.Massachusetts, 1868–1943), elected mayor of Seattle in 1926, was the first woman to be elected mayor of a large US city.

Famous entrepreneurs from Washington include merchandiser Eddie Bauer (1899–1986), and William Henry "Bill"

Gates III (b.1955), cofounder of the Microsoft Corporation.

Hans Georg Dehmelt (b.Germany, 1922) was a recipient of the 1989 Nobel Prize for physics as a member of the University of Washington faculty. William E. Boeing (b.Michigan, 1881–1956) pioneered Washington's largest single industry, aerospace technology.

Washington authors have made substantial contributions to American literature. Mary McCarthy (1912–89) was born in Seattle, and one of her books, *Memories of a Catholic Girlhood* (1957), describes her early life there. University of Washington faculty member Theodore Roethke (b.Michigan, 1908–63), won the Pulitzer Prize for poetry in 1953. Max Brand (Frederick Schiller Faust, 1892–1944) wrote hundreds of Western novels. Washington has also been the birthplace of several prominent cartoonists, including Chuck Jones (b.1912), who created the Road Runner and other animated characters; Hank Ketcham (b.1920), who created the comic strip *Dennis the Menace*; and Gary Larson (b.1950), creator of *The Far Side*.

Singer-actor Harry Lillis "Bing" Crosby (1904–77), born in Tacoma, remained a loyal alumnus of Spokane's Gonzaga University. Modern dance chore-ographers Merce Cunningham (b.1919) and Robert Joffrey (1930–88) are both Washington natives. Modern artist Robert Motherwell (1915–91) was born in Aberdeen. Washington's contribution to popular music is rock-guitarist Jimi Hendrix (James Marshall Hendrix, 1943–70).

40 BIBLIOGRAPHY

Aylesworth, Thomas G. *The Northwest: Alaska, Idaho, Oregon, Washington.* New York: Chelsea House, 1996.

Bancroft, H. H. *History of Washington, Idaho, and Montana.* San Francisco: History Co., 1890.

Blashfield, Jean F. *Washington.* New York: Children's Press, 2001.

Clark, Norman H. *Washington: A Bicentennial History.* New York: Norton, 1976.

McAuliffe, Emily. *Washington Facts and Symbols.* Mankato, Minn.: Hilltop Books, 1999.

Stefoff, Rebecca. *Washington.* New York: Benchmark Books, 1999.

Thompson, Kathleen. *Washington.* Austin: Raintree Steck-Vaughn, 1996.

Web sites

Access Washington Home Page. Just for Kids. [Online] Available http://access.wa.gov/kids/ Accessed May 31, 2001.

Access Washington. Washington State Government Information & Services. [Online] Available http://access.wa.gov/ Accessed May 31, 2001.

State Legislature. The Symbols of Washington State. [Online] Available http://www.leg.wa.gov/legis/symbols/symbols.htm Accessed May 31, 2001.

Washington State Tourism Home Page. Washington State Online Travel Information. [Online] Available http://www.tourism.wa.gov/ Accessed May 31, 2001.

WEST VIRGINIA

State of West Virginia

ORIGIN OF STATE NAME: The state was originally the western part of Virginia.

NICKNAME: The Mountain State.

CAPITAL: Charleston.

ENTERED UNION: 20 June 1863 (35th).

SONGS: "The West Virginia Hills"; "West Virginia, My Home Sweet Home"; "This Is My West Virginia."

MOTTO: *Montani semper liberi* (Mountaineers are always free).

COAT OF ARMS: A farmer stands to the right and a miner to the left of a large ivy-draped rock bearing the date of the state's admission to the Union. In front of the rock are two hunters' rifles upon which rests a Cap of Liberty. The state motto is beneath and the words "State of West Virginia" above.

FLAG: The flag has a white field bordered by a strip of blue, with the coat of arms in the center, wreathed by rhododendron leaves; across the top of the coat of arms are the words "State of West Virginia."

OFFICIAL SEAL: The obverse is the same as the coat of arms; the reverse is no longer in common use.

ANIMAL: Black bear.

BIRD: Cardinal.

FISH: Brook trout.

FLOWER: *Rhododendron maximum* ("big laurel").

TREE: Sugar maple.

FRUIT: Apple.

COLORS: Old gold and blue.

TIME: 7 AM EST = noon GMT.

1 LOCATION AND SIZE

Located in the eastern US, in the South Atlantic region, West Virginia ranks 41st in size among the 50 states. The area of West Virginia totals 24,231 square miles (62,758 square kilometers). The state extends 265 miles (426 kilometers) east-west; its maximum north-south extension is 237 miles (381 kilometers). Its total boundary length is 1,180 miles (1,899 kilometers).

2 TOPOGRAPHY

Most of West Virginia's eastern panhandle, crossed by the Allegheny Mountains, is in the Ridge and Valley region of the Appalachian Highlands. The remainder is part of the Allegheny Plateau. The state's highest point, Spruce Knob, towers 4,861 feet (1,482 meters) above sea level. Major lowlands lie along the rivers, especially the Potomac, Ohio, and Kanawha.

3 CLIMATE

West Virginia has a humid continental climate, with hot summers and cool to cold winters. Mean annual temperatures vary from 56°F (13°C) in the southwest to 48°F (9°C) in higher elevations. The highest recorded temperature was 112°F (44°C) in 1936; the lowest, –37°F (–38°C), occurred in 1917.

Precipitation averages 45 inches (114 centimeters) annually and is slightly heavier on the western slopes of the Alleghenies.

4 PLANTS AND ANIMALS

Oak, maple, poplar, and such softwoods as hemlock and pine are the common forest trees. Rhododendron, dogwood, and pussy willow are among the more than 200 flowering trees and shrubs. The white-tailed (Virginia) deer, black bear, and wildcat are still found in the deep timber of the Allegheny ridges. Common birds include the cardinal, scarlet tanager, and catbird. Notable among more than 100 species of fish are smallmouth bass, rainbow trout, and brook trout (the state fish). The southern bald eagle and American and American peregrine falcons are among the 14 species on the endangered list.

5 ENVIRONMENTAL PROTECTION

Major responsibility for environmental protection in West Virginia rests with the Division of Environmental Protection (DEP). Environmental issues confronting the state of West Virginia include the restoration of about 2,000 miles of streams

West Virginia Population Profile

Total population in 2000:	1,808,344
Population change, 1990–2000:	0.8%
Hispanic or Latino†:	0.7%
Population by race	
One race:	99.1%
White:	95.0%
Black or African American:	3.2%
American Indian/Alaska Native:	0.2%
Asian:	0.5%
Native Hawaiian/Pacific Islander:	—
Some other race:	0.2%
Two or more races:	0.9%

Population by Age Group

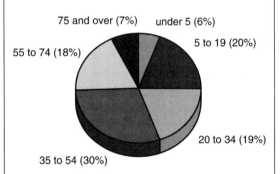

75 and over (7%)   under 5 (6%)
55 to 74 (18%)
5 to 19 (20%)
20 to 34 (19%)
35 to 54 (30%)

Top Cities by Population

City	Population	% change 1990–2000
Charleston	53,421	–6.7
Huntington	51,475	–6.1
Parkersburg	33,099	–2.3
Wheeling	31,419	–9.9
Morgantown	26,809	3.6
Weirton	20,411	–7.7
Fairmont	19,097	–5.5
Beckley	17,254	–5.7
Clarksburg	16,743	–7.3
Martinsburg	14,972	6.4

Notes: †A person of Hispanic or Latino origin may be of any race. NA indicates that data are not available.
Sources: U.S. Census Bureau. Public Information Office. *Demographic Profiles.* [Online] Available http://www.census.gov/Press-Release/www/2001/demoprofile.html. Accessed June 1, 2001. U.S. Census Bureau. *Census 2000: Redistricting Data.* Press release issued by the Redistricting Data Office. Washington, D.C., March, 2001.

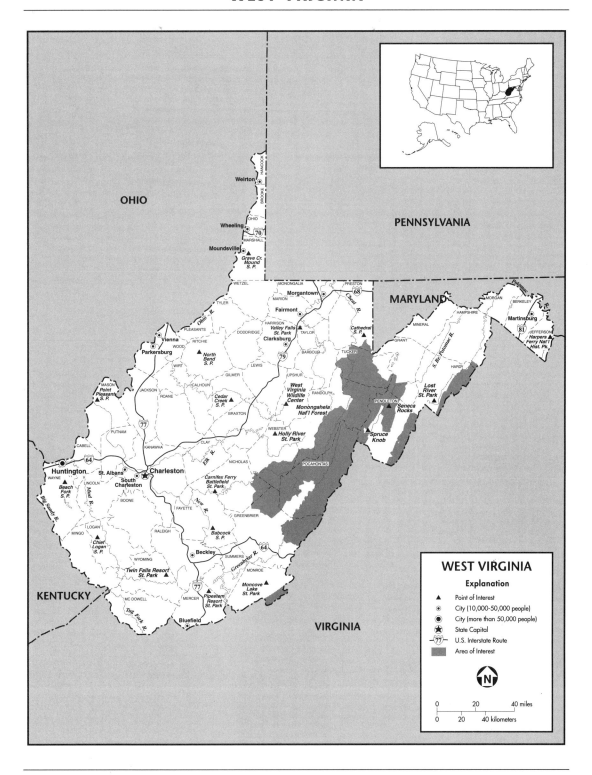

WEST VIRGINIA

Explanation

▲ Point of Interest
◉ City (10,000-50,000 people)
◉ City (more than 50,000 people)
★ State Capital
–⟨77⟩– U.S. Interstate Route
▨ Area of Interest

N

0   20   40 miles
0 20 40 kilometers

West Virginia Population by Race

Census 2000 was the first national census in which the instructions to respondents said, "Mark one or more races." This table shows the number of people who are of one, two, or three or more races. For those claiming two races, the number of people belonging to the various categories is listed. The U.S. government conducts a census of the population every ten years.

	Number	Percent
Total population	1,808,344	100.0
One race	1,792,556	99.1
Two races	14,846	0.8
White *and* Black or African American	4,159	0.2
White *and* American Indian/Alaska Native	5,966	0.3
White *and* Asian	1,704	0.1
White *and* Native Hawaiian/Pacific Islander	214	—
White *and* some other race	1,690	0.1
Black or African American *and* American Indian/Alaska Native	367	—
Black or African American *and* Asian	142	—
Black or African American *and* Native Hawaiian/Pacific Islander	27	—
Black or African American *and* some other race	228	—
American Indian/Alaska Native *and* Asian	35	—
American Indian/Alaska Native *and* Native Hawaiian/Pacific Islander	9	—
American Indian/Alaska Native *and* some other race	52	—
Asian *and* Native Hawaiian/Pacific Islander	66	—
Asian *and* some other race	167	—
Native Hawaiian/Pacific Islander *and* some other race	20	—
Three or more races	942	0.1

Source: U.S. Census Bureau. *Census 2000: Redistricting Data.* Press release issued by the Redistricting Data Office. Washington, D.C., March, 2001. A dash (—) indicates that the percent is less than 0.1.

that are being affected by damage caused from mining. The state mandates that cities with populations of 10,000 or more develop recycling programs. The state had seven hazardous waste sites as of 1998.

6 POPULATION

With a 2000 census total of 1,808,344, West Virginia ranked 37th among the 50 states in population, losing its rank of 34th in 1990 to Utah. The population projection for 2005 is 1.85 million. The density in 2000 was 75.1 persons per square mile (29 persons per square kilometer). In 1990, only 36.1% of West Virginia's population was urban—a smaller proportion than any other state but Vermont. In 2000, Charleston, the largest city, had 53,421 residents; Huntington, 51,475; Parkersburg, 33,099; and Wheeling, 31,419. All four of these cities lost population between 1990 and 2000. The state has one of the oldest populations in the country. Its median age is nearly 39 years, almost 4 years older than the national average.

7 ETHNIC GROUPS

According to a 1997 federal estimate, about 1.75 million whites lived in the state, accounting for 96.2% of the population. Persons reporting at least one specific

Aerial view of Charleston, West Virginia's capital city.

ancestry group in 1990 included 269,798 English, 468,927 Germans, 348,448 Irish, and 74,877 Dutch. In the 1997 estimate, the state only had about 2,500 Native Americans (0.1%). The estimated 57,600 blacks in the state in 1997 constituted about 3.2% of the population; 8,500 persons of Asian and Pacific origin accounted for 0.5%. There were about 10,100 West Virginians with Hispanic origins.

8 LANGUAGES

West Virginia maintains Midland speech. But there are speech differences between the northern and southern halves of the state—the former influenced by Pennsylvania and the latter by western Virginia. In 1990, 1,642,729 West Virginians—97.4% of the population—spoke only English at home. Other languages spoken at home, and the number of persons who spoke them, included Spanish, 13,337; Italian, 4,691; French, 7,695; and German, 5,280.

9 RELIGIONS

Throughout its history, West Virginia has been overwhelmingly Protestant. In 1990, the major Protestant denominations and the number of their members were United Methodist, 182,731; American Baptist USA, 132,325; Presbyterian Church, 37,586; the Church of the Nazarene, 25,811; and Church of God, 19,814. The Catholic population was 108,529 in 1990;

the Jewish population was estimated at 2,000 in 1994.

10 TRANSPORTATION

Total rail mileage of track in 1998 was 2,616 miles (4,166 kilometers). At the end of 1997, there were 35,271 miles (56,751 kilometers) of public roads, 91% in rural areas. Major navigable inland rivers are the Ohio, Kanawha, and Monongahela; each has locks and dams. Yeager Airport in Charleston is the state's main air terminal.

11 HISTORY

When European settlers arrived in present-day West Virginia, only a few Shawnee, Tuscarora, and Delaware Indian villages remained, but the area was still actively used as hunting and warring grounds, and European possession was hotly contested.

The fur trade stimulated early exploration by both the English and French. England eventually prevailed as a result of the French and Indian War. It is thought that the first settlement was founded at Bunker Hill in 1731. By 1750, several thousand settlers were living in the eastern panhandle, and there was movement into the Greenbriar, Monongahela, and upper Ohio river valleys after 1769, although wars with the Native Americans occurred sporadically until the 1790s. The area that is now West Virginia was part of Virginia at the time of that state's entry into the Union on 25 June 1788.

Serious differences between eastern and western Virginia developed after the War of 1812. Eastern Virginia was dominated by large farms that used slave labor, while small diversified farms and infant industries predominated in western Virginia. Westerners resented property qualifications for voting, inadequate representation in the Virginia legislature, and undemocratic county governments, and were dissatisfied with the quality of government operations. In 1859, abolitionist John Brown led a raid at Harpers Ferry, seizing the US Armory there. Brown was convicted and hanged for treason, which made him a hero for the antislavery movement.

Statehood

When Virginia seceded from the Union in 1861, western counties remaining loyal to the Union set up the Reorganized Government and consented to the separation of present West Virginia from Virginia. After approval by Congress and President Lincoln, West Virginia entered the Union on 20 June 1863 as the 35th state.

Both Bourbon Democratic and Republican governors after the Civil War sought to improve transportation, foster immigration, and provide tax structures attractive to business. Republican governors of the early 20th century, attuned to Progressive ideas, were instrumental in the adoption of the direct primary, safety legislation for the coal mines, revision of corporate tax laws, and improvements in highways and education.

The Great Depression of the 1930s, from which West Virginia suffered acutely, ushered in a Democratic era. West Virginians embraced the liberal philosophies of

Presidents Franklin D. Roosevelt and Harry S Truman. World Wars I and II produced significant changes in West Virginia, particularly through stimulation of chemical, steel, and textile industries, which lessened the state's dependence on mining, historically the backbone of its economy.

Post–World War II

After World War II, mechanization and strip-mining displaced thousands of miners and resulted in a large exodus to other states. By 1960, West Virginia was considered one of the most economically depressed areas of the country, primarily because of conditions in the mining regions. Antipoverty programs of the Kennedy and Johnson administrations provided some relief, but much of it was temporary.

Over the last several decades, West Virginia's manufacturing and mining sectors have shrunk dramatically. Automation, foreign competition, and the recession of the early 1980s caused employment in steel, glass, chemical manufacturing, and coal mining to drop by a third between 1979 and 1985. On the other hand, tourism, centered on skiing and whitewater rafting, has provided West Virginia with a growing source of income. The same technological advances which forced a restructuring of the economy of West Virginia have produced social change. Electronic communications have largely eliminated the cultural isolation long felt by West Virginia residents.

12 STATE GOVERNMENT

The legislature consists of a senate with 34 members and a house of delegates with 100 members. Elected officials of the executive branch of government include the governor, secretary of state, auditor, and attorney general. Bills passed by the legislature become law when signed by the governor. Those the governor vetoes may become law if repassed by majorities of both house memberships—except for revenue and appropriations bills, which require a two-thirds majority of both houses.

West Virginia Governors: 1863–2001

1863–1869	Arthur Inghram Boreman	Republican
1869	Daniel Duane Farnsworth	Republican
1869–1871	William Erskine Stevenson	Republican
1871–1877	John Jeremiah Jacob	Dem/Indep
1877–1881	Henry Mason Matthews	Democrat
1881–1885	Jacob Beeson Jackson	Democrat
1885–1889	Emanuel Willis Wilson	Democrat
1889–1893	Aretas Brooks Fleming	Democrat
1893–1897	William Alexander MacCorkle	Democrat
1897–1901	George Wesley Atkinson	Republican
1901–1905	Albert Blakeslee White	Republican
1905–1909	William Mercer Owens Dawson	Republican
1909–1913	William Ellsworth Glasscock	Republican
1913–1917	Henry Drury Hatfield	Republican
1917–1921	John Jacob Cornwell	Democrat
1921–1925	Ephraim Franklin Morgan	Republican
1925–1929	Howard Mason Gore	Republican
1929–1933	William Gustavus Conley	Republican
1933–1937	Herman Guy Kump	Democrat
1937–1941	Homer Adams Holt	Democrat
1941–1945	Matthew Mansfield Neely	Democrat
1945–1949	Clarence Watson Meadows	Democrat
1949–1953	Okey Leonidas Patteson	Democrat
1953–1957	William Casey Marland	Democrat
1957–1961	Cecil Harland Underwood	Republican
1961–1965	William Wallace Barron	Democrat
1965–1969	Hulett Carlson Smith	Democrat
1969–1977	Arch Alfred Moore, Jr.	Republican
1977–1985	John Davidson Rockefeller IV	Democrat
1985–1989	Arch Alfred Moore, Jr.	Republican
1989–1997	Gaston Caperton	Democrat
1997–2000	Cecil Underwood	Republican
2000–	Bob Wise	Democrat

Democrat/Independent – Dem/Indep

An abandoned coal mine.

13 POLITICAL PARTIES

The Republican Party presided over the birth of West Virginia, but the Democrats have generally been in power for the past five decades. In 1998, West Virginia had over 1 million registered voters, of whom 63% were Democrats, 29% were Republicans, and 8% belonged to minor parties or were unaffiliated. Since the 1930s, Republican presidential candidates have carried West Virginia only in 1956, 1972, 1984, and 2000. The state is even more firmly Democratic in elections for other offices. Robert Byrd, who has served in the Senate since 1959 and was majority leader from 1977–80, is a Democrat and was reelected to the Senate in 2000. John D. Rockefeller IV is also a Democrat. As of 2001, West Virginia's US Representatives consist of two Democrats and one Republican.

West Virginia Presidential Vote by Major Political Parties, 1948–2000

YEAR	WEST VIRGINIA WINNER	DEMOCRAT	REPUBLICAN
1948	*Truman (D)	429,188	316,251
1952	Stevenson (D)	453,578	419,970
1956	*Eisenhower (R)	381,534	449,297
1960	*Kennedy (D)	441,786	395,995
1964	*Johnson (D)	538,087	253,953
1968	Humphrey (D)	374,091	307,555
1972	*Nixon (R)	277,435	484,964
1976	*Carter (D)	435,914	314,760
1980	Carter (D)	367,462	334,206
1984	*Reagan (R)	328,125	405,483
1988	Dukakis (D)	341,016	310,065
1992**	*Clinton (D)	331,001	241,974
1996**	*Clinton (D)	327,812	233,946
2000	*Bush (R)	295,497	336,475

* Won US presidential election.
** Independent candidate Ross Perot received 108,829 votes in 1992 and 71,639 votes in 1996.

14 LOCAL GOVERNMENT

West Virginia has 55 counties. The chief county officials are the three commissioners, who comprise the county court; the sheriff, assessor, county clerk, and prosecuting attorney; and the five-member board of education. There were 232 cities, towns, and villages as of 1997.

15 JUDICIAL SYSTEM

The highest court in West Virginia, the supreme court of appeals, has five justices, including the chief justice. The court has broad appeals jurisdiction in both civil and criminal cases, and original jurisdiction in certain other cases. West Virginia is divided into 31 judicial circuits, each with anywhere from one to seven judges. Circuit courts had jurisdiction over juvenile, domestic relations, and administrative proceedings. Local courts include the county magistrate courts and municipal courts. West Virginia's crime rate was 2,547 per 100,000 population in 1998. As of 1999 prisoners in state or federal correctional facilities totaled 3,699. The state abolished the death penalty in 1965.

16 MIGRATION

Between 1950 and 1970, West Virginia suffered a 13% loss in population, chiefly from the coal-mining areas; but between 1970 and 1980, population rose by almost 12%. According to federal estimates, the state had a net migration loss of about 81,000 in the 1980s. During 1990–98, West Virginia had a net gain of 8,000 from interstate migration and 3,300 from migration abroad, an overall increase of 1%.

17 ECONOMY

Agriculture was the backbone of West Virginia's economy until the 1890s, when coal, oil, natural gas, and timber began to play a major role. World War I stimulated important industries such as chemicals, steel, glass, and textiles. The beauty of West Virginia's mountains and forests has attracted an increasing number of tourists, but the state's rugged terrain and relative isolation from major markets continue to hamper its economic development.

18 INCOME

Total personal income was $36.6 billion in 1998. The state's per capita (per person) income of $20,185 ranked last in the US. In 1999, about 17.6% of all West Virginians lived below the federal poverty level.

19 INDUSTRY

Known for its rich natural resources and strong industrial presence, the value of shipments by manufacturers in 1997 totaled $19 billion. Major industries included organic chemicals, primary metals, fabricated metal products, and lumber and wood products.

Major industrial areas are the Kanawha, Ohio, and Monongahela valleys and the eastern panhandle. The largest industrial corporations with headquarters in West Virginia are Weirton Steel and Wheeling-Pittsburgh. Other major industrial companies with operations in West Virginia include E. I. du Pont de Nemours, Union Carbide, Ravenswood Aluminum, and Rhone Poulenc.

20 LABOR

The state's total civilian labor force averaged 807,600 in mid-1998, when unemployment was about 6.6%. Some 12.6% of all workers belonged to labor unions in 1998, down from 47% in 1970.

21 AGRICULTURE

With estimated farm marketing of $382 million, West Virginia ranked 46th among the 50 states in 1999. In 1998, 24% of the state's land was devoted to farming. Leading crops produced in 1998 were hay, 1.2 million tons; corn for grain, 0.7 million bushels; commercial apples, 115 million pounds; and tobacco, 2.4 million pounds. Its 21,000 farms average 176 acres in size.

22 DOMESTICATED ANIMALS

Livestock in 1995 accounted for 81% of West Virginia's agricultural cash receipts. The largest component was the poultry industry. Broilers accounted for 34% of agricultural receipts in 1995; cattle products, 19%; turkeys, 11%; dairy products, 9%; and chicken eggs, 6%. In 1996, West Virginia had 1.8 million chickens, 470,000 cattle, 55,000 sheep, 19,000 hogs, and 21,000 milk cows.

23 FISHING

West Virginia fishing has little commercial importance. In 1998, federal hatcheries distributed nearly 2.2 million trout within the state. West Virginia issued 282,750 sport fishing licenses in that year.

24 FORESTRY

West Virginia has four-fifths, or 12.1 million acres (4.9 million hectares), of its land area in forestland, making it the third-most forested state in the nation. In all, West Virginia's forests contain more than 100 species of trees, all but 12 being hardwoods. In 1998, approximately 737 million board feet of timber was harvested.

The state is encouraging the professional management of its forests so they will continue to produce a sustained array of benefits, such as wood products, jobs, clean water, oxygen, scenery, and diverse recreational opportunities like hunting, hiking, and tourism.

25 MINING

The value of nonfuel mineral production in 1998 was about $182 million. Crushed stone accounted for about 43% of the state's total value of nonfuel minerals. In 1998, construction sand and gravel production was 1.6 million short tons, worth $7.86 million.

26 ENERGY AND POWER

West Virginia has long been an important supplier of energy in the form of electric power and fossil fuels. In 1999, net generation of electric energy was 89.6 billion kilowatt hours, of which 99% was produced by coal-fired steam units. The state has no nuclear power plants. In 1998, West Virginia was second to Wyoming in coal production, producing 171 million tons (15% of the national total). Demonstrated reserves came to 35.4 billion tons. In 1999, West Virginia produced 1.5 million barrels of crude oil and 172 billion cubic feet (4.8 billion cubic meters) of natural gas.

Photo credit: David Fattaleh, West Virginia Division of Tourism.

Architecture of Harpers Ferry National Historical Park in Jefferson.

27 COMMERCE

Wholesale sales totaled $65 billion in 1997; retail sales were also $65 billion in the same year. In 1998, West Virginia exported $2.1 billion in products originating within the state, ranking it 37th.

28 PUBLIC FINANCE

In 1997, revenues totaled $7.47 billion and expenditures amounted to $7.15 billion. The state's outstanding debt totaled $3.04 billion as of 1997, or $1,673 per capita (per person).

29 TAXATION

West Virginia's tax receipts totaled more than $2.9 billion in 1997, or $1,600 per person (25th among the states). The state taxes personal and corporate income. There are consumers' sales taxes of 6% on goods and services excluding food. Counties and localities mainly tax property.

30 HEALTH

West Virginia had the nation's second highest death rate (after the District of Columbia) in 1997, at 1,155.5 per 100,000 population. Its birth rate of 11.4 per 1,000 population that year was lower than the national rate of 14.6. The death rate from heart disease, 380 per 100,000, was highest among the states in 1998. Other leading causes of death were cancer, stroke, accidents, chronic obstructive pulmonary diseases, pneumonia and flu, and diabetes. Pneumoconiosis (black lung) is an occupational hazard among coal miners. In 1998, the state's 58 hospitals had 8,117 beds. Some 17.2% of state residents did not have health insurance in 1998.

31 HOUSING

In 1999, West Virginia had an estimated 716,000 housing units. In 1998, 3,800 new housing units valued at $323 million were authorized for construction by the state. In 1990, West Virginia had the lowest median monthly costs of any state for both owners (with a mortgage) and renters, at $498 and $303, respectively. The median home value in 1990 was $47,900. West Virginia had the highest rate of home ownership in 1994, at 73.7%.

32 EDUCATION

West Virginia has generally ranked below national standards in education. In 1998, 76.4% of adult West Virginians were high school graduates. In 1997, the state's public schools enrolled 301,419 students. Expenditures on education averaged $6,878 per pupil in 1999/2000. The state supports West Virginia University (Morgantown), Marshall University (Huntington), and the West Virginia College of Graduate Studies (various locations in central and southern West Virginia). In the fall of 1997, total higher educational institutions had enrolled 87,965 students.

33 ARTS

West Virginia is known for the quilts, pottery, and woodwork of its mountain artisans. Huntington Galleries, the Sunrise Foundation at Charleston, and Oglebay Park, Wheeling, are major art centers. Musical attractions include the Charleston Symphony Orchestra, the Wheeling Symphony, and a country music program at Wheeling. In 1996, West Virginia had 150 arts associations and 30 local arts groups.

34 LIBRARIES AND MUSEUMS

In 1999, West Virginia's public libraries had 4.8 million volumes in 14 systems; the largest being the Kanawha County Public Library system at Charleston. Of college and university libraries, the largest collection was West Virginia University's (Morgantown). There were 51 museums in 2000, including the State and Sunrise museums in Charleston, and Oglebay Institute-Mansion Museum in Wheeling. Harpers Ferry is the site of John Brown's historic abolitionist raid.

35 COMMUNICATIONS

In 1999, 92.7% of West Virginia's occupied households had telephones. In 2000, broadcasting facilities included 67 AM and 103 FM radio stations, 15 commercial television stations, and 3 public television stations. Almost 14,000 domain names had been registered on the Internet in 2000.

36 PRESS

In 1998, West Virginia had 22 daily newspapers and 12 Sunday newspapers. Leading West Virginia newspapers with their 1998 daily circulations are the *Charleston Gazette* (50,828); the *Charleston Daily*

Mail (unknown) and the *Huntington Her-ald-Dispatch* (38,305).

37 TOURISM, TRAVEL, AND RECREATION

Major attractions are Harpers Ferry National Historical Park, Canaan Valley State Park in Tucker County, and White Sulphur Springs, a popular mountain resort.

There are 37 state parks and 9 state forests. Among state parks and state forests are Cass Scenic Railroad, which includes a restoration of an old logging line, and Prickett's Fort, with re-creations of pioneer life. The state drew 19 million visitors in 1998, many participating in the whitewater rafting and skiing activities for which this state is known.

38 SPORTS

No major league professional teams are based in West Virginia. West Virginia University's basketball team was NCAA Division I runner-up in 1959. In football, West Virginia produced a string of national contenders in the late 1980s and early 1990s, winning the Peach Bowl in 1981. Horse-racing tracks operate in Chester and Charles Town; attendance totaled 294,000 in 1996.

39 FAMOUS WEST VIRGINIANS

Newton D. Baker (1871–1937) was secretary of war during World War I. Lewis L. Strauss (1896–1974) was commerce secretary and chairman of the Atomic Energy Commission, and Cyrus R. Vance (b.1917) served as secretary of state. John W. Davis (1873–1955), an ambassador to Great Britain, ran as the Democratic presi-

Photo credit: EPD Photos.

Fly fishers.

dential nominee in 1924. Prominent members of the US Senate have included Robert C. Byrd (b.1917) and John D. "Jay" Rockefeller IV (b.New York, 1937).

Major state political leaders, all governors (though some have held federal offices), have been E. Willis Wilson (1844–1905), Henry D. Hatfield (1875–1962), and Arch A. Moore, Jr. (b.1923).

Brigadier General Charles E. "Chuck" Yeager (b.1923), a World War II ace, became the first person to fly faster than the speed of sound.

Photo credit: EPD Photos/National Archives

Thomas J. "Stonewall" Jackson (1824–63) was a leading Confederate general during the Civil War.

The state's only Nobel Prize winner has been Pearl S. Buck (Pearl Sydenstricker, 1893–1973), who won the Nobel Prize for literature for her novels about China. Alexander Campbell (b.Ireland, 1788–1866), with his father, founded the Disciples of Christ Church. Major labor leaders have included Walter Reuther (1907–70), president of the United Automobile Workers; and Arnold Miller (b.1923), president of the United Mine Workers.

Entertainers include musician George Crumb (b.1929), a Pulitzer Prize-winning composer; opera singers Eleanor Steber (1916–90) and Phyllis Curtin (b.1922);

and comedy actor Don Knotts (b.1924). Important writers of the modern period include Mary Lee Settle (b.1918) and John Knowles (b.1926).

Jerry West (b.1938) was a collegiate and professional basketball star, and a pro coach after his playing days ended; Rod Hundley (b.1934) and Hal Greer (b.1936) also starred in the National Basketball Association. Mary Lou Retton (b.1968) won a gold medal in gymnastics at the 1984 Olympics. Another West Virginian of note is Anna Jarvis (1864–1948), founder of Mother's Day.

40 BIBLIOGRAPHY

Aylesworth, Thomas G. *Atlantic: District of Columbia, Virginia, West Virginia.* New York: Chelsea House, 1996.

Conley, Phil, and William Thomas Doherty. *West Virginia History.* Charleston: Education Foundation, 1974.

Fazio, Wende. *West Virginia.* New York: Children's Press, 1999.

Hoffman, Nancy. *West Virginia.* New York: Benchmark Books, 1999.

Rice, Otis K. *West Virginia: The State and Its People.* Parsons, W. Va.: McClain, 1972.

Williams, John Alexander. *West Virginia: A Bicentennial History.* New York: Norton, 1976.

Web sites

State of West Virginia. Welcome to West Virginia. [Online] Available http://www.state.wv.us/ Accessed May 31, 2001.

West Virginia Division of Culture and History. [Online] Available http://www.wvculture.org/ Accessed May 31, 2001.

West Virginia State Auditor's Office. General West Virginia Information. [Online] Available http://www.wvauditor.com/wvinfo/ Accessed May 31, 2001.

West Virginia Travel. West Virginia – It's You! [Online] Available http://www.westvirginia.com/home.cfm Accessed May 31, 2001.

WISCONSIN

State of Wisconsin

ORIGIN OF STATE NAME: Probably from the Ojibwa word *wishkonsing,* meaning "place of the beaver."

NICKNAME: The Badger State.

CAPITAL: Madison.

ENTERED UNION: 29 May 1848 (30th).

SONG: "On, Wisconsin!"

MOTTO: Forward.

COAT OF ARMS: Surrounding the US shield is the shield of Wisconsin, which is divided into four parts symbolizing agriculture, mining, navigation, and manufacturing. Flanking the shield are a sailor, representing labor on water; and a yeoman or miner, labor on land. Above is a badger and the state motto; below, a horn of plenty and a pyramid of pig lead.

FLAG: A dark-blue field, fringed in yellow on three sides, surrounds the state coat of arms on each side, with "Wisconsin" in white letters above the coat of arms and '1848' below.

OFFICIAL SEAL: Coat of arms surrounded by the words "Great Seal of the State of Wisconsin" and 13 stars below.

ANIMAL: Badger.

WILD ANIMAL: White-tailed deer.

DOMESTIC ANIMAL: Dairy cow.

BIRD: Robin.

DOG: American water spaniel.

FISH: Muskellunge.

FLOWER: Wood violet.

TREE: Sugar maple.

SYMBOL OF PEACE: Mourning dove.

ROCK: Red granite.

MINERAL: Galena.

FOSSIL: Trilobite.

INSECT: Honeybee.

SOIL: Antigo silt loam.

TIME: 6 AM CST = noon GMT.

1 LOCATION AND SIZE

Located in the eastern north-central US, Wisconsin ranks 26th in size among the 50 states. The total area of Wisconsin is 56,153 square miles (145,436 square kilometers). The state extends 295 miles (475 kilometers) east-west and 320 miles (515 kilometers) north-south. The state's boundaries have a total length of 1,379 miles (2,219 kilometers). Important islands belonging to Wisconsin are the Apostle Islands in Lake Superior and Washington Island in Lake Michigan.

2 TOPOGRAPHY

Wisconsin can be divided into four main geographical regions, each covering roughly one-quarter of the state's land area. The most highly elevated of these is the Superior Upland, with heavily forested rolling hills but no high mountains. A second upland region, called the Driftless Area, has a more rugged terrain. The third region is a large, crescent-shaped plain in central Wisconsin. Finally, in the east and southeast along Lake Michigan lies a large, lowland plain.

Timms Hill, in north-central Wisconsin, is the state's highest point, at 1,952 feet (595 meters). The lowest elevation is 581 feet (177 meters), along the Lake Michigan shoreline. There are more than 14,000 lakes in Wisconsin. By far the largest inland lake is Lake Winnebago, in eastern Wisconsin, covering an area of 215 square miles (557 square kilometers).

The Mississippi River, which forms part of the border with Minnesota and the entire border with Iowa, is the main navigable river. The major river flowing through the state is the Wisconsin, which meets the Mississippi at the Iowa border. Other tributaries of the Mississippi are the St. Croix, Chippewa, and Black rivers.

3 CLIMATE

Wisconsin has a continental climate. Summers are warm and winters very cold. The

Wisconsin Population Profile

Total population in 2000:	5,363,675
Population change, 1990–2000:	9.6%
Hispanic or Latino†:	3.6%
Population by race	
One race:	98.8%
White:	88.9%
Black or African American:	5.7%
American Indian/Alaska Native:	0.9%
Asian:	1.7%
Native Hawaiian/Pacific Islander:	—
Some other race:	1.6%
Two or more races:	1.2%

Population by Age Group

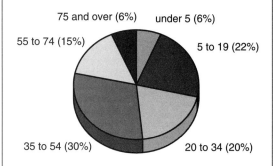

75 and over (6%)
under 5 (6%)
55 to 74 (15%)
5 to 19 (22%)
35 to 54 (30%)
20 to 34 (20%)

Top Cities by Population

City	Population	% change 1990–2000
Milwaukee	596,974	–5.0
Madison	208,054	8.8
Green Bay	102,313	6.1
Kenosha	90,352	12.4
Racine	81,855	–2.9
Appleton	70,087	6.7
Waukesha	64,825	13.8
Oshkosh	62,916	14.4
Eau Claire	61,704	8.5
West Allis	61,254	–3.1

Notes: †A person of Hispanic or Latino origin may be of any race. NA indicates that data are not available.
Sources: U.S. Census Bureau. Public Information Office. *Demographic Profiles.* [Online] Available http://www.census.gov/Press-Release/www/2001/demoprofile.html. Accessed June 1, 2001. U.S. Census Bureau. *Census 2000: Redistricting Data.* Press release issued by the Redistricting Data Office. Washington, D.C., March, 2001.

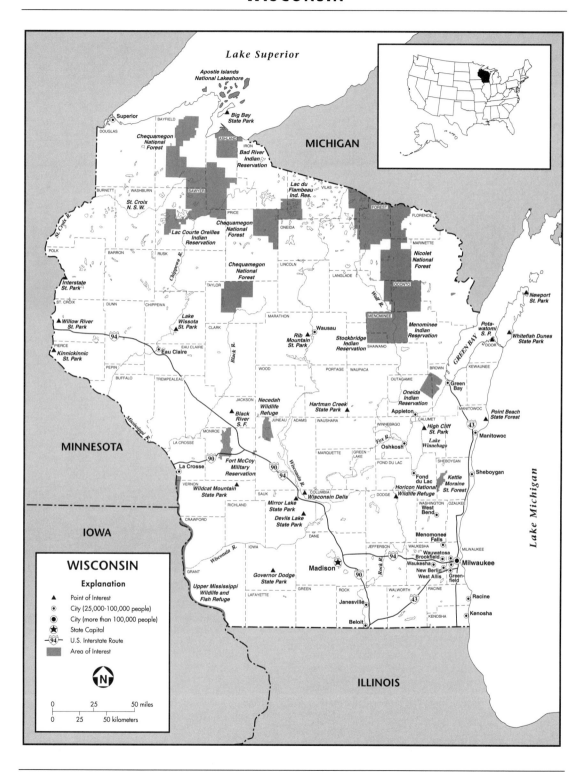

Lake Superior

Apostle Islands
National Lakeshore

Big Bay
State Park

Superior

BAYFIELD

DOUGLAS

Chequamegon
National
Forest

ASHLAND

IRON

MICHIGAN

Bad River
Indian
Reservation

BURNETT | WASHBURN

St. Croix
N. S. W.

SAWYER

Lac du
Flambeau
Ind. Res.

VILAS

PRICE

Lac Courte Oreilles
Indian
Reservation

Chequamegon
National
Forest

ONEIDA

FOREST

FLORENCE

POLK

BARRON

RUSK

LINCOLN

MARINETTE

Nicolet
National
Forest

Interstate
St. Park

ST. CROIX

DUNN

CHIPPEWA

TAYLOR

Chequamegon
National
Forest

CLARK

LANGLADE

OCONTO

Newport
St. Park

Willow River
St. Park

Lake
Wissota
St. Park

MARATHON

MENOMINEE

Wolf R.

Potawatomi
S. P.

Whitefish Dunes
State Park

DOOR

PIERCE

Kinnickinnic
St. Park

Eau Claire

EAU CLAIRE

Rib
Mountain
St. Park

Wausau

Menominee
Indian
Reservation

PEPIN

Black R.

WOOD

Stockbridge
Indian
Reservation

SHAWANO

BUFFALO

TREMPEALEAU

PORTAGE

WAUPACA

BROWN

GREEN BAY

KEWAUNEE

JACKSON

Necedah
Wildlife
Refuge

JUNEAU

ADAMS

Hartman Creek
State Park

WAUSHARA

Oneida
Indian
Reservation

OUTAGAMIE

Appleton

CALUMET

Green
Bay

MANITOWOC

Point Beach
State Forest

Black
River
S. F.

Fox R.

High Cliff
St. Park

Lake
Winnebago

43

Manitowoc

LA CROSSE

MONROE

MARQUETTE

GREEN
LAKE

WINNEBAGO

Oshkosh

FOND DU LAC

SHEBOYGAN

Sheboygan

MINNESOTA

La Crosse

Fort McCoy
Military
Reservation

90

VERNON

Wildcat Mountain
State Park

SAUK

Wisconsin R.

94

COLUMBIA

Wisconsin Dells

DODGE

Fond
du Lac

Horicon National
Wildlife Refuge

Kettle
Moraine
St. Forest

RICHLAND

Mirror Lake
State Park

Devils Lake
State Park

WASHINGTON

West
Bend

OZAUKEE

CRAWFORD

DANE

JEFFERSON

Menomonee
Falls

WAUKESHA

MILWAUKEE

IOWA

Wisconsin R.

IOWA

Governor Dodge
State Park

GRANT

Upper Mississippi
Wildlife and
Fish Refuge

LAFAYETTE

GREEN

Madison

90

Rock R.

Wauwatosa
Brookfield

Waukesha

New Berlin

West Allis

Green-
field

Milwaukee

ROCK

WALWORTH

RACINE

Racine

Janesville

43

KENOSHA

Kenosha

Beloit

Lake Michigan

ILLINOIS

Milwaukee's four-theater Performing Arts Center.

average annual temperature ranges from 39°F (4°C) in the north to about 50°F (10°C) in the south. Over a 30-year period, the state's largest city, Milwaukee, had average daily temperatures ranging from 11°F (–12°C) to 26°F(–3°C) in January, and from 61°F (16°C) to 80°F (27°C) in July. The lowest temperature ever recorded in Wisconsin was –54°F (–48°C) in 1922; the highest, 114°F (46°C), occurred in 1936.

Annual precipitation in the state ranges from about 34 inches (86 centimeters) for parts of the northwest to about 28 inches (71 centimeters) in the south-central region and the areas bordering Lake Superior and Lake Michigan.

4 PLANTS AND ANIMALS

Common trees of Wisconsin include oaks, black cherry, and hickory. Pines, yellow birch, and moosewood are among the trees that grow in the north. Characteristic of southern Wisconsin are sugar maple (the state tree), white elm, and basswood. Prairies are thick with grasses. Forty-five varieties of orchid have been identified, as well as 20 types of violet, including the wood violet (the state flower).

White-tailed deer (the state wild animal), black bear, and chipmunk are mammals typical of forestlands. The striped skunk, and red and gray foxes, are characteristic of upland fields, while wetlands harbor such mammals as the muskrat, mink, and river otter. Game birds include the ring-necked pheasant, bobwhite quail, and ruffed grouse. Some 336 bird species are native to Wisconsin. Muskellunge (the state fish), northern pike, and brook trout are found in Wisconsin waterways. The bald eagle and Kirtland's warbler are among the nine species on the endangered list.

5 ENVIRONMENTAL PROTECTION

The Department of Natural Resources (DNR) brings together conservation and environmental protection responsibilities. The department supervises air, water, and solid-waste pollution control programs and deals with the protection of forest, fish, and wildlife resources.

Southeastern Wisconsin has experienced serious air quality problems since the 1970s. Reductions in industrial emissions have been offset by increases in emissions from transportation sources and consumer products. Six counties in the area must reduce ozone enough to meet health standards early in the next century.

Contaminated stormwater and run-off from agriculture, development, and other sources remain the most serious threats to Wisconsin's lakes, rivers, and streams. The state currently is adopting rules to limit stormwater contamination in large municipalities, construction sites over five acres, and 10,000 industrial facilities.

A 1984 groundwater protection law requires identification and clean-up of groundwater-damaging contamination sources, such as abandoned, leaking landfills, underground gasoline storage tanks, and illegal hazardous-waste dumps. Wisconsin has identified over 16,000 contamination sites that must be cleaned up to prevent environmental contamination and safety hazards.

In 1993, 400,000 Milwaukee residents became ill from inadequately treated water drawn from Lake Michigan. The water was found to contain the bacteria *Cryptosporidium*. Water treatment procedures were changed immediately at 21 community drinking-water treatment plants that drew water from the Great Lakes.

In 1989 Wisconsin passed a comprehensive waste reduction and recycling law requiring local governments to set up effective programs to recycle more than 11 different items.

6 POPULATION

Wisconsin fell behind Tennessee and Missouri to rank 18th in population among the 50 states in 2000, with a census population of over 5.36 million. The population projection for 2005 is 5.48 million.

Average population density in 2000 was 98.8 persons per square mile (38.1 persons per square kilometer). Almost two-thirds (65.7%) of all Wisconsinites lived in urban areas in 1990. Milwaukee, the largest city in Wisconsin (and 19th largest in the country), had a population of 596,974 in 2000. Other large cities, with their 2000 populations, were Madison, 208,054; Green Bay, 102,313;

Wisconsin Population by Race

Census 2000 was the first national census in which the instructions to respondents said, "Mark one or more races." This table shows the number of people who are of one, two, or three or more races. For those claiming two races, the number of people belonging to the various categories is listed. The U.S. government conducts a census of the population every ten years.

	Number	Percent
Total population	5,363,675	100.0
One race	5,296,780	98.8
Two races	62,793	1.2
White *and* Black or African American	14,437	0.3
White *and* American Indian/Alaska Native	16,157	0.3
White *and* Asian	8,484	0.2
White *and* Native Hawaiian/Pacific Islander	688	—
White *and* some other race	14,068	0.3
Black or African American *and* American Indian/Alaska Native	2,003	—
Black or African American *and* Asian	600	—
Black or African American *and* Native Hawaiian/Pacific Islander	82	—
Black or African American *and* some other race	1,860	—
American Indian/Alaska Native *and* Asian	610	—
American Indian/Alaska Native *and* Native Hawaiian/Pacific Islander	56	—
American Indian/Alaska Native *and* some other race	597	—
Asian *and* Native Hawaiian/Pacific Islander	1,104	—
Asian *and* some other race	1,946	—
Native Hawaiian/Pacific Islander *and* some other race	101	—
Three or more races	4,102	0.1

Source: U.S. Census Bureau. *Census 2000: Redistricting Data.* Press release issued by the Redistricting Data Office. Washington, D.C., March, 2001. A dash (—) indicates that the percent is less than 0.1.

Kenosha, 90,352; and Racine, 81,855. Approximately 28% of the population is 19 years of age and younger.

7 ETHNIC GROUPS

According to a 1997 federal estimate, whites numbered 4.76 million, or 92.1% of the population. That year, blacks were the largest racial minority in the state, numbering about 286,100 (5.5% of Wisconsin's population). Most black Wisconsinites live in Milwaukee, which was 30% black in 1990. As of 1997 there were an estimated 127,700 state residents of Hispanic origin, most of whom were of Mexican ancestry or of Puerto Rican descent.

Asians are few in number: in 1997 there were an estimated 77,100 (1.5%), primarily Hmong, Chinese, Koreans, Laotians, and Filipinos. Wisconsin had an estimated 46,000 Native Americans in 1997 (0.9%). The principal tribes are Oneida, Menominee, Ojibwa (Chippewa), and Winnebago.

8 LANGUAGES

Wisconsin English is almost entirely Northern, similar to the areas that provided Wisconsin's first settlers—Michigan, northern Ohio, New York State, and western New England. In 1990, 94.2% of the state population five years old and older spoke only English in the home. Other languages spoken at home and the number of speakers included Spanish, 75,931; German, 61,929; and Polish, 10,386.

9 RELIGIONS

The largest religious groups in Wisconsin are Roman Catholics and Lutherans. As of the end of 1990, there were 1,554,278 Roman Catholics in Wisconsin. Of Protestant denominations in 1990, the Evangelical Lutheran Church in America had the most members, 460,168; followed by the Lutheran Church–Missouri Synod, 248,876; and the United Methodists, 152,426. There were an estimated 35,000 Jews in 1994, 76% of them in Milwaukee.

10 TRANSPORTATION

Wisconsin's first rail line was built across the state, from Milwaukee to Prairie du Chien, in the 1850s. Communities soon began vying with one another to be included on proposed railroad routes. Several thousand farmers mortgaged property to buy railroad stock. The state had to rescue them from ruin when companies went bankrupt. By the late 1860s, two railroads—the Chicago and North Western and the Chicago, Milwaukee, and St. Paul—had become dominant in the state. However, Chicago, Illinois, eventually emerged as the major rail center of the Midwest because of its proximity to eastern markets.

In 1920 there were 35 railroads operating on 11,615 miles (18,693 kilometers) of track. By 1996, there were just 10 railroads operating on 4,170 rail miles (6,710 kilometers) of track, but only 40% was for Class I lines. The state was third-highest in the amount of terminated rail–tons of metallic ores in 1995, at 14.5 million tons. Freight tonnage hauled by rail in 1995 was 142.9 million tons. Amtrak provides passenger service to Milwaukee, La Crosse, and several other cities on Chicago–Milwaukee and Chicago–Seattle runs. Amtrak's 1995/96 Wisconsin riders numbered 341,464.

As of 1997, Wisconsin had 111,950 miles (180,128 kilometers) of roadway; about 55% of this mileage consisted of town roads, 28% state or county highways, 11% city streets, 4% village streets, and 1% park and forest roads. Registered vehicles included 2.55 million automobiles and 1.67 million trucks in 1997, when the state had 3.6 million licensed drivers. In 1996, the Milwaukee County Transit System provided rides for 60 million people, and Madison Metro had nearly 10 million riders.

The opening of the St. Lawrence Seaway in 1959 allowed oceangoing vessels access to Wisconsin via the Great Lakes but failed to stimulate traffic to the extent anticipated. Overall, the state has 15 cargo-handling ports. The port of Superior (shared with Duluth, Minnesota) on Lake Superior handled about 37.2 million tons of cargo in 1996. This made it the busiest of all US Great Lakes ports. Iron ore was the chief commodity. Other important Wisconsin ports, all on Lake Michigan, are Milwaukee, Green Bay, Marinette (shared with Menominee, Michigan), Port Washington, Oconto, Kewaunee, Manitowoc, Sturgeon Bay, and Sheboygan. Manitowoc and Kewaunee offer ferry service across Lake Michigan to Michigan. Ashland on Lake Superior and La Crosse on the Mississippi River are other important ports.

As of 1997, Wisconsin had 691 airports. In 1996, 2.73 million passengers were boarded at General Mitchell Field, in Milwaukee.

11 HISTORY

During the 17th century, the Ojibwa, Sauk, Fox, Potawatomi, Kickapoo, and other tribes came to the area that is now Wisconsin. These tribes engaged in agriculture, hunting, and fishing, but with the arrival of Europeans, they became increasingly dependent on the fur trade. The first European believed to have reached Wisconsin was the Frenchman Jean Nicolet, who in 1634 landed on the shores of Green Bay. After 1673, Jesuits established missions, and French fur traders opened up posts. The French were succeeded by the British after the French and Indian War. Although ceded to the US in 1783, the region remained British in all but name until 1816, when the US built forts at Prairie du Chien and Green Bay.

Under the Ordinance of 1787, Wisconsin became part of the Northwest Territory; it was subsequently included in the Indiana Territory, the Territory of Illinois, and then the Michigan Territory. The Wisconsin Territory was formed in 1836. In the 1830s, the region's population and economy began to expand rapidly. Wisconsin voters endorsed statehood in 1846, and on 29 May 1848, President James K. Polk signed the bill that made Wisconsin the 30th state.

Wisconsinites took a generally abolitionist stand. In the Civil War, 96,000 Wisconsin men fought on the Union side, and 12,216 died. During the late 19th century, Wisconsin was generally prosperous; dairying, food processing, and lumbering emerged as major industries, and Milwaukee grew into an important industrial center.

20th Century

Under Republican governor Robert "Fighting Bob" La Follette in the early 20th century, the legislature passed a law providing for the nation's first direct statewide primary. Other measures that La Follette championed provided for increased taxation of railroads, regulation of lobbyists, creation of a civil service, and establishment of a railroad commission to regulate rates.

After La Follette left the governor's office to become a US senator, his progressivism was carried on by his Republican successors. During one session in 1911, legislators enacted the first state income tax in the US and one of the first workers' compensation programs.

Between the world wars, Wisconsin's tradition of reform continued. A pioneering old-age pension act was passed in 1925; seven years later, Wisconsin enacted the nation's first unemployment compensation act. In the 1930s, La Follette's son, Philip, serving as governor, successfully pressed for the creation of state agencies to develop electric power, arbitrate labor disputes, and set rules for fair business competition. His so-called Little New Deal

Wisconsin Governors: 1848–2001

1848–1852	Nelson Dewey	Democrat
1852–1854	Leonard James Farwell	Whig
1854–1856	William Augustus Barstow	Democrat
1856	Arthur MacArthur	Democrat
1856–1858	Coles Bashford	Republican
1858–1862	Alexander Williams Randall	Republican
1862	Louis Powell Harvey	Republican
1862–1864	Edward P. Salomon	Republican
1864–1866	James Taylor Lewis	Republican
1866–1872	Lucius Fairchild	Republican
1872–1874	Cadwallader Colden Washburn	Republican
1874–1876	William Robert Taylor	Democrat
1876–1878	Harrison Ludington	Republican
1878–1882	William E. Smith	Republican
1882–1889	Jeremiah McLain Rusk	Republican
1889–1891	William Dempster Hoard	Republican
1891–1895	George Wilbur Peck	Democrat
1895–1897	William Henry Upham	Republican
1897–1901	Edward Scofield	Republican
1901–1906	Robert Marion LaFollette	Republican
1906–1911	James Ole Davidson	Republican
1911–1915	Francis Edward McGovern	Republican
1915–1921	Emanuel Lorenz Philipp	Republican
1921–1926	John James Blaine	Republican
1927–1929	Fred R. Zimmerman	Republican
1929–1931	Walter Jodok Kohler, Sr.	Republican
1931–1933	Philip Fox LaFollette	Republican
1933–1935	Albert George Schmedeman	Democrat
1935–1939	Philip Fox LaFollette	Progressive
1939–1943	Julius Peter Heil	Republican
1943–1947	Walter Samuel Goodland	Republican
1947–1951	Oscar Rennebohm	Republican
1951–1957	Walter Jodok Kohler, Jr.	Republican
1957–1959	Vernon Wallace Thompson	Republican
1959–1963	Gaylord Anton Nelson	Democrat
1963–1965	John Whitcome Reynolds	Democrat
1965–1971	Warren Perley Knowles	Republican
1971–1977	Patrick Joseph Lucey	Democrat
1977–1979	Martin James Schreiber	Democrat
1979–1983	Lee Sherman Dreyfus	Republican
1983–1987	Anthony Scully Earl	Democrat
1987–2001	Tommy George Thompson	Republican
2001–	Scott McCallum	Republican

corresponded to the New Deal policies of the Roosevelt administration.

After World War II, the state continued a trend toward increased urbanization, and its industries prospered. The major figure on the national scene in the postwar era was Senator Joseph R. McCarthy, who began unsubstantiated attacks in 1950 on alleged Communists and other subversives in the federal government. After McCarthy's censure by the US Senate in 1954 and his death in 1957, the progressive tradition began to recover strength, and the liberal Democratic Party grew increasingly influential in state politics.

There was student unrest at the University of Wisconsin during the 1960s and early 1970s, and growing discontent among Milwaukee's black population. In 1984, the Milwaukee school board filed suit in federal court against the state and Milwaukee's suburbs, charging that the policies of the state and suburban schools had resulted in an unconstitutionally segregated school system. Two years later, the Milwaukee School Board and nine suburban districts agreed on a plan in which 2,700 city minority students would transfer voluntarily to the nine suburbs, and 9,000–10,000 suburban students would attend Milwaukee schools.

12 STATE GOVERNMENT

The Wisconsin legislature consists of a senate with 33 members elected for four-year terms, and an assembly of 99 representatives elected for two-year terms. There are six elected state officers: governor and lieutenant governor (elected jointly), secretary of state, state treasurer, attorney general, and superintendent of public instruction. As the chief executive officer, the governor exercises authority by the power of appointment, by presenting a budget bill and major addresses to the legislature, and by the power to veto bills and call special legislative sessions.

A bill may be introduced in either house of the legislature but must be passed by both houses to become law. The governor has six days (Sundays excluded) to sign or veto a measure. If the governor fails to act and the legislature is still in session, the bill automatically becomes law. Vetoes can be overridden by a two-thirds majority of both houses.

13 POLITICAL PARTIES

Beginning in the late 1850s, the newly founded Republican Party held sway for over 100 years. More recently, the Democrats held a substantial edge at the state level in the 1970s and 1980s. Socialist parties have won some success in Wisconsin's political history. In 1910, Emil Seidel was elected mayor of Milwaukee, becoming the first Socialist mayor of a major US city; and Victor Berger became the first Socialist ever elected to Congress.

Democratic candidate Al Gore won 48% of the vote in the 2000 presidential election, although Republican George W. Bush also received 48%. Gore won by a

Wisconsin Presidential Vote by Political Party, 1948–2000

YEAR	WISCONSIN WINNER	DEMOCRAT	REPUBLICAN	PROGRESSIVE	SOCIALIST	SOC. WORKERS	SOCIALIST LABOR
1948	*Truman (D)	647,310	590,959	25,282	12,547	—	399
1952	*Eisenhower (R)	622,175	979,744	2,174	1,157	1,350	770
				CONSTITUTION			
1956	*Eisenhower (R)	586,768	954,844	6,918	754	564	710
1960	Nixon (R)	830,805	895,175	—	—	1,792	1,310
1964	*Johnson (D)	1,050,424	638,495	—	—	1,692	1,204
1968	*Nixon (R)	748,804	809,997	—	—	1,222	1,338
				AMERICAN IND.	AMERICAN		
1972	*Nixon (R)	810,174	989,430	127,835	47,525	—	998
					SOCIALIST		LIBERTARIAN
1976	*Carter (D)	1,040,232	1,004,967	8,552	4,298	1,691	3,814
						CITIZENS	
1980	*Reagan (R)	981,584	1,088,845	**1,519	—	7,767	29,135
1984	*Reagan (R)	995,740	1,198,584	—	—	—	4,883
				POPULIST	SOC. WORKERS	N. ALLIANCE	
1988	Dukakis (D)	1,126,794	1,047,499	3,056	2,574	1,953	5,157
				IND. (Perot)		TAXPAYERS	
1992	*Clinton (D)	1,041,066	930,855	2,311	544,479	1,772	2,877
					IND. (Nader)		
1996	*Clinton (D)	1,071,971	845,029	—	227,339	28,723	7,929
				REFORM			LIBERTARIAN
2000	Gore (D)	1,242,987	1,237,279	94,070	11,446	306	6,640

*Won US presidential election.
**Listed as Constitution Party on Wisconsin ballot.

A farm in Dane County, Wisconsin.

narrow margin. Wisconsin's senators, both Democrats, are Russell Feingold, reelected in 1998, and Herbert Kohl, reelected in 2000. Wisconsin's US Representatives consist of four Republicans and five Democrats. As of 2001, there were 15 Republicans and 18 Democrats in the state senate, and 43 Democrats and 56 Republicans in the state assembly. Wisconsin's governor, Republican Scott McCallum, began his first term in 2001.

14 LOCAL GOVERNMENT

Wisconsin has 72 counties, 583 city and village governments, 1,266 towns, and 442 school districts. Each county is governed by a board of supervisors. Nine counties, including Milwaukee County,

have elected county executives. Other county officials include district attorneys, sheriffs, clerks, treasurers, and coroners. Most cities are governed by a mayor-council system. Executive power in a village is vested in an elected president, who presides over an elected board but has no veto power. Wisconsin towns are generally governed by a board of supervisors.

15 JUDICIAL SYSTEM

The judicial branch is headed by a supreme court consisting of seven justices. The supreme court, which is the final authority on state constitutional questions, hears appeals at its own discretion and has original jurisdiction in limited areas. The state's next-highest court is the court of appeals, whose decisions may be reviewed by the supreme court. Circuit courts are Wisconsin's trial courts and have original jurisdiction in civil and criminal cases. Wisconsin's 200 municipal courts have jurisdiction over violations of local ordinances.

Wisconsin's crime rate in 1998 was 3,543.1 per 100,000 population, below the national average. Inmates in federal and state prisons totaled 19,447 in 1999. Wisconsin does not have the death penalty.

16 MIGRATION

Wisconsin suffered a net population loss from migration beginning in 1900, as Wisconsinites moved to other states. Between 1970 and 1983 alone, this loss totaled 154,000. As of 1990, 76.4% of state residents were born in Wisconsin; only six other states had a higher percentage. During 1990–98, Wisconsin had a net gain of 84,400 from interstate migration and 21,400 from international migration.

A significant trend since 1970 has been the decline in population in Milwaukee and other large cities. At the same time, suburbs have continued to grow, as have many other areas, especially in parts of northern Wisconsin.

17 ECONOMY

Although farming—especially dairying—remains important, manufacturing is the mainstay of today's economy. Wisconsin's industries are diversified, with nonelectrical machinery and food products the lead-

ing items. Other important industries are paper and pulp products, transportation equipment, electrical and electronic equipment, and fabricated metals. Economic growth has been concentrated in the southeast. There, soils and climate are favorable for agriculture; a skilled labor force is available to industry; and capital, transportation, and markets are most readily accessible.

In the 1997, gross state product was $147 billion, contributed by manufacturing, services, financial institutions, and government employment.

18 INCOME

In 1998, Wisconsin ranked 22d among the 50 states in per capita (per person) income, which was $26,284. Total personal income was $137.3 billion in 1998. An estimated 8.6% of the population lived below the federal poverty level in that same year.

19 INDUSTRY

The total value of shipments by manufacturers was $119 billion in 1997. Of that total, food products (especially cheese, meat, and canned fruits and vegetables), industrial machinery and equipment, paper and allied products, and transportation equipment contributed.

Industrial activity is concentrated in the southeast, especially in the Milwaukee metropolitan area. Major corporations based in Milwaukee include Johnson Controls and Allen-Bradley, makers of electric and electronic components; and Harley-

Photo credit: Wisconsin Division of Tourism.

Wisconsin farmland.

Davidson, best known for its touring and custom motorcycles.

20 LABOR

The civilian labor force (seasonally adjusted) numbered 2.97 million persons in mid-1998. Of these, 3.4% were unemployed. Labor union membership was 17.7% of all workers in 1995.

21 AGRICULTURE

Farm marketing in 1999 amounted to $5.6 billion, tenth among the 50 states. Over $4.1 billion came from dairy products and livestock. Wisconsin led the US in 1998 in the production of corn for silage, snap beans for processing, cranberries, and cabbage for kraut. Farmland is concentrated in the southern two-thirds of the state, especially in the southeast. Leading field crops (in bushels) in 1998 were corn for grain, 404 million; oats, 18.3 million; barley, 3.3 million; and wheat, 7.6 million.

22 DOMESTICATED ANIMALS

Wisconsin has more milk cows than any other state (1.4 million in 1997) and ranks first in the production of cheese, and second in butter and milk. About 30% of the nation's cheese—and at least 60% of all

Muenster cheese—is produced in the state. Wisconsin ranchers also raise livestock for meat production.

In 1999 there were 3.4 million head of cattle, along with 690,000 hogs in 1998. Dairy products account for over 50% of all cash receipts from agriculture. In 1995, the state produced over two billion pounds of cheese (30% of the US total). Wisconsin farms also yielded 23 billion pounds (10.4 billion kilograms) of milk (15% of the US total) and 280.5 million pounds (127.2 million kilograms) of butter (22% of the national total).

23 FISHING

In 1998, 6.9 million pounds of fish were landed at a total value of $4.4 million, ranking it 2d in the Great Lakes. The muskellunge is the primary game fish of Wisconsin's inland waters; Coho and chinook salmon introduced to Lake Michigan now thrive there. The largest concentration of lake sturgeon in the US is in Lake Winnebago. Wisconsin issued about 1.47 million sport fishing licenses in 1998.

24 FORESTRY

Wisconsin has about 15.9 million acres (6.3 million hectares) of forest, covering 46% of the state's land area, as of 1997. Hardwoods make up about two-thirds of the saw timber. The most heavily forested region is in the north. The lumber and paper industries together employed 78,100 people and had manufactured shipments worth $18.3 billion in 1995. Wisconsin's woods have recreational as well as commercial value. There are two national forests—Chequamegon and Nicolet—and ten state forests.

25 MINING

The estimated value of nonfuel mineral commodities produced in Wisconsin was $296 million in 1998. Crushed stone continued to be the leading mineral commodity produced in Wisconsin, followed by construction sand and gravel, and lime. These three accounted for an estimated 84% of the state's total mineral value. Production of metals—copper, gold, and silver—accounted for 27%.

26 ENERGY AND POWER

In 1998, electrical energy production totaled 52.5 billion kilowatt hours. As of 1999, there were 21 steam-generating plants, accounting for 61% of the state's total installed generating capacity, and 47 combination turbine/internal combustion plants, accounting for 22%. The 69 hydroelectric plants accounted for about 4%. The remaining 13% was attributable to the state's three nuclear power plants: Point Beach Units 1 and 2, at Two Creeks; and Kewaunee Unit 1, at Carlton Township. Wisconsin has no oil, natural gas, or coal resources of its own.

27 COMMERCE

Wholesale sales totaled $61 billion in 1997; retail sales were $51 billion in the same year. Wisconsin exported about $10 billion in goods (18th in the US) in 1998. Foreign trade is conducted through the Great Lakes ports of Superior-Duluth, Milwaukee, Green Bay, and Kenosha.

28 PUBLIC FINANCE

Expenditures by state and local governments alike have risen dramatically since 1960. As of 1997, state indebtedness exceeded $9.83 billion, or $1,902 per capita (per person). Total revenues for 1997 were $23.86 billion; total expenditures were $18.2 billion.

29 TAXATION

In 1997, state taxes amounted to $1,970 per capita (per person), 9th highest in the nation. The largest single source of state revenue is the income tax on individuals. Most local tax revenue comes from property taxes, and most of that goes for education. The general sales tax in 1996 was 5%, and an estate tax was levied. Other state taxes are those on gasoline, cigarettes, liquor, wine, beer, public utilities, and real estate transfers. In 1996, total federal individual income tax receipts from Wisconsin were nearly $11.6 billion.

30 HEALTH

As of 1998, Wisconsin ranked above the nation as a whole in death rates for cerebrovascular disease, cancer, accidents, and suicide, but below the national average for heart disease. Wisconsin had 123 community hospitals, with 16,693 beds. The average hospital cost per inpatient day in 1998 came to $1,028, or $6,364 for an average cost per stay. There were 11.8% of residents who did not have health insurance in this same year.

31 HOUSING

In 1999, there were an estimated 2.3 million housing units. Rural areas had a higher proportion of deficient housing than urban areas, and substandard conditions were three times as common in units built before 1940. In 1998, 35,400 new housing units valued at $3.6 billion were authorized. As of 1990, the median home value was $62,500. Median monthly costs for owners (with a mortgage) and renters in 1990 were $678 and $399, respectively, throughout the state.

32 EDUCATION

Wisconsin has a tradition of leadership in education. As of 1998, 88% of all Wisconsinites 25 years or older had completed high school, well above the US average. In the 1997 school year, Wisconsin's elementary and secondary schools had a total enrollment of 881,780 students. Expenditures on education averaged $6,474 per pupil (12th in the nation) in 1995/96.

The University of Wisconsin (UW) system is comprised of 13 degree-granting campuses, 13 two-year centers, and the UW-Extension. During the 1996/97 academic year, UW-Madison enrolled 39,306 students. UW-Milwaukee, the system's second largest campus, enrolled 25,819 students. The 11 other sites included Eau Claire, Green Bay, and Oshkosh. The University of Wisconsin's 13 two-year centers enrolled 17,325 students in 1996/97.

Wisconsin's private institutions of higher education encompass a broad range of schools and had a combined enrollment of 50,011 in 1996/97. There are 21 colleges and universities, including leading institutions such as Marquette University (Milwaukee), Lawrence University (Appleton), Ripon College, and Beloit College. In addition, there are four technical and professional schools, and five theological seminaries.

[33] ARTS

Wisconsin offers numerous facilities for drama, music, and other performing arts, including a four-theater Performing Arts Center in Milwaukee and the Dane County Exposition Center in Madison. Milwaukee has a repertory theater. Summer plays are performed at an unusual garden theater at Fish Creek, on the Door Peninsula, and American Players Theater (Shakespeare) in Spring Green.

The Pro Arte String Quartet in Madison and the Fine Arts Quartet in Milwaukee have been sponsored by the University of Wisconsin. Milwaukee is the home of the Florentine Opera Company, the Milwaukee Ballet Company, and the Milwaukee Symphony. In 1996, Wisconsin had 1,154 arts associations and 193 local arts groups.

[34] LIBRARIES AND MUSEUMS

In 1998, the state public libraries had a total of 18 million volumes and circulation of 47 million. The Milwaukee Public Library maintained 12 branches and had 2.5 million bound volumes. The largest academic library is that of the University of Wisconsin at Madison. The best-known specialized library is that of the State Historical Society of Wisconsin at Madison.

Wisconsin had 208 museums and historical sites in 2000. The State Historical Society maintains a historical museum in Madison and other historical sites and museums around the state. The Milwaukee Art Center, a major museum of the visual arts, emphasizes European works of the 17th to 19th centuries. Historical sites in Wisconsin include the Taliesin estate of architect Frank Lloyd Wright, in Spring Green. The Circus World Museum at Baraboo occupies the site of the original Ringling Brothers Circus.

[35] COMMUNICATIONS

About 95.7% of the state's households had telephones in 1999. In 2000 there were 112 AM and 196 FM radio stations. The state also had 46 television stations. In 2000, 77,862 Internet domain names were registered.

[36] PRESS

In 1998, Wisconsin had 10 morning papers, 25 evening papers, and 17 Sunday papers. The leading papers, with their late 1998 daily circulations, were the *Milwaukee Journal Sentinel* (285,776); the *Wisconsin State Journal* (87,305); and the *Green Bay Press-Gazette* (61,184). As of 1997, there were more 27 semiweekly newspapers and weeklies, as well as 318 periodicals directed to a wide variety of special interests.

[37] TOURISM, TRAVEL, AND RECREATION

The state has ample scenic attractions and outdoor recreational opportunities. In addition to the famous Wisconsin Dells gorge, visitors are attracted to the Cave of the Mounds at Blue Mounds, the sandstone cliffs along the Mississippi River, the lakes and forests of the Rhinelander and

Taste of Madison, a gastronomic extravaganza held every Labor Day weekend.

Minocqua areas in the north, and Lake Geneva, a resort, in the south.

There are three national parks in Wisconsin: Apostle Islands National Lakeshore, on Lake Superior, and the St. Croix and Lower St. Croix scenic riverways. In 2000, there were 48 state parks with 4,208 campsites.

38 SPORTS

Wisconsin has three major league teams: the Milwaukee Brewers of Major League Baseball, the Green Bay Packers of the National Football League, and the Milwaukee Bucks of the National Basketball Association. The University of Wisconsin Badgers compete in the Big Ten Confer-

ence, winning the Rose Bowl in 1994. The Badger ice hockey team won the NCAA championship in 1990. Marquette University's basketball team won the NCAA Division I title in 1977.

Other annual sporting events include ski jumping tournaments in Iola, Middleton, and Wetsby; the World Championship Snowmobile Derby in Eagle River in January; and the Great Wisconsin Dells Balloon Race in the Dells.

39 FAMOUS WISCONSINITES

Wisconsinites who have won prominence as federal judicial or executive officers include Jeremiah Rusk (b.Ohio, 1830–93), a Wisconsin governor selected as the first head of the Agriculture Department in 1889; Melvin Laird (b.Nebraska, 1922–92), a congressman who served as secretary of defense from 1969–73; and William Rehnquist (b.1924), named to the Supreme Court in 1971, and now Chief Justice.

Joseph R. McCarthy (1908–57) won attention in the Senate and throughout the nation for his anti-Communist crusade. William Proxmire (b.Illinois, 1915), a Democrat, succeeded McCarthy in the Senate and eventually chaired the powerful Senate Banking Committee.

Wisconsin was the birthplace of several Nobel Prize winners, including Herbert S. Gasser (1888–1963), who shared a 1944 Nobel Prize for research into nerve impulses; John Bardeen (1908–91), who shared the physics award in 1956 for his contribution to the development of the transistor; and Herbert A. Simon (b.1916), who won the 1978 prize in economics.

Thornton Wilder (1897–1975), a novelist and playwright best known for *The Bridge of San Luis Rey* (1927), *Our Town* (1938), and *The Skin of Our Teeth* (1942), each of which won a Pulitzer Prize, heads the list of literary figures born in the state. Hamlin Garland (1860–1940), a novelist and essayist, was also a native, as was the poet Ella Wheeler Wilcox (1850–1919). The novelist Edna Ferber (b.Michigan, 1887–1968) spent her early life in the state.

Wisconsin is the birthplace of architect Frank Lloyd Wright (1869–1959) and the site of his famous Taliesin estate (Spring Green). The artist Georgia O'Keeffe (1887–1986) was born in Sun Prairie.

Wisconsin natives who have distinguished themselves in the performing arts include Spencer Tracy (1900–67) and Orson Welles (1915–85). Magician and escape artist Harry Houdini (Ehrich Weiss, b.Hungary, 1874–1926) was raised in the state.

Speed-skater Eric Heiden (b.1958), a five-time Olympic gold medalist in 1980, is another Wisconsin native.

40 BIBLIOGRAPHY

Abrams, Lawrence, and Kathleen Abrams. *Exploring Wisconsin.* Skokie, Ill: Rand McNally, 1983.

Aylesworth, Thomas G. *Western Great Lakes: Illinois, Iowa, Minnesota, Wisconsin.* New York: Chelsea House, 1996.

Blashfield, Jean F. *Wisconsin.* New York: Children's Press, 1998.

Legislative Reference Bureau. *The 1995–1996 Wisconsin Blue Book.* Madison: 1995.

Nesbit, Robert C. *Wisconsin: A History.* Madison: University of Wisconsin Press, revised, 1989.

Parker, Janice. *Wisconsin.* Mankato, Minn.: Weigl Publishers, 2001.

Zeinert, Karen. *Wisconsin.* New York: Benchmark Books, 1998.

Web sites

State of Wisconsin. State of Wisconsin Information Server-BADGER. [Online] Available http://www.wisconsin.gov/state/home/ Accessed May 31, 2001.

Wisconsin Department of Tourism. Wisconsin. [Online] Available http://tourism.state.wi.us/ Accessed May 31, 2001.

———. Wisconsin – "Gathering of the Waters" – Wisconsin Facts. [Online] Available http://www.travelwisconsin.com/d2k/servlet/internet.Intro Accessed May 31, 2001.

WYOMING

State of Wyoming

ORIGIN OF STATE NAME: Derived from the Delaware Indian words *maugh-wau-wa-ma,* meaning "large plains."

NICKNAME: The Equality State (Also: Big Wyoming; The Cowboy State).

CAPITAL: Cheyenne.

ENTERED UNION: 10 July 1890 (44th).

SONG: "Wyoming."

MOTTO: Equal Rights.

FLAG: A blue field with a white inner border and a red outer border (symbolizing, respectively, the sky, purity, and the Native Americans) surrounds a bison with the state seal branded on its side.

OFFICIAL SEAL: A female figure holding the banner "Equal Rights" stands on a pedestal between pillars topped by lamps symbolizing the light of knowledge. Two male figures flank the pillars, on which are draped banners that proclaim "Livestock," "Grain," "Mines," and "Oil." At the bottom is a shield with an eagle, star, and Roman numerals XLIV, flanked by the dates 1869 and 1890. The whole is surrounded by the words "Great Seal of the State of Wyoming."

MAMMAL: Bison.

BIRD: Meadowlark.

FLOWER: Indian paintbrush.

FISH: Cutthroat trout.

TREE: Cottonwood.

GEM: Jade.

FOSSIL: Knightia.

TIME: 5 AM MST = noon GMT.

1 LOCATION AND SIZE

Located in the Rocky Mountain region of the northwestern US, Wyoming ranks ninth in size among the 50 states. The total area of Wyoming is 97,914 square miles (253,596 square kilometers). It has a maximum east-west extension of 365 miles (587 kilometers); its extreme distance north-south is 265 miles (426 kilometers). The state's boundary length is 1,269 miles (2,042 kilometers).

2 TOPOGRAPHY

The eastern third of Wyoming forms part of the Great Plains; the remainder belongs to the Rocky Mountains. Wyoming's mean elevation is 6,700 feet (2,042 meters), second only to Colorado's among the 50 states. Gannett Peak, at 13,804 feet (4,207 meters), is the highest point in the state. Wyoming's largest lake—Yellowstone—lies in the heart of Yellowstone National Park. Major rivers include the Green, Yellowstone, and Big Horn.

3 CLIMATE

Wyoming is generally semiarid, with local desert conditions. Daily temperatures in Cheyenne range from 14°F (–10°C) to 37°F (3°C) in January, and 44°F (7°C) to 80°F (27°C) in July. The record low temperature, –63°F (–53°C), was set in 1933; the record high, 114°F (46°C), occurred in 1900. Normal precipitation in Cheyenne is 13 inches (33 centimeters) a year.

4 PLANTS AND ANIMALS

Wyoming has more than 2,000 species of ferns, conifers, and flowering plants. Prairie grasses dominate the eastern third of the state; desert shrubs, primarily sagebrush, cover the Great Basin in the west. Rocky Mountain forests consist largely of pine, spruce, and fir. Game mammals include the mule deer, elk, and moose. The jackrabbit and antelope are plentiful. Wild turkey and sage grouse are leading game birds, while rainbow trout is the favorite game fish. Endangered species (10 in 1997) include the black-footed ferret and the Wyoming toad.

5 ENVIRONMENTAL PROTECTION

The state's principal environmental concerns are conservation of scarce water resources and preservation of air quality. The Department of Environmental Quality runs 21 air-monitoring sites to maintain air quality. Programs to dispose of hazardous waste and assure safe drinking water are administered by the state. Wyoming had three hazardous waste sites as of 1998.

Wyoming Population Profile

Total population in 2000:	493,782
Population change, 1990–2000:	8.9%
Hispanic or Latino†:	6.4%
Population by race	
One race:	98.2%
White:	92.1%
Black or African American:	0.8%
American Indian/Alaska Native:	2.3%
Asian:	0.6%
Native Hawaiian/Pacific Islander:	0.1%
Some other race:	2.5%
Two or more races:	1.8%

Population by Age Group

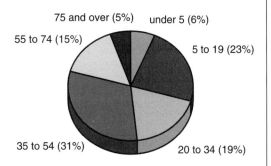

75 and over (5%) under 5 (6%)
55 to 74 (15%)
5 to 19 (23%)
35 to 54 (31%)
20 to 34 (19%)

Top Cities by Population

City	Population	% change 1990–2000
Cheyenne	53,011	6.0
Casper	49,644	6.2
Laramie	27,204	1.9
Gillette	19,646	11.4
Rock Springs	18,708	–1.8
Sheridan	15,804	13.7
Green River	11,808	–7.1
Evanston	11,507	5.5
Riverton	9,310	1.2
Cody	8,835	11.9

Notes: †A person of Hispanic or Latino origin may be of any race. NA indicates that data are not available.
Sources: U.S. Census Bureau. Public Information Office. *Demographic Profiles.* [Online] Available http://www.census.gov/PressRelease/www/2001/demoprofile.html. Accessed June 1, 2001. U.S. Census Bureau. *Census 2000: Redistricting Data.* Press release issued by the Redistricting Data Office. Washington, D.C., March, 2001.

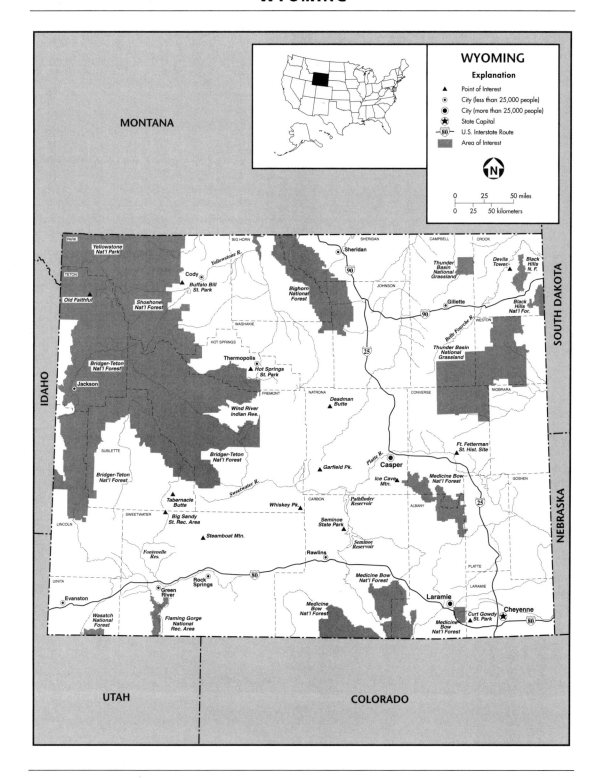

The Grand Teton Peak, tallest of the Grand Teton National Park's 19 peaks.

6 POPULATION

Wyoming has maintained its rank as 50th in the US in population and 49th in population density. Only Alaska is more sparsely populated. In 2000, the state's population was 493,782 (less than the 2000 population of Oklahoma City, Oklahoma), with a density of 5.1 persons per square mile (2 persons per square kilometer). Leading cities in 2000 were Cheyenne, 53,011; Casper, 49,644; and Laramie, 27,204. Approximately 29% of the population is 19 years of age and younger.

7 ETHNIC GROUPS

The population is mostly of European descent, the largest groups being German, English, and Irish. The white population was estimated at 461,400 in 1997, accounting for 96.2% of the state total (the 7th highest proportion of whites for any state). There were an estimated 10,500 Native Americans in Wyoming in 1997 (2.2%). The state also had about 4,000 blacks and 3,900 persons of Asian-Pacific Island descent, about half of whom were of Japanese or Chinese ancestry.

8 LANGUAGES

Generally, Wyoming English is North Midland with some South Midland elements, especially along the Nebraska border. In 1990, 394,904 Wyomingites—94.3% of the residents five years old or older—spoke only English at home. Residents who spoke other languages at home, and number of speakers, included Spanish, 13,790; and various Native American languages, 1,654.

9 RELIGIONS

Wyoming's churchgoing population is mostly Protestant. The largest denominations in 1990 were United Methodist, 13,099; Episcopal, 9,894; Southern Baptist Convention, 18,674; Evangelical Lutheran Church in America, 9,088; and Presbyterian, 8,749. There were 59,565 Roman Catholics in that year. Wyoming also had 45,793 Mormons and an estimated 330 Jews in 1990.

10 TRANSPORTATION

Wyoming is served chiefly by the Burlington Northern, Chicago and Northwestern, and Union Pacific railroads. The total trackage of these three Class I railroads in 1998 was 1,928 miles (3,102 kilometers). Trackage increased in the 1990s primarily to haul coal from the Powder River Basin. Wyoming leads the nation in the volume of coal transported by rail out of the state. In 1997, public highways and rural and urban roads totaling 33,293 miles (53,568 kilometers) crossed the state. In 1996, Wyoming had 96 airports and heliports.

11 HISTORY

Although the first Europeans to visit Wyoming were French Canadian traders, the first modern exploration of Wyoming was made by an American fur trader, John Colter, who traversed the northwestern

Photo credit: Corel Corporation.

The American Buffalo (bison) were nearly extinct before establishing a stronghold in Yellowstone National Park in the 20th century.

part of the state in 1807–08, probably crossing what is now Yellowstone Park. After Colter, trappers and fur traders crisscrossed Wyoming.

Between 1840 and 1867, thousands of Americans crossed Wyoming on the Oregon Trail, bound for Oregon or California. However, very few stayed in this harsh region. The event that brought population as well as territorial status to Wyoming was the coming of the Union Pacific Railroad. In 1868, Wyoming was organized as a territory. Wyoming in 1869 became the

Wyoming Population by Race

Census 2000 was the first national census in which the instructions to respondents said, "Mark one or more races." This table shows the number of people who are of one, two, or three or more races. For those claiming two races, the number of people belonging to the various categories is listed. The U.S. government conducts a census of the population every ten years.

	Number	Percent
Total population	493,782	100.0
One race	484,899	98.2
Two races	8,476	1.7
White *and* Black or African American	739	0.1
White *and* American Indian/Alaska Native	3,289	0.7
White *and* Asian	934	0.2
White *and* Native Hawaiian/Pacific Islander	141	—
White *and* some other race	2,737	0.6
Black or African American *and* American Indian/Alaska Native	86	—
Black or African American *and* Asian	44	—
Black or African American *and* Native Hawaiian/Pacific Islander	5	—
Black or African American *and* some other race	102	—
American Indian/Alaska Native *and* Asian	34	—
American Indian/Alaska Native *and* Native Hawaiian/Pacific Islander	11	—
American Indian/Alaska Native *and* some other race	192	—
Asian *and* Native Hawaiian/Pacific Islander	49	—
Asian *and* some other race	102	—
Native Hawaiian/Pacific Islander *and* some other race	11	—
Three or more races	407	0.1

Source: U.S. Census Bureau. *Census 2000: Redistricting Data.* Press release issued by the Redistricting Data Office. Washington, D.C., March, 2001. A dash (—) indicates that the percent is less than 0.1.

first territory or state that allowed women to vote.

Wyoming became a center for cattle ranchers and foreign investors who hoped to make a fortune from free grass and the high price of cattle. The struggle between the large landowners and small ranchers culminated in the so-called Johnson County War of 1891–92.

Statehood

Wyoming became a state in 1890, but growth remained slow. Attempts at farming proved unsuccessful in this high, arid region, and Wyoming to this day remains a sparsely settled ranching state. What growth has occurred has been primarily through the minerals industry, especially the development of coal, oil, and natural-gas resources during the 1970s' national energy crisis.

However, the worldwide oil glut in the early 1980s slowed the growth of the state's energy industries. In 1984, the growth of the state's nonfuel mineral industry slowed as well. Since then, the state has looked to tourism as an effective means of expanding its economy.

12 STATE GOVERNMENT

The legislature consists of a 30-member senate and a 60-member house of representatives. Heading the executive branch are five elected officials: the governor, secretary of state, auditor, treasurer, and superintendent of public instruction.

Wyoming Governors: 1890–2001

1890	Francis Emroy Warren	Republican
1890–1893	Amos Walker Barber	Republican
1893–1895	John Eugene Osborne	Democrat
1895–1899	William Alford Richards	Republican
1899–1903	DeForest Richards	Republican
1903–1905	Fenimore Chatterton	Republican
1905–1911	Bryant Butler Brooks	Republican
1911–1915	Joseph Maull Carey	Republican
1915–1917	John Benjamin Kendrick	Democrat
1917–1919	Frank L. Houx	Democrat
1919–1923	Robert Davis Carey	Republican
1923–1924	William Bradford Ross	Democrat
1924–1925	Franklin Earl Lucas	Republican
1925–1927	Nellie Tayloe Ross	Democrat
1927–1931	Frank Collins Emerson	Republican
1931–1933	Alonzo Monroe Clark	Republican
1933–1939	Leslie Andrew Miller	Democrat
1939–1943	Nels Hanson Smith	Republican
1943–1949	Lester Calloway Hunt	Democrat
1949–1951	Arthur Griswold Crane	Republican
1951–1953	Frank Aloysius Barrett	Republican
1953–1955	Clifford Joy Rogers	Republican
1955–1959	Milward Lee Simpson	Republican
1959–1961	John Joseph Hickey	Democrat
1961–1963	Jack Robert Gage	Democrat
1963–1967	Clifford Peter Hansen	Republican
1967–1975	Stanley Knapp Hathaway	Republican
1975–1987	Edgar J. Herschler	Democrat
1987–1995	Michael John Sullivan	Democrat
1995–	Jim Geringer	Republican

13 POLITICAL PARTIES

The Republicans currently dominate Wyoming politics at the federal level. Until recently, Democrats were more likely to be elected for state office. There are 125,336 registered Republicans, or 54%; 83,091 registered Democrats, or 36%; and 25,806 independents, or 11%. The governor, Jim Geringer, who was elected in 1994, is a Republican. Both of Wyoming's senators, Mike Enzi and Craig Thomas (who was reelected in 2000), are Republicans, as is Wyoming's US Representative, Barbara Cubin (who was also reelected in 2000). In 2001, there were 20 Republicans and 10 Democrats in the state senate; in the state house, there are 46 Republicans and 14 Democrats. Republican George W. Bush received 69% of the vote in the 2000 presidential election, while Democrat Al Gore won 28%.

Wyoming Presidential Vote by Major Political Parties 1948–2000

YEAR	WYOMING WINNER	DEMOCRAT	REPUBLICAN
1948	*Truman (D)	52,354	47,947
1952	*Eisenhower (R)	47,934	81,049
1956	*Eisenhower (R)	49,554	74,573
1960	Nixon (R)	63,331	77,451
1964	*Johnson (D)	80,718	61,998
1968	*Nixon (R)	45,173	70,927
1972	*Nixon (R)	44,358	100,464
1976	Ford (R)	62,239	92,717
1980	*Reagan (R)	49,427	110,700
1984	*Reagan (R)	53,370	133,241
1988	*Bush (R)	67,113	106,867
1992**	Bush (R)	68,160	79,347
1996**	Dole (R)	77,934	105,388
2000	*Bush (R)	60,481	147,947

* Won US presidential election.
** Independent candidate Ross Perot received 51,263 votes in 1992 and 25,928 votes in 1996.

14 LOCAL GOVERNMENT

Wyoming is subdivided into 23 counties and 97 municipalities. County officials include a clerk, treasurer, assessor, sheriff, attorney, three commissioners, and from one to five county judges.

15 JUDICIAL SYSTEM

Wyoming's judicial branch consists of a supreme court with a chief justice and four other justices, nine district courts, county courts, justice of the peace courts, and municipal courts. Wyoming's total crime rate in 1998 was 3,808 per 100,000 persons. Wyoming's prison population totalled 1,634 in 1999.

16 MIGRATION

Many people have passed through Wyoming, but relatively few have come to stay. Not until the 1970s, a time of rapid economic development, did the picture change. Between 1970 and 1983, Wyoming gained a net total of 45,500 residents through migration. In the 1980s, however, there was a net loss of 52,000 persons. From 1990 to 1998, there was a net gain of about 1,700 residents due to migration.

17 ECONOMY

The economic life of Wyoming is largely sustained by agriculture—chiefly feed grains and livestock—and mining, including petroleum and gas production. Mining and petroleum production grew rapidly during the 1970s, leading to a powerful upsurge in population. The absence of personal and corporate income taxes has helped foster a favorable business climate.

18 INCOME

In income per capita (per person), Wyoming ranked 35th among the 50 states in 1998 with $24,312. Total personal income in the same year was $11.7 billion. In 1998, 12% of the state's residents lived below the federal poverty level.

19 INDUSTRY

Manufacturing increased strikingly in Wyoming from 1977 to 1991. Value of

Photo credit: Pete Saloutos/Wyoming Division of Tourism.

Shoshone dancer from the Wind River Indian Reservation, home to 3,700 Arapahos and 2,800 Shoshones.

shipments by manufacturers more than doubled from $1,287 million to $2,733 million. But these figures remain very small by national standards.

20 LABOR

In 1998, Wyoming's civilian labor force was about 258,000. Of that total, about 4.8% were unemployed. In the same year, 9.6% of all workers belonged to labor unions.

21 AGRICULTURE

Agriculture—especially livestock and grain—is one of Wyoming's most important industries. In 1998, Wyoming had about 9,200 farms and ranches covering almost 34.6 million acres (14 million hectares). Total farm marketing in 1999 amounted to $854 million. Field crops in 1998 included 6.7 million bushels of wheat; 1.4 million bushels of oats; 120,000 tons of sugar beets; and 7.3 million bushels of barley.

22 DOMESTICATED ANIMALS

For most of Wyoming's territorial and state history, cattle ranchers have dominated the economy. In 1999, Wyoming had 1.56 million head of cattle and 140,000 hogs. In 1995, cattle products accounted for 50% of Wyoming's agricultural receipts.

23 FISHING

There is no important commercial fishing in Wyoming. Fishing is largely recreational in the state, and fish hatcheries and fish-planting programs keep the streams and lakes well stocked.

24 FORESTRY

Wyoming has 10.9 million acres (4.4 million hectares) of forested land, equal to 18% of the state's land area. Shipments by the lumber industry were valued at $15.2 million in 1997. Ponderosa pine accounted for 50% of the annual cut; and lodgepole pine, 41%.

25 MINING

The estimated value of nonfuel mineral production for Wyoming in 1998 was nearly $1.06 billion. Three commodities—clays, grade-A helium, and soda ash—accounted for over 90% of the state's non-fuel mineral production. In 1996, Wyoming produced 3.2 million metric tons of clays. The state continued to rank first in bentonite production and leads the nation in soda ash production. Wyoming has the world's largest deposit of trona, the ore from which soda ash is refined.

26 ENERGY AND POWER

In 1998, electric power production totaled 44.7 billion kilowatt hours. The state has no nuclear power plants.

Wyoming is comparatively energy-rich, ranking first among the states in coal production. Wyoming has the three largest producing coal mines in the US and total coal deposits estimated at 7,220 million tons. In 1998, the state's 24 active mines produced 314.4 million tons of coal.

Crude oil production totaled 61.1 million barrels in 1998, and natural gas production totaled 761.3 billion cubic feet (21.6 billion cubic meters).

27 COMMERCE

Wholesale sales totaled $2.5 billion in 1997; retail sales were $3.6 billion. Wyoming's exports of products to other countries were valued at $500 million in 1998.

28 PUBLIC FINANCE

Revenues for Wyoming in 1997 were $2.56 billion; expenditures were $2.13 billion. The outstanding state debt was $872 million as of 1997, or $1,817 per capita (per person).

29 TAXATION

In 1997, the state government collected a total of $654 million in tax revenues, including sales and property taxes. Wyoming has no personal or corporate income tax. The state retail sales tax is 4%.

30 HEALTH

The death rates for heart disease and cancer, were well below the national norm, but accidental deaths and cerebrovascular diseases were above it. Wyoming has the lowest number, ratio, and rate of abortions of all the states—208 in 1996. In 1998, Wyoming's 25 hospitals had 1,935 beds. Some 16.9% of state residents did not have health insurance in 1998.

31 HOUSING

In 1999, there were an estimated 213,000 housing units in Wyoming. In 1998, 1,900 new housing units valued at $251 million were authorized for construction. The median home value was $61,600 in 1990. The median monthly cost for an owner-occupied home with a mortgage was $612 in 1990; renters had a median monthly cost of $333.

32 EDUCATION

Nearly 90% of all adults in the state were high school graduates in 1998, and more than 19% were college graduates. In 1997, there were over 97,000 public school students. Expenditures on education averaged $5,720 per pupil (20th in the nation) in 1995. In the fall of 1997, 30,280 students were enrolled in Wyoming's institutions of higher education.

There are no private colleges or universities in the state.

33 ARTS

The ten-member Wyoming Council on the Arts is appointed by the governor to fund local activities and organizations in the visual arts, including painting, music, theater, and dance. The council supports arts programs such as the Desert School of Wamsutter, the Crest Hill School Writing Center in Casper, and the Grand Teton Music Festival. In 1996, there were 60 arts associations and 100 local arts groups in Wyoming.

34 LIBRARIES AND MUSEUMS

Wyoming was served by 23 county public library systems, with over 2 million volumes, in 1999. Public library circulation exceeded 3.5 million during the same period. The University of Wyoming, in Laramie, had 1.2 million volumes in 1999. There are 53 museums and historical sites, including the Wyoming State Art Gallery and Wyoming State Museum in Cheyenne, and the Buffalo Bill Historical Center in Cody.

35 COMMUNICATIONS

In 1999, 95% of Wyoming households had telephones. In 2000, Wyoming had 88 radio stations, 32 AM and 56 FM, plus 17 commercial television stations. During the same year, over 7,000 Internet domain names were registered.

36 PRESS

There were nine daily newspapers and four Sunday newspapers in Wyoming in

Elk graze in Yellowstone National Park, surrounded by the remains of trees killed ten years earlier when massive forest fires swept through the park. When the fires started in June 1988, the National Park Service allowed them to burn, predicting that they would die out on their own. By September, the fires had raged out of control and were threatening historic tourist facilities. The Park Service was forced to call in an army of over 9,000 firefighters, the largest fire-fighting effort in U.S. history. Over one million acres were burned before the fires were extinguished.

1998. The major daily paper and its 1998 circulation was the *Casper Star–Tribune*, with 31,319 (33,957 on Sunday).

37 TOURISM, TRAVEL, AND RECREATION

There are two national parks in Wyoming—Yellowstone and Grand Teton—9 national forests, and 11 state parks. Devils Tower and Fossil Butte are national monuments, and Fort Laramie is a national his-toric site. Yellowstone National Park is the oldest and largest national park in the US, featuring some 3,000 geysers and hot springs, including the celebrated Old Faithful. Just to the south of Yellowstone is Grand Teton National Park.

38 SPORTS

There are no major league professional sports teams in Wyoming. Rodeos are held throughout the state, and skiing is a major

Photo credit: Corel Corporation.

Every 74 minutes, the Old Faithful geyser erupts in Yellowstone National Park.

sport. Jackson Hole is the largest, best-known resort area. In collegiate sports, the University of Wyoming competes in the Western Athletic Conference.

39 FAMOUS WYOMINGITES

Important federal officeholders from Wyoming include Willis Van Devanter (b.Indiana, 1859–1941), who served on the US Supreme Court from 1910 to 1937; and Richard Cheney (b.Nebraska, 1941), the US secretary of defense from 1989 to 1992, and elected Vice-President on the Republican ticket in 2000. Nellie Taylor

Ross (b.Missouri, 1876–1977) became the first female governor of any state in 1925, serving later as director of the US Mint from 1933 to 1953. Many of Wyoming's better-known individuals are associated with the frontier. William F. "Buffalo Bill" Cody (b.Iowa, 1846–1917) established the town of Cody. A number of outlaws made their headquarters in Wyoming. The most famous were "Butch Cassidy" (Robert Leroy Parker, b.Utah, 1866–1909?) and the "Sundance Kid" (Harry Longabaugh, 1863?–1909?). Wyoming's most famous entrepreneur was James Cash Penney (b. Missouri, 1875–1971), who built a nationwide chain of department stores. Jakson Pollack (1912–56), known for his Impressionistic "all-over drip style" painting, was born in Cody.

40 BIBLIOGRAPHY

Athearn, Robert G. *Union Pacific Country.* New York: Rand McNally, 1971.

Baldwin, Guy. *Wyoming.* New York: Benchmark Books, 1999.

Fradin, Dennis B. *Wyoming.* Chicago: Childrens Press, 1994.

Frisch, Carlienne. *Wyoming.* Minneapolis: Lerner Publications, 1994.

Kent, Deborah. *Wyoming.* New York: Children's Press, 2000.

Larson, T. A. *Wyoming: A History.* New York: Norton, 1984.

Mead, Jean. *Wyoming in Profile.* Boulder, Colo: Pruett, 1982.

Web sites

Secretary of State. Interesting Information About Wyoming. [Online] Available http://soswy.state.wy.us/informat/informat.htm Accessed May 31, 2001.

State of Wyoming. About Wyoming. [Online] Available http://www.state.wy.us/about.html Accessed May 31, 2001.

DISTRICT OF COLUMBIA

District of Columbia

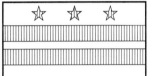

ORIGIN OF NAME: From "Columbia," a name commonly applied to the US in the late 18th century, ultimately deriving from Christopher Columbus.

BECAME US CAPITAL: 1 December 1800, when Congress first assembled in the city.

MOTTO: *Justitia omnibus* (Justice for all).

FLAG: The flag, based on George Washington's coat of arms, consists of three red stars above two horizontal red stripes on a white field.

OFFICIAL SEAL: In the background, the Potomac River separates the District of Columbia from the Virginia shore, over which the sun is rising. In the foreground, Justice, holding a wreath and a tablet with the word "Constitution," stands beside a statue of George Washington. At the left of Justice is the Capitol; to her right, an eagle and various agricultural products. Below is the District motto and the date 1871; above are the words "District of Columbia."

BIRD: Wood thrush.

FLOWER: American beauty rose.

TREE: Scarlet oak.

TIME: 7 AM EST = noon GMT.

1 LOCATION AND SIZE

Located in the South Atlantic region of the US, the District of Columbia has a total area of 69 square miles (179 square kilometers). Its total boundary length is 37 miles (60 kilometers).

2 TOPOGRAPHY

The District of Columbia lies wholly within the Atlantic Coastal Plain. The major physical features are the Potomac River and its nearby marshlands; the Anacostia River; Rock Creek; and the gentle hills of the north. The District's average elevation is about 150 feet (46 meters).

3 CLIMATE

The climate of the nation's capital is characterized by chilly, damp winters and hot, humid summers. The normal daily mean temperature is 58°F (14°C), ranging from 35°F (2°C) in January to 79°F (26°C) in July. Precipitation averages 39 inches (99 centimeters) yearly.

4 PLANTS AND ANIMALS

The District has long been known for its beautiful parks, and about 1,800 varieties of flowering plants and 250 shrubs and trees grow there. Boulevards are shaded by stately sycamores, pine and red oaks,

American lindens, and black walnut trees. Famous among the introduced species are the flowering Japanese cherry trees around the Tidal Basin. Magnolia, dogwood, and gingko are also characteristic. The District's animal life includes squirrels, cottontails, English sparrows, and starlings.

5 ENVIRONMENTAL PROTECTION

The Environmental Regulation Administration (ERA) administers district and federal laws, regulations, and mayoral initiatives governing the environment and natural resources of the District of Columbia and the surrounding metropolitan area. The Metropolitan Washington Council of Governments coordinates water and air pollution control programs.

6 POPULATION

The District of Columbia outranked the state of Wyoming in population in 2000, with a census total of 572,059, similar to that of Nashville, Tennessee. The population density was 9,378 persons per square mile (3,620.8 persons per square kilometer). Considered as a city, the District ranked 21st in the US in 2000. The number of Washington, D.C., metropolitan area residents reached 4.56 million in 1996. Nearly one-quarter of the population is 19 years of age and younger.

7 ETHNIC GROUPS

Since the 1950s, blacks have been the largest ethnic group in the District of Columbia, accounting for an estimated 62.9% of the population in 1997. Blacks comprised about 26.6% of the metropolitan area

District of Columbia Population Profile

Total population in 2000:	572,059
Population change, 1990–2000:	–5.7%
Hispanic or Latino†:	7.9%
Population by race	
One race:	97.6%
White:	30.8%
Black or African American:	60.0%
American Indian/Alaska Native:	0.3%
Asian:	2.7%
Native Hawaiian/Pacific Islander:	0.1%
Some other race:	3.8%
Two or more races:	2.4%

Population by Age Group

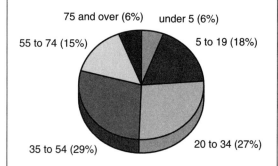

75 and over (6%) under 5 (6%)
55 to 74 (15%)
5 to 19 (18%)
35 to 54 (29%)
20 to 34 (27%)

Top Cities by Population

City	Population	% change 1990–2000
Washington	572,059	–5.7%

Notes: †A person of Hispanic or Latino origin may be of any race. NA indicates that data are not available.
Sources: U.S. Census Bureau. Public Information Office. *Demographic Profiles*. [Online] Available http://www.census.gov/Press-Release/www/2001/demoprofile.html. Accessed June 1, 2001. U.S. Census Bureau. *Census 2000: Redistricting Data*. Press release issued by the Redistricting Data Office. Washington, D.C., March, 2001.

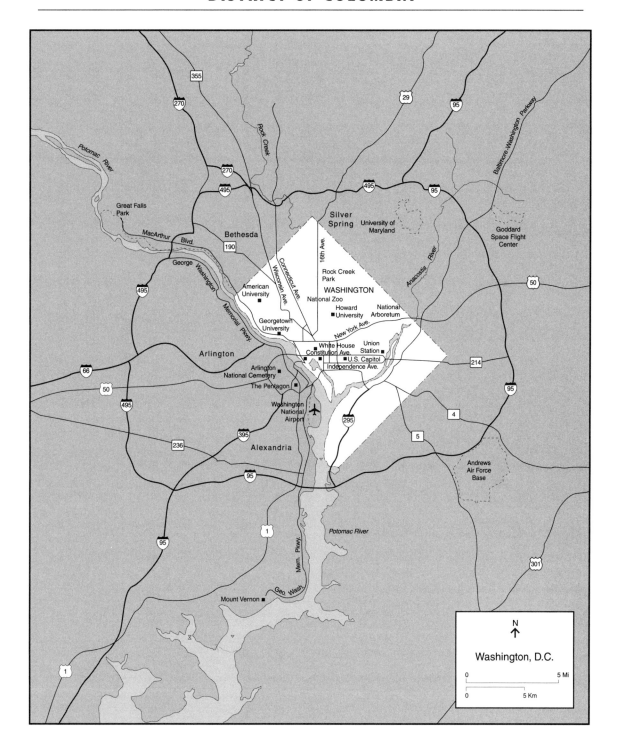

Washington, D.C.

District of Columbia Population by Race

Census 2000 was the first national census in which the instructions to respondents said, "Mark one or more races." This table shows the number of people who are of one, two, or three or more races. For those claiming two races, the number of people belonging to the various categories is listed. The U.S. government conducts a census of the population every ten years.

	Number	Percent
Total population	572,059	100.0
One race	558,613	97.6
Two races	12,179	2.1
White *and* Black or African American	1,679	0.3
White *and* American Indian/Alaska Native	603	0.1
White *and* Asian	1,319	0.2
White *and* Native Hawaiian/Pacific Islander	75	—
White *and* some other race	3,413	0.6
Black or African American *and* American Indian/Alaska Native	1,389	0.2
Black or African American *and* Asian	554	0.1
Black or African American *and* Native Hawaiian/Pacific Islander	108	—
Black or African American *and* some other race	2,312	0.4
American Indian/Alaska Native *and* Asian	48	—
American Indian/Alaska Native *and* Native Hawaiian/Pacific Islander	4	—
American Indian/Alaska Native *and* some other race	133	—
Asian *and* Native Hawaiian/Pacific Islander	98	—
Asian *and* some other race	401	0.1
Native Hawaiian/Pacific Islander *and* some other race	43	—
Three or more races	1,267	0.2

Source: U.S. Census Bureau. *Census 2000: Redistricting Data.* Press release issued by the Redistricting Data Office. Washington, D.C., March, 2001. A dash (—) indicates that the percent is less than 0.1.

population in 1990, a proportion that has been fairly constant for over 200 years. In 1997, the District had an estimated 178,800 whites (33.8%), 15,600 Asians and Pacific Islanders (2.9%), and 1,600 Native Americans (0.3%). That year, there were an estimated 178,800 residents with Hispanic origins. The 1990 census count included 12,353 Russians, 8,547 Salvadorans, 3,184 Jamaicans, and 2,574 Chinese.

8 LANGUAGES

Many different dialects of English are spoken in the Washington, D.C., area. In 1990, 87% of all District of Columbia residents spoke only English at home. Other languages spoken at home included Spanish, Chinese, French, Italian, German, and Greek.

9 RELIGIONS

As of 1990, Washington, D.C. had 77,532 Roman Catholics. The leading Protestant denominations in 1990 were Episcopal, 16,273; American Baptist Convention, 33,744; United Methodist, 18,321; and Southern Baptist Convention, 17,597. The Jewish population in 1990 was estimated at 25,400 in the District.

10 TRANSPORTATION

In 1995/96, Amtrak operated about 75 trains per day into Union Station, with a total of 3.14 million riders. Within the District as of 1996 were 1,424 miles (2,291 kilometers) of public streets and roads. About 40% of working District residents commute by public transportation, which includes a highly developed rail system that extends to suburban Maryland and Virginia. Three major airports handle the District's commercial air traffic: Ronald Reagan Washington National Airport (renamed in 1998) and Dulles International Airport in Virginia; and the Baltimore–Washington International Airport in Maryland.

11 HISTORY

The English founded the Jamestown, Virginia, settlement in 1607. Originally part of the Maryland Colony, the region of the present-day capital had been carved up into plantations by the latter half of the 17th century. After the US Constitution (1787) provided that a tract of land be reserved for the seat of the federal government, Congress authorized George Washington to choose a site along the Potomac River in 1791. Washington made his selection and appointed Andrew Ellicott to survey the area. He then employed Pierre Charles L'Enfant, a French military engineer, to draw up plans for the federal city.

L'Enfant's design called for a wide roadway (now called Pennsylvania Avenue) to connect the Capitol with the President's House (the White House), a mile away. L'Enfant was dismissed before completion of the work, and Ellicott carried out the plans. Although construction was delayed by lack of adequate financing, President John Adams and some 125 gov-

Photo credit: Corel Corporation.

Looking down Pennsylvania Avenue.

ernment officials moved into the District in 1800.

On 3 May 1802, the city of Washington was incorporated, with an elected council and a mayor appointed by the president. In August 1814, during the War of 1812, British forces invaded and burned the Capitol, the President's House, and other public buildings. These were rebuilt within five years. At the request of its residents, Virginia took back its portion of the District in 1846, thus confining the District to the eastern shore of the Potomac. The Civil War brought a large influx of

Union soldiers, workers, and freed slaves. The District's population rose sharply, spurring the development of modern Washington.

In 1874, a new form of government was established, headed by three commissioners appointed by the president. The 1930s brought a rise in public employment, growth of federal facilities, and the beginnings of large-scale public housing construction. The White House was completely renovated in the late 1940s, and a huge building program coincided with the expansion of the federal bureaucracy during the 1960s.

1960s–1990s

In recent years, the District's form of government has undergone significant changes. The 23d Amendment to the US Constitution, ratified on 3 April 1961, permits residents to vote in presidential elections. In 1964, residents of the District voted for a president for the first time since 1800. Beginning in 1971, the District was allowed to send a nonvoting delegate to the US House of Representatives, and a local school board was also elected. Local self-rule began in 1975, when an elected mayor and council took office. There has been a movement for statehood which won local approval, but was defeated by the US Senate in 1992, when they refused to consider the bill.

The District has both prospered and suffered in the last two decades. An expanding economy increased the city's office space by 25%. At the same time, the city has been wracked by drug-related crime and by corruption in high places. In 1990, the District's mayor of twelve years, Marion Barry, was videotaped smoking crack and convicted of possessing cocaine. Barry was succeeded that year by Sharon Pratt Dixon, who promised to clean house "with a shovel, not a broom."

In 1994, Democrat Marion Barry, returning to political life after serving a six-month jail term for his drug conviction, defeated Republican Carol Schwartz in the mayoral contest. Elected in 1999, Anthony A. Williams serves as the District's mayor. Eleanor Holmes Norton serves as the District's delegate to the House of Representatives.

12 STATE GOVERNMENT

The District of Columbia is the seat of the federal government and houses the principal parts of the legislative, executive, and judicial branches. The District of Columbia committees of the US Senate and House of Representatives oversee affairs within Washington, D.C. The District elects a delegate to the US House who participates in discussions and votes on bills within the District of Columbia Committee, but who may not vote on measures on the actual floor of the House.

13 POLITICAL PARTIES

Washington, D.C., is the headquarters of the Democratic and Republican parties, the nation's major political organizations. The District itself is overwhelmingly Democratic, unfailingly casting their votes for the Democratic nominee in every election since 1964. In 1998 there were 353,503 registered voters.

D.C. Presidential Vote by Major Parties, 1964–96

Year	D.C. Winner	Democrat	Republican
1964	*Johnson (D)	169,796	28,801
1968	Humphrey (D)	139,566	31,012
1972	McGovern (D)	127,627	35,226
1976	*Carter (D)	137,818	27,873
1980	Carter (D)	124,376	21,765
1984	Mondale (D)	180,408	29,009
1988	Dukakis (D)	159,407	27,590
1992	*Clinton (D)	192,619	20,698
1996	*Clinton (D)	158,220	17,339
2000	Gore (D)	171,923	18,073

* Won US presidential election.

14 LOCAL GOVERNMENT

In 1973, Congress provided the District with a home-rule charter, allowing Washington, D.C., residents to elect their own mayor and a city council of 13 members, all serving four-year terms. The mayor is the District's chief executive, and the council is the legislative branch. However, under constitutional authority, Congress can enact laws on any subject affecting the District, and all legislation enacted by the District is subject to congressional veto.

15 JUDICIAL SYSTEM

The US Court of Appeals for the District of Columbia functions in a manner similar to that of a state supreme court. It also has original jurisdiction over federal crimes. The Superior Court of the District of Columbia is its trial court. The District of Columbia is the only US jurisdiction where the US Attorney's Office, and not the local government, prosecutes criminal offenders for nonfederal crimes. According to the FBI Crime Index, the crime rate in the District of Columbia was 8,836 per 100,000 population in 1998, over two times greater than the national average.

16 MIGRATION

The principal migrations have been an influx of southern blacks after the Civil War and, more recently, the rapid growth of the Washington, D.C., metropolitan area. These migrations have been coupled with a shrinkage in the population of the District itself since the mid-1960s. From 1985 to 1990, the District had a net loss from migration of over 30,000 people. During 1990–98, there was a net loss of 139,000 residents to various states, and a net gain of 27,900 from migration abroad.

17 ECONOMY

The city enjoyed an economic boom in the 1980s which increased its office space from 52,000 square feet in 1985 to 69,000 square feet in 1990. The federal government is the District's largest employer, followed by services, professional associations, and tourism. Between 1980 and 1990, the number of jobs in the service industry grew 43.5%. Other industries, however, suffered in that decade.

18 INCOME

With a per capita (per person) income of $36,415 in 1998, the District of Columbia ranked second in the US. Total personal income was $19 billion in 1998. The proportion of District of Columbia residents below the federal poverty level was 22.7% in 1998.

19 INDUSTRY

The Government Printing Office operates one of the largest printing plants in the US. Also in the District is the Washington Post

Company, publisher of the newspaper of that name and of *Newsweek* magazine; the company also owns television stations. Services, federal civilian government, and finance, insurance and real estate were the largest industries in 1998.

20 LABOR

The civilian labor force in the District of Columbia was about 267,000 in 1998, of whom 8.8% were unemployed. The District of Columbia is the headquarters of the American Federation of Labor and Congress of Industrial Organizations (AFL-CIO), the largest US labor organization. Some 13.5% of all workers were union members in 1998. Services and government accounted for 44% and 36% of all employment, respectively, in mid-1998.

21 AGRICULTURE

There is no commercial farming in the District of Columbia.

22 DOMESTICATED ANIMALS

The District of Columbia has no livestock industry.

23 FISHING

There is no commercial fishing in the District of Columbia. Recreational fishing is accessible via a boat-launching facility on the Anacostia River.

24 FORESTRY

There is no forestland or forest products industry in the District of Columbia.

25 MINING

There is no mining in the District of Columbia, although a few mining firms have offices there.

26 ENERGY AND POWER

The District of Columbia had an electrical output totaling 244 million kilowatt hours from four oil-fired plants in 1998.

27 COMMERCE

Wholesale sales totaled $3.3 billion in 1997; retail sales were $3.6 billion in that same year; exports totaled $350 million in merchandise in 1998.

28 PUBLIC FINANCE

The local tax base is limited by a shortage of taxable real estate, much of the District being occupied by government buildings. Also, Congress has not allowed the District to tax the incomes of people who work in Washington but live in the suburbs. Annual budgets in recent years have exceeded $3 billion.

29 TAXATION

In 1999, the District of Columbia's personal income tax ranged from 5% to 9.5%. The District levies a 5.75% general sales and use tax, plus real and personal property taxes, an inheritance tax, and various excise taxes. As of 1995, federal individual income taxes from the District totaled nearly $1.74 billion.

30 HEALTH

In 1998, the District's death rate was higher than any state's—1,157 per

100,000 population. Its infant mortality rate of 14.9 per 1,000 live births exceeded that of every state in 1996. In that same year, some 66.1% of all births were to unmarried women, higher than in any state. Death rates from heart disease were well above the national rates, and the death rate from diabetes mellitus (37.2 per 100,000) was the highest in the country after Louisiana. The homicide rate, 41.9 per 100,000, also remains the highest in the country.

In 1998, there were 12 hospitals with 3,552 beds. The average hospital expense per inpatient day was $1,417, or $9,694 for an average cost per stay—the highest in the US. In 1996, the District had 3,968 nonfederal physicians. The 8,000 registered nurses in 1994 gave the District a ratio of 1,428 employed nurses per 100,000 population, higher than in any state. Some 20% of residents in the District did not have health insurance in 1995.

31 HOUSING

The District of Columbia in 1999 had an estimated 265,000 housing units. Over 10% of all housing units are condominiums, third-highest after Hawaii and Florida. Housing prices were high; the median monthly cost for an owner (including mortgage) in 1990 was $950; renters had a median monthly cost of $479. The median home value was $123,900 in 1990, ninth-highest in the nation.

32 EDUCATION

In the fall of 1997 the public schools had a total enrollment of 77,111 students, minorities making up 96% of total enrollment. Most white and many black students attend private schools. Expenditures on education averaged $7,067 per pupil (sixth in terms of the states) in 1995/96. In 1998 over 83% of all residents 25 years of age or older were high school graduates, and 36.5% were college graduates.

The District had 18 institutions of higher education in 1997. Some of the best-known private universities are American, Georgetown, George Washington, and Howard. The University of the District of Columbia has an open admissions policy for District freshman undergraduate students.

33 ARTS

The John F. Kennedy Center for the Performing Arts is the District's principal performing arts center. The District's leading symphony is the National Symphony Orchestra, which performs from October through April at the Concert Hall of the Kennedy Center. The National Gallery of Art and the Library of Congress offer concerts and recitals. The Washington Opera performs at the Kennedy Center's Opera House.

34 LIBRARIES AND MUSEUMS

Washington, D.C. is the site of the world's largest library, the Library of Congress, with a 1998 collection of more than 80 million items, including 26 million books and pamphlets. The Library has on permanent display Thomas Jefferson's first draft of the Declaration of Independence, and Abraham Lincoln's first two drafts of the Gettysburg Address. The Folger Shakespeare Library contains not only rare Renaissance manuscripts but also a full size re-creation of an Elizabethan theater. In all, the District has over 600 public, private, and special libraries.

The District was home to at least 93 museums in 2000. The Smithsonian Institution operates a vast museum and research complex that includes the National Air and Space Museum and many other facilities. Among the art museums operated by the Smithsonian is the National Gallery of Art, housing one of the world's outstanding collections of Western art.

35 COMMUNICATIONS

Washington, D.C. is the home of the US Postal Service. As of 1999, 92.4% of the District's households had telephones. As of 2000, the District had 7 AM and 13 FM radio stations, and 13 television stations. A total of 47,433 Internet domain names were registered in 2000.

36 PRESS

The District has one major newspaper, the *Washington Post*. In 1998, the *Post*, a morning paper, had an average daily circulation of 759,122 and a Sunday circulation over 1 million. There are many active Press clubs in the District. There are more than 30 major Washington-based periodicals and many ethnic and neighborhood papers. Among the best-known are the *National Geographic*, *U.S. News & World Report*, *Smithsonian*, and *New Republic*.

Photo credit: Corel Corporation.

The "Castle"—the Smithsonian Museum.

37 TOURISM, TRAVEL, AND RECREATION

The District of Columbia is one of the world's leading tourist centers. The capital's extraordinary attractions include the Washington Monument, Lincoln Memorial, Jefferson Memorial, Vietnam Veterans Memorial, White House, Capitol, Smithsonian Institution, Library of Congress, and many more. Across the Potomac, in Virginia, are Arlington National Cemetery, site of the Tomb of the Unknown Soldier and the grave of John F.

Photo credit: National Archives.

Bandmaster, composer, and inventor of the sousaphone, John Philip Sousa was born in Washington D.C. He is best known for his popular marches including Stars and Stripes Forever *and* Semper Fidelis.

Kennedy, and George Washington's home at Mt. Vernon.

38 SPORTS

There are five major league professional sports teams in Washington, D.C.: the Redskins of the National Football League, the Wizards (formerly the Bullets) of the National Basketball Association, the Mystics of the Women's National Basketball Association, the Capitals of the National Hockey League, and the DC United of Major League Soccer. In collegiate sports

the Georgetown Hoyas were a dominant force in basketball during the 1980s.

39 FAMOUS WASHINGTONIANS

Although no US president has been born in the District of Columbia, all but George Washington (b.Virginia, 1732–99) lived there while serving as chief executive.

Inventor Alexander Graham Bell (b. Scotland, 1842–1922) was president of the National Geographic Society in his later years. The designer of the nation's capital was Pierre Charles L'Enfant (b. France, 1754–1825), whose grave is in Arlington National Cemetery. Also involved in laying out the capital were surveyor Andrew Ellicott (b.Pennsylvania, 1754–1820) and mathematician-astronomer Benjamin Banneker (b.Maryland, 1731–1806), a black who was an early champion of equal rights.

Among Washingtonians to achieve distinction in the creative arts were John Philip Sousa (1854–1932), bandmaster and composer; and composer-pianist-bandleader Edward Kennedy "Duke" Ellington (1899–1974).

40 BIBLIOGRAPHY

Brill, Marlene Targ. *Building the Capital City.* New York: Children's Press, 1996.

Feeney, Kathy. *Washington, D.C. Facts and Symbols.* Mankato, Minn.: Bridgestone Books, 2000.

Goldish, Meish. *Our Capital.* New York: Newbridge Educational, 2001.

Gutheim, Frederick. *Worthy of the Nation: The Planning and Development of the National Capital City.* Washington, D.C.: Smithsonian, 1977.

Kummer, Patricia K. *Washington, D.C.* Mankato, Minn.: Capstone Press, 1998.

Levy, Debbie. *Kidding Around Washington, D.C.: What to Do, Where to Go, and How to Have*

Fun in Washington D.C. Emeryville CA: John Muir Publications, 2000.

Lewis, David L. *District of Columbia: A Bicentennial History.* New York: Norton, 1976.

Mitchell, Alexander D. *Washington Then & Now.* San Diego: Thunder Bay Press, 2000.

Sanders, Mark C. *Washington, D.C.* Austin, TX: Steadwell Books, 2000.

Stein, R. Conrad. *Washington, D.C.* New York: Children's Press, 2000.

Web sites

The Washington Post. Home page. [Online] Available http://www/washingtonpost.com/ Accessed March 15, 1999.

PUERTO RICO

Commonwealth of Puerto Rico
Estado Libre Asociado de Puerto Rico

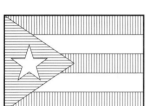

ORIGIN OF NAME: Spanish for "rich port."

NICKNAME: Island of Enchantment.

CAPITAL: San Juan.

BECAME A COMMONWEALTH: 25 July 1952.

SONG: "La Borinquena."

MOTTO: *Joannes est nomen ejus.* (John is his name.)

FLAG: From the hoist extends a blue triangle, with one white star; five horizontal stripes—three red, two white—make up the balance.

OFFICIAL SEAL: In the center of a green circular shield, a lamb holding a white banner reclines on the book of the Apocalypse. Above are a yoke, a cluster of arrows, and the letters "F" and "I," signifying King Ferdinand and Queen Isabella, rulers of Spain at the time of discovery; below is the commonwealth motto. Surrounding the shield, on a white border, are the towers of Castile and lions symbolizing Spain, crosses representing the conquest of Jerusalem, and Spanish banners.

ANIMAL: Coqui.

BIRD: Reinita.

FLOWER: Maga.

TREE: Ceiba.

TIME: 8 AM Atlantic Standard Time = noon GMT.

1 LOCATION AND SIZE

Situated on the northeast periphery of the Caribbean Sea, about 1,000 miles (1,600 kilometers) southeast of Miami, Puerto Rico is the easternmost and smallest island of the Greater Antilles group. Its total area is 3,515 square miles (9,104 square kilometers), including 3,459 square miles (8,959 square kilometers) of land and 56 square miles (145 square kilometers) of inland water. The main island measures 111 miles (179 kilometers) east-west and 36 (58 kilometers) north-south. Offshore and to the east are two major islands, Vieques and Culebra. Puerto Rico's total boundary length is 378 miles (608 kilometers).

2 TOPOGRAPHY

About 75% of Puerto Rico's land area consists of hills or mountains too steep for intensive commercial cultivation. The Cordillera Central range, separating the northern coast from the semiarid south, has the island's highest peak, Cerro de Punta (4,389 feet—1,338 meters). Puerto Rico's best-known peak, El Yunque (3,496 feet—1,066 meters), stands to the east, in the Luquillo Mountains (Sierra de Luquillo). The north coast consists of a level strip about 100 miles (160 kilometers) long and 5 miles (8 kilometers) wide.

Principal valleys are located along the east coast, from Fajardo to Cape Mala Pascua, and around Caguas, in the east-central region. Off the eastern shore are two small islands: Vieques, with an area of 51 square miles (132 square kilometers), and Culebra, covering 24 square miles (62 square kilometers).

The longest river is the Rio de la Plata, extending 46 miles (74 kilometers) from Cayey to Dorado, where it empties into the Atlantic. There are few natural lakes but numerous artificial ones, of which Dos Bocas, south of Arecibo, is one of the most beautiful.

Like many other Caribbean islands, Puerto Rico is the crest of an extinct submarine volcano. About 45 miles (72 kilometers) north of the island lies the Puerto Rico Trench, at over 28,000 feet (8,500 meters) one of the world's deepest chasms.

3 CLIMATE

Tradewinds from the northeast keep Puerto Rico's climate steady, although tropical. San Juan has a normal daily mean temperature of 80°F (27°C), ranging from 77°F (25°C) in January to 82°F (28°C) in July; the normal daily minimum is 73°F (23°C), the maximum 86°F (30°C). The lowest temperature ever recorded on the island is 39°F (4°C); the highest was 103°F (39°C). The recorded temperature in San Juan has never been lower than 60°F (16°C) or higher than 98°F (37°C).

Rainfall varies by region. Ponce, on the south coast, averages only 32 inches (81 centimeters) a year, while the highlands

Puerto Rico Population Profile

Total population in 2000:	3,808,610
Population change, 1990–2000:	10.4%
Hispanic or Latino†:	98.8%
Population by race	
One race:	95.8%
White:	80.5%
Black or African American:	8.0%
American Indian/Alaska Native:	0.4%
Asian:	0.2%
Native Hawaiian/Pacific Islander:	—
Some other race:	6.8%
Two or more races:	4.2%

Population by Age Group

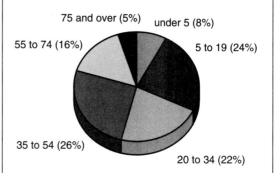

75 and over (5%) under 5 (8%)
55 to 74 (16%) 5 to 19 (24%)
35 to 54 (26%) 20 to 34 (22%)

Top Cities by Population

City	Population	% change 1990–2000
San Juan	421,958	–1.1
Bayamón	203,499	0.7
Carolina	168,164	3.5
Ponce	155,038	–2.6
Caguas	88,680	–4.1
Guaynabo	78,806	7.4
Mayagüez	78,647	–5.3
Trujillo Alto	50,841	14.7
Arecibo	49,318	–0.5
Fajardo	33,286	5.1

Notes: †A person of Hispanic or Latino origin may be of any race. NA indicates that data are not available.
Sources: U.S. Census Bureau. Public Information Office. *Demographic Profiles.* [Online] Available http://www.census.gov/Press-Release/www/2001/demoprofile.html. Accessed June 1, 2001. U.S. Census Bureau. *Census 2000: Redistricting Data.* Press release issued by the Redistricting Data Office. Washington, D.C., March, 2001.

average 108 inches (274 centimeters); the rain forest on El Yunque receives an annual average of 183 inches (465 centimeters). San Juan's average annual rainfall is 54 inches (137 centimeters), with its rainiest months being May through November.

The word "hurricane" derives from *hurakán,* a term the Spanish learned from Puerto Rico's Taino Indians. Several hurricanes have struck Puerto Rico in this century, most recently in 1998.

4 PLANTS AND ANIMALS

During the 19th century, forests covered about three-fourths of Puerto Rico. Today, however, only one-fourth of the island is forested. Flowering trees still abound, and the butterfly tree, African tulip, and flamboyán (royal poinciana) add bright reds and pinks to Puerto Rico's lush green landscape. Among hardwoods, now rare, are nutmeg, satinwood, Spanish elm, and Spanish cedar.

The only mammal found by the conquistadores on the island was a kind of barkless dog, now extinct. Virtually all present-day mammals have been introduced, including horses, cattle, cats, and dogs. The only troublesome mammal is the mongoose, brought in from India to control reptiles in the cane fields and now wild in remote rural areas.

Mosquitoes and sand flies are common pests, but the only dangerous insect is the giant centipede, whose sting is painful but rarely fatal.

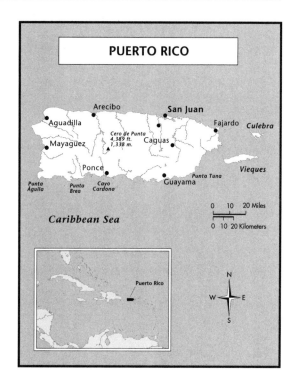

Perhaps the island's best-known inhabitant is the golden coqui, a tiny threatened tree frog. Marine life is extraordinarily abundant, including many tropical fish, crabs, and corals. Puerto Rico has some 200 bird species, many of which live in the rain forest. Thrushes, orioles, grosbeaks, and hummingbirds are common, and the reinita and pitirre are distinctive to the island. Several parrot species are rare, and the Puerto Rican parrot is endangered. Also on the endangered list are the yellow-shouldered blackbird and the Puerto Rican plain pigeon, Puerto Rican whippoorwill. The Mona boa and Mona ground iguana are threatened. There are three national wildlife refuges, covering over 2,000 acres.

5 ENVIRONMENTAL PROTECTION

US environmental laws and regulations are applicable in Puerto Rico. Land-use planning, overseen by the Puerto Rico Planning Board, is an especially difficult problem, since residential, industrial, and recreational developers are all competing for about 30% of the total land area on an island that is already more densely populated than any state of the US except New Jersey. Pollution from highland latrines and septic systems and from agricultural and industrial wastes is a potential hazard. The rum industry, for example, has traditionally dumped its wastes into the ocean. Sewage discharges into the ocean remain a problem.

About 300,000 tons of hazardous waste are generated annually, and 16,000 tons of chemical substances are released into the air, water, and soil each year. As of 1996, the island had nine hazardous waste sites.

6 POPULATION

Puerto Rico's population amounted to over 3.8 million in 2000, up from 3.52 million in 1990. The population projection for 2010 is 4.09 million. With a population density of 1,025 per square mile (465 per square kilometer), Puerto Rico is one of the most densely populated areas of the world.

According to the 1990 census, the population was 71% urban and 29% rural. About 33% of the population was 19 years of age or younger in 1998, and 10.3% was 65 or older. San Juan is Puerto Rico's capital and largest city, with a 2000 population estimate of 421,958, followed by Bayamon, 203,499; Carolina, 168,164; Ponce, 155,038; Caguas, 88,680; Guaynabo, 78,806; and Mayaguez, 78,647.

7 ETHNIC GROUPS

Three main ethnic strands are the heritage of Puerto Rico: the Taino Indians, most of whom fled or perished after the Spanish conquest; black Africans, imported as slaves under Spanish rule; and the Spanish themselves. With an admixture of Dutch, English, Corsicans, and other Europeans, Puerto Ricans today enjoy a distinct Hispanic-Afro-Antillean heritage.

Less than two thirds of all ethnic Puerto Ricans live on the island. Virtually all the remainder reside on the US mainland. In 1990, there were 1.96 million people who identified themselves as Puerto Rican in the 50 states. The State of New York has almost half the US ethnic Puerto Rican population.

8 LANGUAGES

Spanish is the official language of Puerto Rico; English is required in schools as a second language. From 1898 through the 1920s, US authorities unsuccessfully sought to make English the island's primary language.

Taino Indian terms that survive in Puerto Rican Spanish include such place-names as Arecibo, Guayama, and Mayagüez, as well as *hamaca* (hammock) and *canoa* (canoe). Among many African borrowings are food terms like *quimbombó*

Puerto Rico Population by Race

Census 2000 was the first national census in which the instructions to respondents said, "Mark one or more races." This table shows the number of people who are of one, two, or three or more races. For those claiming two races, the number of people belonging to the various categories is listed. The U.S. government conducts a census of the population every ten years.

	Number	Percent
Total population	3,808,610	100.0
One race	3,650,195	95.8
Two races	146,453	3.8
White *and* Black or African American	88,324	2.3
White *and* American Indian/Alaska Native	1,255	—
White *and* Asian	1,533	—
White *and* Native Hawaiian/Pacific Islander	410	—
White *and* some other race	31,963	0.8
Black or African American *and* American Indian/Alaska Native	1,378	—
Black or African American *and* Asian	574	—
Black or African American *and* Native Hawaiian/Pacific Islander	156	—
Black or African American *and* some other race	11,879	0.3
American Indian/Alaska Native *and* Asian	1,156	—
American Indian/Alaska Native *and* Native Hawaiian/Pacific Islander	46	—
American Indian/Alaska Native *and* some other race	3,701	0.1
Asian *and* Native Hawaiian/Pacific Islander	52	—
Asian *and* some other race	3,239	0.1
Native Hawaiian/Pacific Islander *and* some other race	787	—
Three or more races	11,962	0.3

Source: U.S. Census Bureau. *Census 2000: Redistricting Data*. Press release issued by the Redistricting Data Office. Washington, D.C., March, 2001. A dash (—) indicates that the percent is less than 0.1.

(okra), *guince* (banana), and *mondongo* (a spicy stew).

9 RELIGIONS

During the first three centuries of Spanish rule, Roman Catholicism was the only religion permitted in Puerto Rico. More than 80% of the population was still Roman Catholic at the end of 1992, and the Church maintains numerous hospitals and schools on the island. Most of the remaining Puerto Ricans belong to other Christian denominations, which have been allowed on the island since the 1850s. By 2010, Protestants may outnumber Roman Catholics in Puerto Rico, according to some projections. Pentecostal churches have attracted a significant following, particularly among the urban poor of the barrios.

10 TRANSPORTATION

Rivers are not navigable, and the only function of narrow-gauge rural railroads is to haul sugarcane to the mills during the harvesting season. Other goods are transported by truck. A few public bus systems provide intercity passenger transport, the largest being the Metropolitan Bus Authority (MBA), a government-owned company serving San Juan and nearby cities. The predominant form of public transportation outside the San Juan metropolitan area is the *público,* or privately owned jitney, a small bus that carries passengers between fixed destinations. In many rural areas, this is the only form of public transit.

In 1996, Puerto Rico had 14,535 miles (23,387 kilometers) of streets and roads, 77% of which were small local roads. Of the total mileage, 52% was rural, and 250 miles (402 kilometers) were classified as interstate highways. A rail transit system is under construction and is scheduled to begin operations in fall 2001 in San Juan.

San Juan, the island's principal port handled 15.5 million tons of cargo in 1998. Crude oil and gasoline were the leading items. Ponce handled 1.14 million tons, and Mayagüez 407,000 tons. Ferries link the main island with Vieques and Culebra.

Puerto Rico receives flights from the US mainland and from the Virgin Islands, the British West Indies, Jamaica, and the Dominican Republic, as well as from Great Britain, France, Spain, and the Netherlands. Puerto Rico had 30 airports in 1998. Luis Muñoz Marin International Airport serviced 4.7 million passengers and handled 145,607 tons of freight in 1996.

11 HISTORY

Archaeological finds indicate that at least three Indian cultures settled on the island now known as Puerto Rico long before its discovery by Christopher Columbus on 19 November 1493. The first group, belonging to the Archaic Culture, is believed to have come from Florida and relied on the products of the sea. The second group, the Igneri, came from northern South America and brought agriculture and pottery to the island. The third culture, the Taino, combined fishing with agriculture. A peaceful, sedentary tribe, the Taino were adept at stonework and lived in many parts of the island. To the Indians, the island was known as Boriqúen.

Columbus, accompanied by a young nobleman named Juan Ponce de León, landed at the western end of the island—which he called San Juan Bautista (St. John the Baptist)—and claimed it for Spain. Not until colonization was well under way would the island acquire the name Puerto Rico (literally, "rich port"), with the name San Juan Bautista applied to the capital city. The first settlers arrived on 12 August 1508, under the able leadership of Ponce de León, who sought to transplant and adapt Spanish civilization to Puerto Rico's tropical habitat. The small contingent of Spaniards compelled the Taino, numbering perhaps 30,000, to mine for gold; the rigors of forced labor and the losses from rebellion reduced the Taino population to about 4,000 by 1514, by which time the mines were nearly depleted. With the introduction of slaves from Africa, sugarcane growing became the leading economic activity. Since neither mining or sugarcane was able to provide sufficient revenue to support the struggling colony, the treasury of New Spain began a subsidy which until the early 19th century defrayed the cost of the island's government and defense.

16th–18th Centuries

From the early 16th century onward, an intense power struggle for the control of the Caribbean marked Puerto Rico as a strategic base of the first magnitude. After a French attack in 1528, construction of La Fortaleza (still in use today as the governor's palace) was begun in 1533, and work on El Morro fortress in San Juan commenced six years later. The new fortifications helped repel a British attack led by Sir Francis Drake in 1595; a second force, arriving in 1598 under George Clifford, Earl of Cumberland, succeeded in capturing San Juan, but the British were forced to withdraw by tropical heat and disease. In 1625, a Dutch attack under the command of Boudewijn Hendrikszoon was repulsed, although much of San Juan was sacked and burned by the attackers. By the 18th century, Puerto Rico had become a haven for pirates, and smuggling was the major economic activity. A Spanish envoy who came to the island in 1765 was appalled, and his report to the crown inaugurated a period of economic, administrative, and military reform. The creation of a native militia helped Puerto Rico withstand a fierce British assault on San Juan in 1797, by which time the island had more than 100,000 inhabitants.

Long after most of the Spanish colonies in the New World had obtained independence, Puerto Rico and Cuba remained under Spanish rule. Despite several rebellions, most of them inspired by the Latin American liberator, Simón Bolivar, Spain's military might concentrated on these islands halted any revolution.

Puerto Rico became a shelter for refugees from Santo Domingo, Haiti, and Venezuela who were faithful to Spain, fearful of disturbances in their own countries, or both. As in Cuba, the sugar industry developed in Puerto Rico during this period under policies that favored the institution of slavery in the island.

19th Century

The 19th century also gave birth, however, to a new Puerto Rican civil and political consciousness. Puerto Rican participation in the short-lived constitutional experiments in Spain (1812–14 and 1820–23) fostered the rise of a spirit of liberalism. The Spanish constitution of 1812 declared that the people of Puerto Rico were no longer colonial subjects but were full-fledged citizens of Spain. Nevertheless, the Spanish crown maintained an alert, centralized, absolutist government in Puerto Rico with all basic powers concentrated in the captain general.

Toward the middle of the 19th century, a *criollo* generation with strong liberal roots began a new era in Puerto Rican history. This group, which called for the abolition of slavery and the introduction of far-reaching economic and political reforms, at the same time developed and strengthened Puerto Rican literary tradition. The more radical reformers espoused the cause of separation from Spain and joined in a propaganda campaign in New York on behalf of Cuban independence. An aborted revolution began in the town of Lares in September 1868 (and coincided with an insurrection in Spain that deposed Queen Isabella II). Though it was soon quelled, this rebellion awakened among Puerto Ricans a dormant sense of national identity.

The major reform efforts after 1868 revolved around abolitionism and *autonomia,* or self-government. Slavery was abolished in 1873 by the First Spanish Republic, which also granted new political rights to the islanders. The restoration of the Spanish monarchy two years later, however, was a check to Puerto Rican aspirations. During the last quarter of the century, leaders such as Luis Muñoz Rivera sought unsuccessfully to secure vast new powers of self-government.

The imminence of war with the US over Cuba, coupled with autonomist agitation within Puerto Rico, led Spain in November 1897 to grant to the island a charter with broad powers of self-rule. No sooner had an elected government begun to function in July 1898 than US forces, overcoming Spanish resistance, took over the island. A cease-fire was proclaimed on 13 August, and sovereignty was formally transferred to the US with the signing in December of the Treaty of Paris, ending the Spanish-American War. The US government swept aside the self-governing charter granted by Spain and established military rule from 1898 to 1900. Civilian government was restored in 1900 under a colonial law, the Foraker Act, that gave the federal government full control of the executive and legislative branches, leaving some local representation in the lower chamber, or house of delegates. Under the Jones Act, Congress extended US citizenship to the islanders and granted an elective senate, but still reserved vast powers over Puerto Rico to the federal bureaucracy.

20th Century

The early period of US rule saw an effort to Americanize local institutions, and even tried to substitute English for the Spanish language. In the meantime, American corporate capital took over the sugar industry, developing a plantation economy so pervasive that, by 1920, 75% of the population relied on the cane crop for its livelihood. Glaring irregularities of wealth resulted, sharpening social and political divisions. This period also saw the development of three main trends in Puerto Rican political thinking. One group favored the incorporation of Puerto Rico into the US as a state; a second group, fearful of cultural assimilation, favored self-government; while a third group spoke for independence.

The Depression hit Puerto Rico especially hard. With a population approaching two million by the late 1930s, and with few occupational opportunities outside the sugar industry, the island's economy deteriorated. Mass unemployment and near-starvation were the results. Controlling the Puerto Rican legislature from 1932 to 1940 was a coalition of the Socialist Party, led by Santiago Iglesias, a Spanish labor leader who became a protégé of the American Federation of Labor; and the Republican Party, which had traditionally espoused statehood and had been founded in Puerto Rico by José Celso Barbosa, a black physician who had studied in the US. The coalition was unable to produce any significant improvement, although under the New Deal a US government effort was made to supply emergency relief for the "stricken island."

Agitation for full political and economic reform or independence gained ground during this period. Great pressure was put on Washington for a change in the island's political status, while social and economic reform was carried to the fullest extent possible within the limitations of the Jones Act. Intensive efforts were made to centralize economic planning, attract new industries through local tax exemptions (Puerto Rico was already exempt from federal taxation), reduce inequalities of income, and improve housing, schools, and health conditions. By 1955, income from manufacturing surpassed that from agriculture and was five times as great by 1970.

The Popular Democratic Party (PDP), the dominant force in Puerto Rican politics from 1940 to 1968, favored a new self-governing relationship with the US, distinct from statehood or independence. The party succeeded not only in bringing about significant social and economic change but also in obtaining from Congress, in 1950, a law allowing Puerto Ricans to draft their own constitution with full local self-government. This new constitution, approved in a general referendum on 3 March 1952, led to the establishment on 25 July of the Commonwealth of Puerto Rico (Estado Libre Asociado de Puerto Rico), which was constituted as an autonomous political entity in voluntary association with the United States.

More advanced than most Caribbean countries in education, health, and social development, Puerto Rico suffered from growing political tensions in the early 1980s, with occasional terrorist attacks on US military installations and personnel. These tensions may have been exacerbated by the national recession of 1980–81, which had a particularly severe impact on Puerto Rico. At the same time, the island's economy experienced a structural shift. Whereas 50% of jobs in Puerto Rico had been in agriculture in 1940, by 1989 that figure had dropped to 20%. Manufacturing jobs, in contrast, rose from 5 to 15% of total employment between 1940 and 1989.

The 51st State?

Puerto Rico's political status remains a source of controversy. Statehood would give Puerto Rico representation in the US Congress and would make the island eligible for billions of dollars more a year in food stamps, medical insurance, and income support payments, which are currently set at levels far below those of states. However, statehood would also incur the loss of tax benefits. Under current federal tax law for the commonwealth, individuals pay no federal income tax. More importantly, corporations pay no federal tax on profits, which has persuaded many companies, particularly manufacturers of pharmaceuticals, chemicals and electronics, to build plants in Puerto Rico. In a 1993 plebiscite, a slight majority of Puerto Rican voters chose to maintain the island's status as an American commonwealth. The vote was conditioned, however, by a request that Congress modify the terms of the island's commonwealth status. Specifically, Puerto Ricans asked for such "enhancements" as removing the federal ceiling on food stamps and extending Supplemental Security Income, a federal aid program, to elderly and handicapped Puerto Ricans. They also requested that federal tax law, recently amended to reduce by 60% the exemptions corporations could claim from taxes on profits, be restored to its original form.

12 STATE GOVERNMENT

Since 1952, Puerto Rico has been a commonwealth of the US, governed under the Puerto Rican Federal Relations Act and under a constitution based on the US model.

The commonwealth legislature comprises a senate (Senado) of 29 members, 2 from each of 8 senatorial districts and 11 elected at large, and a house of representatives (Cámara de Representantes) of 52 members, 1 from each of 40 districts and 11 at large. Each senate district consists of five house districts. If a single party wins two-thirds or more of the seats in either house, the number of seats can be expanded (up to a limit of 9 in the senate and 17 in the house) to assure representation for minority parties. The governor, who may serve an unlimited number of four-year terms, is the only elected executive.

Residents of Puerto Rico may not vote in US presidential elections. A Puerto Rican who settles in one of the 50 states automatically becomes eligible to vote for president; conversely, a state resident who migrates to Puerto Rico forfeits such eligibility. Puerto Rico has no vote in the US

Senate or House of Representatives, but a nonvoting resident delegate, elected every four years, may speak on the floor of the House, introduce legislation, and vote in House committees.

13 POLITICAL PARTIES

The Popular Democratic (PDP), founded in 1938, favors the strengthening and development of commonwealth status. The New Progressive Party (NPP), created in 1968 as the successor to the Puerto Rican Republican Party, is pro-statehood. Two smaller parties, each favoring independence for the island, are the Puerto Rican Independence Party, founded in the mid-1940s and committed to democratic socialism, and the more radical Puerto Rican Socialist Party, which has close ties with Cuba. A breakaway group, the Renewal Party, led by the mayor of San Juan, Hernán Padilla, left the NPP and took part in the 1984 elections.

In 1980, Governor Carlos Romero Barceló of the NPP, who had pledged to seek actively Puerto Rico's admission to the Union if elected by a large margin, retained the governorship by a plurality of fewer than 3,500 votes. Former governor Rafael Hernández Colón defeated Romero Barceló's bid for reelection in 1984 by more than 54,000 votes. Colon was reelected in 1988 and was succeeded in 1992 by Pedro Rossello, a New Progressive and a supporter of statehood, and who was reelected in 1996.

Although Puerto Ricans have no vote in US presidential elections, the island does send voting delegates to the national conventions of the Democratic and Republican parties.

14 LOCAL GOVERNMENT

The Commonwealth of Puerto Rico had 78 *municipios* (municipalities) in 1997, each governed by a mayor and municipal assembly elected every four years. In fact, these governments resemble US county governments in that they perform services for both urban and rural areas. Many of the functions normally performed by municipal governments in the US—for instance, fire protection, education, water supply, and law enforcement—are performed by the commonwealth government directly.

15 JUDICIAL SYSTEM

Puerto Rico's highest court, the Supreme Court, consists of a chief justice and six associate justices. They are appointed, like all other judges, by the governor with the consent of the senate and serve until compulsory retirement at age 70. The court may sit in separate panels for some purposes, but not in cases dealing with the constitutionality of commonwealth law, for which the entire body convenes. Decisions of the Supreme Court of Puerto Rico regarding US constitutional questions may be appealed to the US Supreme Court.

The nine superior courts are the main trial courts; superior court judges are appointed to 12-year terms. There are 111 superior court justices in 12 districts. Superior courts hear appeals from the 38 district courts, which have 111 judges. These courts have original jurisdiction in civil cases not exceeding $10,000 and in

Photo Credit: © Bernaed Boutrit/Woodfin Camp.

A modern office building in San Juan.

minor criminal cases. District courts also hear preliminary motions in more serious criminal cases. Municipal judges, serving for five years, and justices of the peace, in rural areas, decide cases involving local ordinances.

San Juan is the seat of the US District Court for Puerto Rico, which has the same jurisdiction as federal district courts on the US mainland.

16 MIGRATION

Although migration from Puerto Rico to the US mainland is not an entirely new phenomenon—several Puerto Rican merchants were living in New York City as early as 1830—there were no more than 70,000 islanders in the US in 1940. Mass migration, spurred by the booming postwar job market in the US, began in 1947. The out-migration was particularly large from 1951 through 1959, when the net outflow of migrants from the island averaged more than 47,000 a year. According to the 1990 census, 1,955,323 ethnic Puerto Ricans were living in the 50 states, including 1,190,533 native-born Puerto Ricans. At least 32 cities had Puerto Rican communities of 5,000 or more. Puerto Ricans are found in significant numbers not only in New York State but also in New Jersey, Illinois, Pennsylvania, California, Florida, Connecticut, and Massachusetts. In 1996, Puerto Rico admitted 8,560 immigrants from countries other than the United States.

17 ECONOMY

Puerto Rico's gross product in 1995 was $28.4 billion. In 1995, agriculture contributed 1% to the total economic output; manufacturing, 41%; construction and mining, 2%; transportation and public utilities, 8%; trade, 14%; finance, insurance, and real estate, 13%; services, 11%; and government, 10%.

The island's most important industrial products are apparel, textiles, pharmaceuticals, petroleum products, rum, refined sugar, computers, instruments, and office machines. Tourism is the backbone of a large service industry, and the government sector has also grown. Tourist revenues and remittances from Puerto Rican workers on the US mainland largely counterbalance the island's chronic trade deficit.

18 INCOME

Per capita (per person) income in Puerto Rico, $9,000 in 1998, was far lower than in any of the 50 states during that year, but still greatly exceeded that of its Caribbean neighbors. Total income increased from $1.3 billion in 1960 to $5 billion in 1972, $9 billion in 1980, and $24.5 billion in 1996. Average family income on the island in 1996 was $27,587.

19 INDUSTRY

In 1992, the value of manufactured shipments was $31 billion. Chemicals accounted for 43%; food and related products, 17%; and electronic equipment, 9%. In 1995, 172,000 Puerto Ricans were employed by manufacturing. The leading employment categories are apparel and textiles, chemicals and allied products, food and food-related products, electric and electronic equipment, and instruments. The growth areas were electric and electronic equipment, up 47% from 1977, and instruments and related products, up 60%.

There are more than 90 pharmaceutical plants representing 20 of the world's leading drug and health companies. The largest included Johnson & Johnson (Rio Piedras), Abbott Chemicals (Barceloneta), Bristol-Myers Squibb (Humacao), Warner-Lambert (Vega Baja), and Schering-Plough (Manati). Baxter International (medical devices) is one of the commonwealth's largest non-locally based manufacturers, with 10 plants; Westinghouse Electric

(electric components) has 15; and Motorola (radio equipment), 4. The Coca-Cola Company operates the world's largest soft drink concentrate and base manufacturing facility in Puerto Rico.

20 LABOR

Puerto Rico's civilian labor force in mid-1998 numbered 1.3 million, of whom 165,900 were employed, yielding an unemployment rate of 12.8%.

In 1997, agriculture, forestry, and fishing accounted for about 3.1% of employment; mining, 0.1%; construction, 5.5%; manufacturing, 15.3%; wholesale and retail trade, 19.5%; finance, insurance, and real estate, 3%; transportation, communication, and public utilities, 5.5%; services, 25.5%; and government, 22.5%.

Approximately 7% of the labor force belonged to trade unions in 1997. Wages tend to adhere closely to the US statutory minimum, which applies to Puerto Rico.

21 AGRICULTURE

Total farm income in 1996 was $663 million. In 1940, agriculture employed 43% of the work force; by 1996, about 3.5% of Puerto Rican labor force had agricultural jobs. Nowhere is this decline more evident than in the sugar industry. Production peaked at 1.3 million tons in 1952. The hilly terrain makes mechanization difficult, and manual cutting contributes to production costs that are much higher than those of Hawaii and Louisiana. Despite incentives and subsidies, tobacco is no longer profitable, and coffee production—well adapted to the highlands—falls far short of domestic consumption, although about half of the crop is exported. In 1996, some 26.5 million pounds (12 million kilograms) of coffee were produced by Puerto Rican farmers, with a value of $56 million. Plantains are also an important crop, with 76 tons produced in 1995. Ornamental plants, tropical fruits, mangoes, vegetables, and bananas are also grown.

22 DOMESTICATED ANIMALS

In early 1996, there were 429,000 cattle and 196,000 hogs on Puerto Rico farms and ranches. Production of meat animals in 1995 included 39.7 million pounds (18 million kilograms) of beef, and 33 million pounds (15 million kilograms) of pork.

Leading dairy and poultry products in 1995 were 822.5 million pounds (373 million kilograms) of milk, 39,690 pounds (18,000 kilograms) of eggs, and 136.7 million pounds (62 million kilograms) of broiler chickens. In 1995, there were about 14 million chickens on Puerto Rican poultry farms.

23 FISHING

Although sport fishing, especially for blue marlin, is an important tourist attraction, the waters surrounding Puerto Rico are too deep to lend themselves to commercial fishery. Tuna brought in from African and South American waters is processed on the western shore that together provide much of the canned tuna sold in eastern US markets. Five aquacultural projects covering some 550 acres (220 hectares) operate, including the largest freshwater prawn farm in the Americas. Other species pro-

A large luxury ocean liner at the tourism terminal in the harbor at San Juan.

duced by Puerto Rican aquaculture include saltwater shrimp, red tilapia fish, and ornamental species. The total catch in 1995 was over 4 million pounds, valued at $7.05 million.

24 FORESTRY

Puerto Rico lost its self-sufficiency in timber production by the mid-19th century, as population expansion and increasing demand for food led to massive deforestation. Today, Puerto Rico must import nearly all of its wood and paper products. The Caribbean National Forest covers 55,665 acres (22,527 hectares), of which 27,846 acres (11,269 hectares) constituted national Forest System lands.

25 MINING

The estimated value of nonfuel mineral commodities produced in Puerto Rico was $217 million in 1997. Portland cement and crushed stone are the most valuable commodities. The latter accounts for approximately 24% of the Commonwealth's mineral value and is the island's second leading mineral commodity. In 1997, 13.2 million metric tons of crushed stone were produced, for a value of $52.5 million. Even with crushed stone being excluded, Puerto Rico's mineral value was greater than that of eleven mainland States.

At least 11 different types of metallic mineral deposits, including copper, iron, gold, manganese, silver, molybdenum, zinc, lead, and other minerals, are found on the island. Also produced are industrial minerals (cement, stone, clay, and sand and gravel).

26 ENERGY AND POWER

Puerto Rico is almost totally dependent on imported crude oil for its energy needs. The island has not yet developed any fossil fuel resources of its own, and its one experimental nuclear reactor, built on the south coast at Rincon in 1964, was shut down after a few years. Solar-powered hot-water heaters have been installed in a few private homes and at La Fortaleza. Inefficiency in the public transport system has encouraged commonwealth residents to rely on private vehicles, thereby increasing the demands for imported petroleum. Of Puerto Rico's total energy requirements, about 90% is supplied by liquid fuels. Puerto Rico imported 5.29 million barrels of refined petroleum products in 1996.

27 COMMERCE

Wholesale trade in Puerto Rico in 1992 included some 2,651 establishments and major distributors, with sales of $10.19 billion. Retail trade consists mainly of food and apparel stores. Two large shopping centers, Plaza las Americas and Plaza Carolina, are in the San Juan area.

Foreign trade is a significant factor in Puerto Rico's economy. Trade between the US and Puerto Rico is unrestricted. In 1996, the island's imports were $19.1 billion, and exports were $22.9 billion. During 1995, the US received 88% of Puerto Rico's exports and supplied about 62% of its imports.

28 PUBLIC FINANCE

Puerto Rico's annual budget is prepared by the Bureau of Budget and Management and submitted by the governor to the legislator, which has unlimited power to amend it. The fiscal year extends from July 1 to June 30. In the 1999/2000 fiscal year, revenues totaled $6.7 billion and expenditures amounted to $9.6 billion.

29 TAXATION

The Puerto Rican Federal Relations Act stipulates that the Commonwealth is exempt from US internal revenue laws. The federal income tax is not levied on permanent residents of Puerto Rico, but federal Social Security and unemployment taxes are deducted from payrolls, and the commonwealth government collects an income tax. Corporations in Puerto Rico are also taxed, though some companies fall into a special category—Section 936 of the federal tax code virtually exempts subsidiaries of US corporations operating in Puerto Rico from paying US corporate federal income taxes.

30 HEALTH

Infant mortality declined from 113 per 1,000 live births in 1940 to 10.8 in 1999. Compared with the United States, the commonwealth's infant mortality rate in 1996 was lower than in the District of Columbia, Mississippi, and North Carolina.

Photo Credit: © Robert Frerck/Woodfin Camp.

A radio telescope on the island of Puerto Rico.

In 1997, Puerto Rico enjoyed one of the lowest death rates in the world—only 692 per 100,000 population. The only states with a lower death rate that year were Alaska and Utah. The leading causes of death were similar to those in most industrialized countries (heart disease, cancer, diabetes mellitus). Alcoholism and drug addiction are among the major public health problems, although suicide occurs less often than it does in most of the states.

In 1991, Puerto Rico had 56 hospitals, with 9,688 beds; average daily occupancy was 6,792, or 70.1% of beds filled. Medical personnel included 7,942 non-federal physicians in 1992.

31 HOUSING

In 1990, there were a total of 1,184,382 housing units with 2.97 persons per unit, versus 867,697 units in 1980 when there were 3.66 persons per occupied unit. Local authorities, however, estimated that from 1990 to 1995, Puerto Rico needed to build about 16,000 units per year in order to satisfy the local housing demand.

32 EDUCATION

Education is compulsory for children between 6 and 16 years of age, and nearly two out of ten commonwealth budget dollars goes to education.

In the 1995/96 academic year there were 621,370 students attending public school. Instruction is carried out in Spanish, but English is taught at all levels.

Puerto Rico had 14 public institutions of higher learning in 1995/96, including 10 four-year institutions. The main state supported institution of higher learning is the University of Puerto Rico with its main campus at Rico Piedras. Total enrollment at higher education institutions was 156,439 in 1994/95.

33 ARTS

The Tapia Theater in Old San Juan is the island's major showcase for local and visiting performers, including the Taller de Histriones group and *zarzuela* (comic opera) troupes from Spain. The Institute of Puerto Rican Culture produces an annual theatrical festival. The Fine Arts Center features entertainment ranging from ballet, opera, and symphonies to drama, jazz, and popular music.

Puerto Rico has its own symphony orchestra and conservatory of music. The Opera de Camara tours several houses. Puerto Rico supports both a classical ballet company (the Ballets de San Juan), and the Areyto Folkloric Group, which performs traditional folk dances. Salsa, a popular style pioneered by such Puerto Rican musicians as Tito Puente, influenced the development of pop music on the US mainland during the 1970s.

34 LIBRARIES AND MUSEUMS

In 1997, Puerto Rico's public libraries contained about 609,391 volumes. The University of Puerto Rico Library at Rio Piedras held 587,270 books; the library of the Puerto Rico Conservatory of Music, in San Juan, has a collection of music written by Puerto Rican and Latin American composers. Among the 21 museums in 1997, the Museo de Arte de Ponce (Luis A. Ferre Foundation) had paintings, sculptures, and archaeological artifacts, as well as a library. The Marine Station Museum in Mayagüez exhibits Caribbean marine specimens and sponsors research and field trips.

35 COMMUNICATIONS

The Puerto Rico Telephone Company was founded in 1914 by the creators of International Telephone and Telegraph (ITT). In 1974, the Puerto Rican government bought the phone company from ITT. In 1997, there were an estimated 1.3 million telephone lines on the island. Two cellular companies provide service to 33,000 customers.

As of 1995, there were 65 AM and 53 FM radio stations and 33 television stations. Television service was provided by 27 stations in 1997, 3 of which originate from the US Armed Forces Radio and Television Service.

36 PRESS

Puerto Rico has three major Spanish-language dailies: 1997 circulation for *El Nuevo Dia* was 223,112 mornings, 239,999 Sundays; and for *El Vocero*, 198,897 mornings. The English-language *San Juan Star,* with a circulation of 33,429 mornings and 35,015 Sundays, won a

Pulitzer Prize in 1961. *El Reportero* is an evening Spanish-language newspaper.

37 TOURISM, TRAVEL, AND RECREATION

Only government and manufacturing exceed tourism in importance to the Puerto Rican economy. The industry has grown rapidly, from 65,000 tourists in 1950 to 1.1 million in 1970 and 4 million in the late 1990s. Tourism accounts for about 5% of the island's gross national product.

Most tourists come for sunning, swimming, deep-sea fishing, and the fashionable shops, night clubs, and casinos of San Juan's Condado Strip. Attractions of old San Juan include two fortresses, El Morro and San Cristobal, San Jose Church (one of the oldest in the New World), and La Fortaleza, the governor's palace. The government has been encouraging tourists to journey outside of San Juan to destinations such as the rain forest of El Yunque, and the bird sanctuary and mangrove forest on the shores of Torrecilla Lagoon.

38 SPORTS

Baseball is very popular in Puerto Rico. There is a 15-team professional winter league, in which many ball players from American and National league teams participate. Horse racing, cockfighting, boxing, and basketball are also popular. Other annual sporting events include the Copa Velasco Regatta, the first leg of the Caribbean Ocean Racing Triangle, and the International Billfish Tournament in San Juan.

39 FAMOUS PUERTO RICANS

Elected to represent Puerto Rico before the Spanish Cortes in 1812, Ramón Power y Giralt (1775–1813), a liberal reformer, was the leading Puerto Rican political figure of the early 19th century. Power, appointed vice president of the Cortes, participated in the drafting of the new Spanish constitution of 1812. Ramón Emeterio Betances (1827–98) became well known not only for his efforts to alleviate a cholera epidemic in 1855, but also for his crusade to abolish slavery in Puerto Rico and for his leadership in a racial separatist movement.

The dominant political figure in 20th-century Puerto Rico was Luis Muñoz Marin (1898–1980), founder of the Popular Democratic Party in 1938 and president of Puerto Rico's senate from 1940 to 1948. Muñoz, the first native-born elected governor of the island (1948–64), devised the commonwealth relationship that has governed the island since 1952.

Women have participated actively in Puerto Rican politics. Ana Roqué de Duprey (1853–1933) led the Asociación Puertorriquena de Mujeres Sufragistas, organized in late 1926, while Milagros Benet de Mewton (1868–1945) presided over the Liga Social Sufragista, founded in 1917. Both groups actively lobbied for the extension of the right to vote to Puerto Rican women, not only in Puerto Rico but in the US and other countries as well.

Manuel A. Alonso (1822–89) blazed the trail for a distinctly Puerto Rican literature with the publication, in 1849, of *El Gibaro,* the first major effort to depict the

Photo credit: EPD Photos/United Nations Photo.

Cellist Pablo Casals (1875–1973) fell in love with Puerto Rico—and with a Puerto Rican cellist, Marta Montañez, whom he married in 1957. He was instrumental in establishing many music institutions, including the Puerto Rico Symphony Orchestra and the Conservatory of Music. In 1957, he established the Casals Festival which attracts top musicians from around the world to the island annually.

traditions and mores of the island's rural society.

In the world of entertainment, Academy Award winners José Ferrer (1912–1992) and Rita Moreno (b.1931) are among the most famous. Notable in classical music is cellist-conductor Pablo Casals (b.Spain, 1875–1973), a long-time resident of Puerto Rico. Well-known popular musicians include Tito Puente (b. New York, 1923-2000) and José Feliciano (b.1945).

Roberto Clemente (1934–72), one of baseball's most admired performers and a member of the Hall of Fame, played on 12 National League All-Star teams and was named Most Valuable Player in 1966.

40 BIBLIOGRAPHY

Carr, Raymond. *Puerto Rico: A Colonial Experiment*. New York: Vintage, 1984.
———. *Puerto Rico: A Political and Cultural History*. New York: Norton, 1984.
Davis, Lucile. *Puerto Rico*. New York: Children's Press, 2000.
Harlan, Judith. *Puerto Rico: Deciding Its Future*. New York: Twenty-First Century Books, 1996.
Landau, Elaine. *Puerto Rico*. New York: Children's Press, 1999.
Milivojevic, JoAnn. *Puerto Rico*. Minneapolis, MN: Carolrhoda Books, 2000.
Moritz, Patricia M. *Puerto Rico*. Vero Beach, Fla.: Rourke, 1998.
Puerto Rico Federal Affairs Administration. *Puerto Rico, U.S.A.* Washington, DC., 1979.
US Department of Commerce. *Economic Study of Puerto Rico*. 2 vols. Washington, D.C., 1979.
Votaw, Carmen Delgado. *Puerto Rican Women: Some Biographical Profiles*. Washington, D.C.: National Conference of Puerto Rican Woman, 1978.
Winslow, Zachery. *Puerto Rico*. Philadelphia: Chelsea House, 1999.

Web sites

Organization of World Heritage Cities. San Juan. [Online] Available http://www.ovpm.org/ovpm/sites/asanju.html Accessed March 15, 1999.

US CARIBBEAN DEPENDENCIES

NAVASSA

Navassa, a 2-square-mile (5-square-kilometer) island between Jamaica and Haiti, was claimed by the US under the Guano Act of 1856. The island, located at 18°24′ north and 75°1′ west, is uninhabited except for a lighthouse station under the administration of the coast guard. Passing Haitian fishers and others occasionally camp on the island.

VIRGIN ISLANDS

The Virgin Islands of the United States lie about 40 miles (64 kilometers) north of Puerto Rico and 1,000 miles (1,600 kilometers) south-southeast of Miami, between 17°40′ and 18°25′ north and 64°34′ and 65°3′ north. The island group extends 51 miles north-south and 50 miles east-west with a total area of at least 136 square miles (353 square kilometers). Only 3 of the more than 50 islands and cays are of significant size: St. Croix, 84 square miles (218 square kilometers) in area; St. Thomas, 32 square miles (83 square kilometers); and St. John, 20 square miles (52 square kilometers). The territorial capital, Charlotte Amalie, on St. Thomas, has one of the finest harbors in the Caribbean.

St. Croix is relatively flat, with a terrain suitable for sugarcane cultivation. St. Thomas is mountainous and little cultivated, but it has many snug harbors. St. John, also mountainous, has fine beaches and lush vegetation; about two-thirds of St. John's area has been declared a national park. The subtropical climate, with temperatures ranging from 70°F to 90°F (21°C to 32°C) and an average temperature of

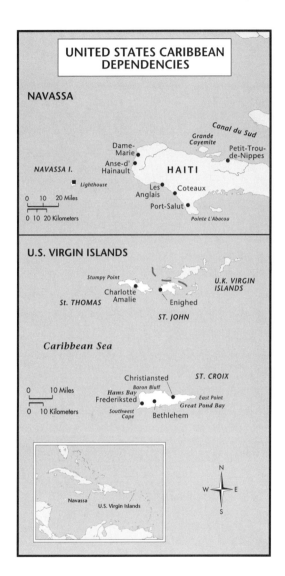

UNITED STATES CARIBBEAN DEPENDENCIES

77°F (25°C), is moderated by northeast trade winds. Rainfall, the main source of fresh water, varies widely, and severe droughts are frequent. The average yearly rainfall is 45 inches, mostly during the summer months.

The population of the US Virgin Islands was 96,569 at the time of the 1980 census, and was estimated at 97,240 in 1997. St. Croix has two principal towns: Christiansted and Frederiksted. Economic development has brought an influx of new residents, mainly from Puerto Rico, other Caribbean islands, and the US mainland. Most of the permanent inhabitants are descendants of slaves who were brought from Africa in the early days of Danish rule, and about 80% of the population is black. English is the official and most widely spoken language.

Some of the oldest religious congregations in the Western Hemisphere are located in the Virgin Islands. A Jewish synagogue there is the second oldest in the New World, and the Lutheran Congregation of St. Thomas, founded in 1666, is one of the three oldest congregations in the US. Baptists make up an estimated 42% of the population, Roman Catholics 34%, and Episcopalians 17%.

Excavations at St. Croix in the 1970s uncovered evidence of a civilization perhaps as ancient as AD 100. Christopher Columbus, who reached the islands in 1493, named them for the martyred virgin St. Ursula. At this time, St. Croix was inhabited by Carib Indians, who were eventually driven from the island by Spanish soldiers in 1555. During the 17th century, the archipelago was divided into two territorial units, one controlled by the British, the other (now the US Virgin Islands) controlled by Denmark. The separate history of the latter unit began with the settlement of St. Thomas by the Danish West India Company in 1672. St. John was claimed by the company in 1683, and St. Croix was purchased from France in 1733. The holdings of the company were taken over as a Danish crown colony in 1754. Sugarcane, cultivated by slave labor, was the backbone of the islands' prosperity in the 18th and early 19th centuries. After brutally suppressing several slave revolts, Denmark abolished slavery in the colony in 1848. A long period of economic decline followed, until Denmark sold the islands to the US in 1917 for $25 million. Congress granted US citizenship to the Virgin Islanders in 1927. In 1931, administration of the islands was transferred from the Department of the Navy to the Department of the Interior, and the first civilian governor was appointed.

Tourism has supplanted agriculture as the islands' principal economic activity. The number of tourists rose dramatically throughout the late 1960s and early 1970s, averaging 2 million annually in the late 1990s. Today, tourism accounts for more than 70% of GDP and 70% of the employment. Rum remains an important manufacture, with petroleum refining (on St. Croix) a major addition in the late 1960s.

Education is compulsory. The College of the Virgin Islands is the territory's first institution of higher learning. In 1997, the Virgin Islands had 12 radio stations and 2 television stations.

US PACIFIC DEPENDENCIES

AMERICAN SAMOA

American Samoa, an unincorporated and unorganized US territory in the South Pacific Ocean, comprises that portion of the Samoan archipelago lying east of longitude 171° west. (The rest of the Samoan islands comprise the independent state of Western Samoa.) While the Samoan group as a whole has an area of 1,205 square miles (3,121 square kilometers), American Samoa consists of only seven small islands (between 14° and 15° south and 168° and 171° west) with a total area (land and water) of 76 square miles (197 square kilometers). Five of the islands are volcanic, with rugged peaks rising sharply, and two are atolls (coral islands made up of a reef around a lagoon).

The climate is hot and rainy. Normal temperatures range from 75°F (24°C) in August to 90°F (32°C) during December–February. Mean annual rainfall is 130 inches (330 centimeters), with the rainy season lasting from December through March. Hurricanes are common. The native plant life includes flourishing tree ferns, coconut, hardwoods, and rubber trees. There are few wild animals.

As of 1999, the estimated population was 63,786, an increase over the 1986 population estimate of 37,500. However, the total population has remained relatively constant for many years because of the substantial number of Samoans who migrate to the United States. The inhabitants, who are concentrated on the island of Tutuila, are almost entirely Polynesian. English is the official language, but Samoan is also widely spoken. Most Samoans are Christians.

The capital of the territory, Pago Pago, on Tutuila, has one of the finest natural harbors in the South Pacific and is a duty-free port. Passenger liners call there on South Pacific tours, and passenger and cargo ships arrive regularly from Japan, New Zealand, Australia, and the US west coast. There are regular air and sea services between American Samoa and Western Samoa, and scheduled flights between Pago Pago and Honolulu.

American Samoa was settled by Melanesian migrants around 1000 BC. The Samoan islands were visited in 1768 by the French explorer Louis-Antoine de Bougainville, who named them the Îles des Navigateurs as a tribute to the skill of their native boatmen. In 1889, the US, the UK, and Germany agreed to share control of the islands. The UK later withdrew its claim, and under the 1899 Treaty of Berlin, the US was internationally acknowledged to have rights extending over all the islands of the Samoan group lying east of 171° west, while Germany was acknowledged to have similar rights to the islands west of that meridian. The islands of American Samoa were officially ceded to the US by the various ruling chiefs in 1900 and 1904, and on 20 February 1929 the US Congress formally accepted sovereignty over the entire group. From 1900 to 1951, the territory was administered by the US Department of the Navy, and thereafter by the Department of the Interior. The basic law is the Constitution of 1966.

The economy is primarily agricultural. Small plantations occupy about one-third of the land area; 70% of the land is communally owned. The principal crops are bananas, breadfruit, taro, papayas, pineapples, sweet potatoes, tapioca, coffee, cocoa, and yams. Hogs and poultry are the principal livestock raised; dairy cattle are few. The principal cash crop is copra. More than half of the total labor force is employed by the federal and territorial government. The largest employers in the private sector, with more than 15% of the labor force, are two modern tuna canneries supplied with fish caught by Japanese, US, and Taiwanese fishing fleets.

Samoans are entitled to free medical treatment, including hospital care. Besides district dispensaries, the government maintains a central hospital, a tuberculosis unit, and a leprosarium. US-trained staff physicians work with Samoan medical practitioners and nurses. The 170 bed LBJ Tropical Medical Center opened in 1986.

Education is a joint undertaking between the territorial government and the villages. School attendance is compulsory for all children from 6 through 18, and about 99% of the population 10 years of age and over is literate. The villages furnish the elementary-school buildings and living quarters for the teachers; the territorial government pays teachers' salaries and provides buildings and supplies for all but

primary schools. Since 1964, educational television has served as the basic teaching tool in the school system. In 1995, total enrollment in elementary and secondary schools was 14,406. American Samoa Community College enrolled 1,249 in 1995.

GUAM

The largest and most populous of the Mariana Islands in the Western Pacific, Guam (13°28′ north and 144°44′ east) has an area, including land and water, of 208 square miles (540 square kilometers) and is about 30 miles (48 kilometers) long and from 4 to 7 miles (6 to 12 kilometers) wide. The island is of volcanic origin; in the south, the terrain is mountainous, while the northern part is a plateau with shallow fertile soil. The central part of the island (where the capital, Agana, is located) features rolling hills.

Guam lies in the typhoon belt of the Western Pacific, and is occasionally subject to widespread storm damage. In May 1976, a typhoon with winds of 190 miles per hour (306 kilometers per hour) struck Guam, causing an estimated $300 million in damage and leaving 80% of the island's buildings in ruins. Guam has a tropical climate with little seasonal variation. Average temperature is 79°F (26°C). Rainfall is substantial, reaching an annual average of more than 80 inches (200 centimeters). Endangered species in 1987 included the giant Micronesian kingfisher and Marianas crow.

The 1999 population, excluding transient US military and civilian personnel and their families, was estimated at

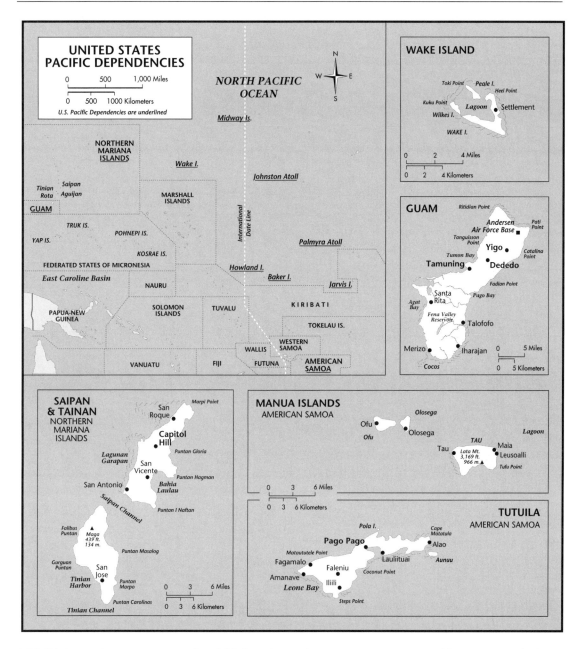

151,716, an increase over the 1986 estimate of 117,500. The increase was attributed largely to the higher birthrate and low mortality rate. The present-day Chamorro, who comprise about 47% of the permanent resident population, descend from the intermingling of the few surviving original Chamorro inhabitants with the Spanish, Filipino, and Mexican settlers, plus later arrivals from the US,

UK, Korea, China, and Japan. Filipinos (25%) are the largest ethnic minority. English is the official language, although Chamorro is taught in the primary schools. The predominant religion is Roman Catholicism.

The earliest known settlers on Guam were the original Chamorro, who migrated from the Malay Peninsula to the Pacific around 1500 BC. When Ferdinand Magellan landed on Guam in 1521, it is believed that as many as 100,000 Chamorro lived on the island; by 1741, their numbers had been reduced to 5,000—most of the population either had fled the island or been killed through disease or war with the Spanish. A Spanish fort was established in 1565, and from 1696 until 1898, Guam was under Spanish rule.

Under the Treaty of Paris that ended the Spanish-American War in 1898, the island was ceded to the US and placed under the jurisdiction of the Department of the Navy. During World War II, Guam was occupied by Japanese forces; the US recaptured the island in 1944 after 54 days of fighting. In 1950, the island's administration was transferred from the Navy to the US Department of the Interior. Under the 1950 Organic Act of Guam, passed by the US Congress, the island was established as an unincorporated territory of the US. Guamanians were granted US citizenship, and internal self-government was introduced.

Guam is one of the most important US military bases in the Pacific, and the island's economy has been profoundly affected by the large sums of money spent by the US defense establishment. During the late 1960s and early 1970s, when the US took the role of a major combatant in the Viet Nam conflict, Guam served as a base for long-range US bombers on missions over Indochina.

Prior to World War II, agriculture and livestock raising were the primary activities. By 1947, most adults were wage earners employed by the US armed forces, although many continued to cultivate small plots to supplement their earnings. Since World War II, agriculture has generally contributed less than 1% of the GNP, partly because a considerable amount of arable land is taken up by military installations. Fruits and vegetables are grown and pigs and poultry are raised for local consumption, but most food is imported. Current fish catches are insufficient to meet local demand. Guam's Kmart store has become a social gathering place; about 10% of the island's population visits the store on any given day.

Tourism has become a major industry and sparked a boom in the construction industry in the mid-1980s. The number of visitors grew rapidly from 6,600 in 1967 to over 900,000 in 1992 and provided $600 million in revenues to the economy. The stagnation in the Japanese economy in the early 1990s slowed the growth of Guam's tourism sector.

Typical tropical diseases are practically unknown today in Guam. Tuberculosis, long the principal killer, was brought under control by the mid-1950s. The Guam Memorial Hospital has a capacity of 147 beds. Village dispensaries serve both as public health units and first-aid stations. In addition, there are a number of physicians in private practice. Specialists from the US Naval Hospital in Guam, assisting on a part-time basis, have made possible a complete program of curative medicine.

School attendance is compulsory from the age of 6 through 16. The number of graduates from the islands' schools is over 1,000 pupils per year. The University of Guam and Guam Community College together had 6,449 students in 1995. There were six radio and five television stations in 1997.

HOWLAND, BAKER, AND JARVIS ISLANDS

Howland Island (0°48′ north and 176°38′ west), Baker Island (0°14′ north and 176°28′ west), and Jarvis Island (0°23′ south and 160°1′ west) are three small coral islands, each about 1 square mile (2.6 square kilometers) in area, belonging to the Line Islands group of the Central Pacific Ocean. All are administered directly from Washington as US unincorporated territories. Howland was discovered in 1842 by US sailors, claimed by the US in 1857, and formally proclaimed a US territory in 1935–36. It was worked for guano (sea bird manure used for fertilizer) by US and British companies until about 1890.

Baker, 40 miles (64 kilometers) south of Howland, and Jarvis, 1,100 miles (1,770 kilometers) east of Howland, also were claimed by the US in 1857, and their guano deposits were similarly worked by

US and British enterprises. The UK annexed Jarvis in 1889. In 1935, the US sent colonists from Hawaii to all three islands, which were placed under the US Department of the Interior in 1936 and are administered as part of the National Wildlife Refuge system. Baker was captured by the Japanese in 1942 and recaptured by the US in 1944. The three islands lack fresh water and have no permanent inhabitants. They are visited annually by the US Coast Guard. A lighthouse on Howland Island is named in honor of the US aviatrix Amelia Earhart, who vanished en route to the island on a round-the-world flight in 1937.

JOHNSTON ATOLL

Johnston Atoll, located in the North Pacific 715 miles (1,151 kilometers) southwest of Honolulu, consists of two islands, Johnston (16°44′ north and 169°31′ west) and Sand (16°45′ north and 169°30′ west), with a total land and water area of about 1 square mile (2.6 square kilometers). The islands are enclosed by a semicircular reef. It was discovered by English sailors in 1807 and claimed by the US in 1858. For many years, it was worked for guano and was a bird reservation. Commissioned as a naval station in 1941, it remains an unincorporated US territory under the control of the US Department of the Air Force. In recent years, it has been used primarily for the testing of nuclear weapons.

As of 1997 there were 1,500 people living on the atoll. The atoll's population was composed entirely of government personnel and contractors.

MIDWAY

The Midway Islands (28°12'–17' north and 177°19'–26' west) consist of an atoll and two small islets, Eastern Island (177°20' west) and Sand Island (177°22'–24' west), 1,300 miles (2,100 kilometers) west-northwest of Honolulu. Total land and water area is 2 square miles (5 square kilometers). Their population was 468 at the 1980 census, a decline from 2,220 in 1970 because of the cessation of US military involvement in Indochina. As of 1995, 453 military personnel lived on the base.

Discovered and claimed by the US in 1859 and formally annexed in 1867, Midway became a submarine cable station early in the 20th century and an airlines station in 1935. Made a US naval base in 1941, Midway was attacked by the Japanese in December 1941 and January 1942. In one of the great battles of World War II, a Japanese naval attack on 3–6 June 1942 was repelled by US warplanes. There is a naval station at Midway, and the islands are important nesting places for seabirds. Midway is a US unincorporated territory under the administrative control of the US Department of the Navy.

NORTHERN MARIANAS

The Northern Marianas, a US commonwealth in the Western Pacific Ocean, is comprised of the Mariana Islands excluding Guam (a separate political entity). Located between 12° and 21° north and 144° and 146° east, it consists of 16 volcanic islands with a total land area of about 183.5 square miles (475 square kilometers). Only six of the islands are inhabited, and most of the people live on the three largest islands—Rota, 33 square miles (85 square kilometers); Saipan, 47 square miles (122 square kilometers); and Tinian, 39 square miles (101 square kilometers).

The climate is tropical, with relatively little seasonal change; temperatures average 70°F to 85°F (21°C to 29°C), and relative humidity is generally high. Rainfall averages 85 inches (216 centimeters) per year. The southern islands, which include Rota, Saipan, and Tinian, are generally lower and covered with moderately heavy tropical vegetation. The northern islands are more rugged, reaching a high point of 3,146 feet (959 meters) on Agrihan, and are generally barren due to erosion and insufficient rainfall. Insects are numerous and ocean birds and animals are abundant. The Marianas mallard is a local endangered species.

The Northern Marianas had an estimated population of 53,552 in 1997. Three-fourths of the population is descended from the original Micronesian inhabitants, known as Chamorros. There are also many descendants of migrants from the Caroline Islands and smaller numbers of Filipino and Korean laborers and settlers from the US mainland. English is the official language and Chamorro and Carolinian are taught in school. About 90% of the people are Roman Catholic.

It is believed that the Marianas were settled by migrants from the Philippines and Indonesia. Excavations on Saipan have yielded evidence of settlement around 1500 BC. The first European to reach the Marianas, in 1521, was Ferdinand Magellan. The islands were ruled by Spain until the Spanish defeat by the US in the Spanish-American War (1898). Guam was then ceded to the US and the rest of the Marianas were sold to Germany. When World War I broke out, Japan took over the Northern Marianas and other German-held islands in the Western Pacific. These islands (the Northern Marianas, Carolines, and Marshalls) were placed under Japanese administration as a League of Nations mandate on 17 December 1920. Upon its withdrawal from the League in 1935, Japan began to fortify the islands, and in World War II they served as important military bases. Several of the islands were the scene of heavy fighting during the war. In the battle for control of Saipan in June 1944, some 23,000 Japanese and 3,500 US troops lost their lives in one day's fighting. As each island was occupied by US troops, it became subject to US authority in accordance with the international law of belligerent occupation. The US planes that dropped atomic bombs on Hiroshima and Nagasaki, bringing an end to the war, took off from Tinian.

On 18 July 1947, the Northern Mariana, Caroline, and Marshall islands formally became a UN trust territory under US administration. This Trust Territory of the Pacific Islands was administered by the US Department of the Navy until 1 July 1951, when administration was transferred to the Department of the Interior. From 1953 to 1962, the Northern Marianas, with the exception of Rota, were administered by the Department of the Navy.

The people of the Northern Marianas voted to become a US commonwealth by a majority of 78.8% in a plebiscite held on 17 June 1975. A covenant approved by the US Congress in March 1976 provided for the separation of the Northern Marianas from the Caroline and Marshall island groups, and for the Marianas' transition to a commonwealth status similar to that of Puerto Rico. The islands became internally self-governing in January 1978. On 3 November 1986, US President Ronald Reagan proclaimed the Northern Marianas a self-governing commonwealth; its people became US citizens. The termination of the trusteeship had been approved by the UN Trusteeship Council in May 1986 but technically required approval from the UN Security Council. Approval from the council was later obtained.

A governor and a lieutenant governor are popularly elected for four-year terms. The legislature consists of 9 senators elected for four-year terms and 14 representatives elected for two-year terms. A district court handles matters involving federal law and a commonwealth court has jurisdiction over local matters.

The traditional economic activities were subsistence agriculture, livestock raising, and fishing. However, much agricultural land was destroyed or damaged during World War II and agriculture has never resumed its prewar importance. Today, government employment and tourism are the mainstays of the economy. Tourism employs about 50% of the workforce, catering primarily to Japanese tourists. The construction industry is also expanding, and there is some small-scale industry, chiefly handicrafts and food processing.

The Northern Marianas is heavily dependent on federal funds; the US government provided $228 million for capital developments, government operations, and special programs between 1986 and 1992. Federal grants to the islands totaled $31 million in 1997. The US also pays to lease property on Saipan, Tinian, and Farallon de Medinilla islands for defense purposes. The principal exports are milk and meat; imports include foods, petroleum, construction materials, and vehicles. US currency is the official medium of exchange.

Health care is primarily the responsibility of the commonwealth government and has improved substantially since 1978. Tuberculosis, once the major health problem, has been controlled. There is a hospital on Saipan and health centers on Tinian and Rota.

PALMYRA ATOLL

Palmyra, an atoll in the Central Pacific Ocean, containing some 50 islets with a total area of some 4 square miles (10 square kilometers), is situated about 1,000 miles (1,600 kilometers) south-southwest of Honolulu at 5°52′ north and 162°5′ west. It was discovered in 1802 by the USS *Palmyra*. It was formally annexed by the US in 1912, and was under the jurisdiction of the city of Honolulu until 1959, when Hawaii became the 50th state of the US. It is now the responsibility of the US Department of the Interior. The atoll is privately owned by the Fullard-Leo family of Hawaii.

Kingman Reef, northwest of Palmyra Atoll at 6°25′ north and 162°23′ north, was discovered by the US in 1874, annexed by the US in 1922, and became a naval reservation in 1934. Now abandoned, it is under the control of the US Department of the Navy.

WAKE ISLAND

Wake Island, actually a coral atoll and three islets (Wake, Peale, and Wilkes) about 5 miles (8 kilometers) long by 2.25 miles (3.6 kilometers) wide, lies in the North Pacific 2,100 miles (3,380 kilometers) west of Honolulu at 19°17′ north and 166°35′ east. The total land and water area is about 3 square miles (8 square kilometers). Discovered by the British in 1796, Wake was long uninhabited.

In 1898, a US expeditionary force en route to Manila landed on the island. The US formally claimed Wake in 1899. It was made a US naval reservation in 1934, and became a civil aviation station in 1935. Captured by the Japanese on 23 December 1941, Wake was subsequently the target of several US air raids. It was surrendered by the Japanese in September 1945 and has thereafter remained a US unincorporated territory under the jurisdiction, since 1972, of the Department of the Air Force.

In 1995, 302 US military personnel and contractors inhabited Wake Island. It is a stopover and fueling station for civilian and military aircraft flying between Honolulu, Guam, and Japan.

UNITED STATES OF AMERICA

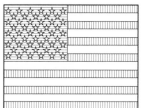

CAPITAL: Washington, D.C. (District of Columbia)

FLAG: The flag consists of 13 alternate stripes, 7 red and 6 white; these represent the 13 original colonies. Fifty 5-pointed white stars, representing the present number of states in the Union, are placed in 9 horizontal rows alternately of 6 and 5 against a blue field in the upper left corner of the flag.

ANTHEM: *The Star-Spangled Banner.*

MONETARY UNIT: The dollar ($) of 100 cents is a paper currency with a floating rate. There are coins of 1, 5, 10, 25, and 50 cents and 1 dollar, and notes of 1, 2, 5, 10, 20, 50, and 100 dollars. Although issuance of higher notes ceased in 1969, a limited number of notes of 500, 1,000, 5,000, and 10,000 dollars remain in circulation.

WEIGHTS AND MEASURES: The imperial system is in common use; however, the use of metrics in industry is increasing, and the metric system is taught in public schools throughout the United States. Common avoirdupois units in use are the avoirdupois pound of 16 ounces or 453.5924277 gram; the long ton of 2,240 pounds or 35,840 ounces; and the short ton, more commonly used, of 2,000 pounds or 32,000 ounces. (Unless otherwise indicated, all measures given in tons are in short tons.) Liquid measures: 1 gallon = 231 cubic inches = 4 quarts = 8 pints. Dry measures: 1 bushel = 4 pecks = 32 dry quarts = 64 dry pints. Linear measures: 1 foot = 12 inches; 1 statute mile = 1,760 yards = 5,280 feet. Metric equivalent: 1 meter = 39.37 inches.

HOLIDAYS: New Year's Day, 1 January; Birthday of Martin Luther King, Jr., 3d Monday in January; Presidents' Day, 3d Monday in February; Memorial or Decoration Day, last Monday in May; Independence Day, 4 July; Labor Day, 1st Monday in September; Columbus Day, 2d Monday in October; Election Day, 1st Tuesday after the 1st Monday in November; Veterans or Armistice Day, 11 November; Thanksgiving Day, 4th Thursday in November; Christmas, 25 December.

TIME: Eastern, 7 AM = noon GMT; Central, 6 AM = noon GMT; Mountain, 5 AM = noon GMT; Pacific (includes the Alaska panhandle), 4 AM = noon GMT; Yukon, 3 AM = noon GMT; Alaska and Hawaii, 2 AM = noon GMT; western Alaska, 1 AM = noon GMT.

1 LOCATION AND SIZE

Located in the Western Hemisphere on the continent of North America, the United States is the fourth-largest country in the world. Its total area, including Alaska and Hawaii, is 9,372,607 square kilometers (3,618,773 square miles). The continental United States has a total boundary length of 17,563 kilometers (10,913 miles).

Alaska, the 49th state, has an area of 1,477,267 square kilometers (570,374 square miles), with a total boundary length of 13,161 kilometers (8,178 miles). The 50th state, Hawaii, consists of islands in the Pacific Ocean with a total area of 16,636 square kilometers (6,423 square miles) and a combined coastline of 1,207 kilometers (750 miles).

2 TOPOGRAPHY

The northeastern coast, known as New England, is rocky, but along the rest of the eastern seaboard the Atlantic Coastal Plain rises gradually from the shoreline, merging with the Gulf Coastal Plain in Georgia. To the west is a plateau, bounded by the Appalachian Mountains, which extend from southwest Maine into central Alabama.

Between the Appalachians and the Rocky Mountains, more than 1,600 kilometers (1,000 miles) to the west, lies the vast interior plain of the United States. Its eastern reaches are bounded on the north by the Great Lakes—Lake Superior, Lake Michigan, Lake Huron, Lake Erie, and Lake Ontario—thought to contain about half the world's total supply of fresh water. The interior plain consists of two major divisions: the fertile Central Plains to the east and the drier Great Plains extending westward to the foothills of the Rocky Mountains. Running south through the center of the interior plain, and draining almost two-thirds of the area of the continental United States, is the Mississippi River.

The Continental Divide runs along the crest of the Rocky Mountains. The Rock-

United States Population Profile

Total population in 2000:	281,421,906
Population change, 1990–2000:	13.2%
Hispanic or Latino†:	12.5%
Population by race	
One race:	97.6%
White:	75.1%
Black or African American:	12.3%
American Indian/Alaska Native:	0.9%
Asian:	3.6%
Native Hawaiian/Pacific Islander:	0.1%
Some other race:	5.5%
Two or more races:	2.4%

Population by Age Group

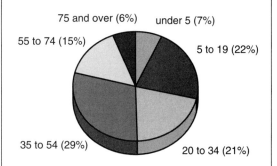

Top Cities by Population

City	Population	% change 1990–2000
New York, NY	8,008,278	9.4
Los Angeles, CA	3,694,820	6.0
Chicago, IL	2,896,016	4.0
Houston, TX	1,953,631	19.8
Philadelphia, PA	1,517,550	–4.3
Phoenix, AZ	1,321,045	34.3
San Diego, CA	1,223,400	10.2
Dallas, TX	1,188,580	18.0
San Antonio, TX	1,144,646	22.3
Detroit, MI	951,270	–7.5

Notes: †A person of Hispanic or Latino origin may be of any race. NA indicates that data are not available.
Sources: U.S. Census Bureau. Public Information Office. *Demographic Profiles.* [Online] Available http://www.census.gov/Press-Release/www/2001/demoprofile.html. Accessed June 1, 2001. U.S. Census Bureau. *Census 2000: Redistricting Data.* Press release issued by the Redistricting Data Office. Washington, D.C., March, 2001.

UNITED STATES OF AMERICA

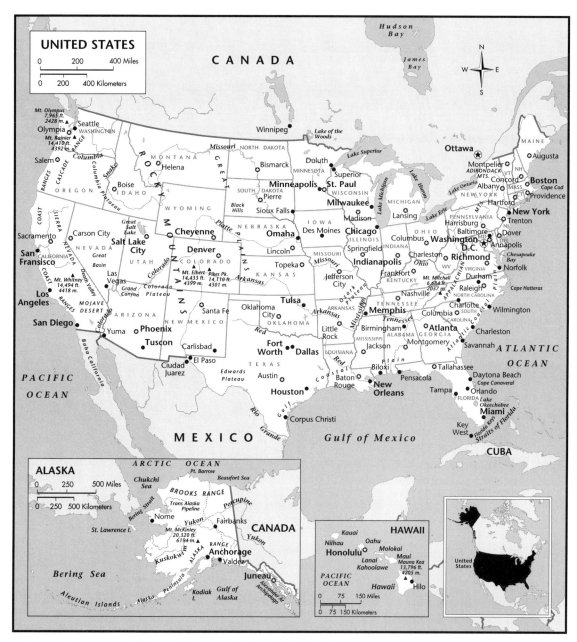

LOCATION: Conterminous US: 66°57′ to 124°44′w; 24°33′ to 49°23′N. Alaska: 130°w to 172°28′E; 51° to 71°23′N. Hawaii: 154°48′ to 178°22′w 18°55′ to 28°25′N. **BOUNDARY LENGTHS:** Conterminous US: Canada, 6,416 kilometers (3,987 miles); Atlantic Ocean, 3,330 kilometers (2,069 miles); Gulf of Mexico coastline, 2,625 kilometers (1,631 miles); Mexico, 3,111 kilometers (1,933 miles); Pacific coastline, 2,081 kilometers (1,293 miles). Alaska: Arctic Ocean coastline, 1,706 kilometers (1,060 miles); Canada, 2,475 kilometers (1,538 miles); Pacific coastline, including the Bering Sea and Strait and Chukchi coastlines, 8,980 kilometers (5,580 miles). Hawaii: coastline, 1,207 kilometers (750 miles).

ies and the ranges to the west—the Sierra Nevada, the Coast, and Cascade ranges — are parts of a larger system of mountains that extends through the western part of Central and South America. Between the Rockies and the Pacific ranges lies a group of vast plateaus containing most of the nation's desert areas, known as the Great Basin. The coastal plains along the Pacific Ocean are narrow, and in many places the mountains plunge directly into the sea. The greatest rivers of the far west are the Colorado in the south and the Columbia in the northwest.

Separated from the continental United States by Canada, the state of Alaska occupies the extreme northwest portion of North America. A series of steep mountain ranges separates the Pacific Ocean coast on the south from Alaska's broad central basin, bounded on the north by the Brooks Range, which slopes down gradually to the Arctic Ocean. The Yukon River flows from Canada in the east through the Central Basin to the Bering Sea in the west. The state of Hawaii consists of a group of Pacific islands formed by volcanoes rising sharply from the ocean floor. The largest of the islands, Hawaii, still has active volcanoes.

The lowest point in the United States is Death Valley in California, at 86 meters (282 feet) below sea level. At 6,194 meters (20,320 feet), Mt. McKinley in Alaska is the highest peak in North America. These topographic extremes show how unstable the Pacific Coast region is geologically. Major earthquakes caused great destruction in San Francisco in 1906 and Anchorage, Alaska, in 1964.

3 CLIMATE

The east coast is affected mostly by masses of air moving from west to east across the continent. Its climate is basically continental, with clear contrasts between seasons. However, because Florida has the Gulf of Mexico lying to its west, it experiences only moderate differences between summer and winter temperatures. Mean annual temperatures vary considerably between north and south, ranging from 11°C (51°F) in Boston to 24°C (76°F) in Miami. Annual rainfall is generally more than 100 centimeters (40 inches). The Gulf and South Atlantic states are often hit by severe tropical storms in late summer and early autumn.

The prairie lands in the middle of the country have more drought than heavy rainfall. The average midwinter temperature in the extreme north—Minnesota and North Dakota—is about –13°C (9°F) or less, while the average July temperature is 18°C (65°F). In the Texas prairie region to the south, January temperatures average 10–13°C (50–55°F) and July temperatures 27–29°C (80–85°F). Rainfall in this region is as low as 46 centimeters (18 inches).

The Great Plains are semiarid. Rainfall in the southern plains averages about 50 centimeters (20 inches) per year and in the northern plains about 25 centimeters (10 inches). The contrast between summer and winter temperatures is extreme throughout the Great Plains. Maximum summer temperatures of over 43°C (110°F) have been recorded, while the average minimum temperature for January is –19°C (–3°F).

The higher reaches of the Rockies and the other western ranges have an alpine climate. The climate of the Western desert region varies considerably from north to south. In New Mexico, Arizona, and southeastern California, mean annual rainfall ranges from 8 centimeters (3 inches) to 76 centimeters (30 inches), while some of the mountainous areas of central Washington and Idaho receive at least 152 centimeters (60 inches) of rain per year. Phoenix, Arizona, has a mean annual temperature of 22°C (71°F).

The Pacific coast has a maritime climate, with mild winters and moderately warm, dry summers. Los Angeles in the south has an average temperature of 13°C (56°F) in January and 21°C (69°F) in July; Seattle in the north has an average temperature of 4°C (39°F) in January and 18°C (65°F) in July. Precipitation ranges from an annual average of 4.52 centimeters (1.78 inches) at Death Valley in California (the lowest in the United States) to more than 356 centimeters (140 inches) in Washington's mountain regions.

Alaska has varied climatic conditions. The Aleutian Islands and the coastal panhandle strip have a moderate maritime climate. The interior is characterized by short, hot summers and long, bitterly cold winters. In the region bordering the Arctic Ocean a polar climate prevails, the soil hundreds of feet below the surface remaining frozen year-round.

Northeast ocean winds give Hawaii a mild, stable climate. The mean temperature in Honolulu is 23°C (73°F) in January and 27°C (80°F) in July. Rainfall is moderate—about 71 centimeters (28 inches) per year—but much greater in the mountains.

The lowest temperature recorded in the United States was –62°C (–79.8°F) in Alaska at Prospect Creek Camp on 23 January 1971; the highest, 57°C (134°F) in California at Greenland Ranch in Death Valley on 10 July 1913. The record annual rainfall is 1,468 centimeters (578 inches) on Maui in Hawaii in 1950.

Between 1980 and 1998, the United States sustained 37 weather-related disasters that each caused over $1 billion in damages. Between 1940 and 1997, floods and flash floods caused 6,390 deaths in the United States. Tornadoes caused 3,877 fatalities during 1953–97. During 1959–97, 3,421 people in the US were killed by lightning.

4 PLANTS AND ANIMALS

At least 7,000 species and subspecies of native United States plants have been categorized. Wildflowers bloom in all areas, from the seldom-seen blossoms of rare desert cacti to the hardiest alpine species. The eastern forests contain a mixture of softwoods and hardwoods that includes pine, birch, maple, and hickory. The central hardwood forest—still an important timber source—contains oak, ash, and walnut among others. Tupelo, pecan, and sycamore are found in the southern forest that stretches along the coast of the Gulf of Mexico into the eastern half of Texas. The forest along the Pacific Ocean coast is spectacular with its enormous redwoods and Douglas firs. In the southwest are

Photo credit: CT Department of Economic Development.

A seal relaxing under the sun's rays at the Mystic Marinelife Aquarium in Connecticut.

saguaro (giant cactus), yucca, candlewood, and the Joshua tree.

Mesquite grass covers parts of west Texas, southern New Mexico, and Arizona. Short grass may be found in the highlands of the latter two states, while tall grass covers large portions of Texas and Louisiana. The Western desert supports sagebrush, creosote, and—near the Great Salt Lake and in Death Valley—saltbrush. Coniferous forests are found on the lower mountain slopes. The central part of the Yukon Basin in Alaska is also a region of softwood forests, while the rest of the state is heath or tundra. Hawaii has extensive forests of bamboo and ferns.

An estimated 1,500 species and subspecies of mammals are found in the continental United States. Among the larger game animals are the white-tailed deer, moose, mountain goat, black bear, and grizzly bear. The Alaskan brown bear often reaches a weight of 540–635 kilograms (1,200–1,400 pounds). Some 25 important furbearers are common, including the muskrat, red and gray foxes, mink, raccoon, and beaver. The American buffalo (bison), millions of which once roamed the plains, is now found only on select reserves.

Year-round and migratory birds abound. Loons, wild ducks, and wild geese are found in lake country; terns, gulls, sandpipers, and other seabirds live along the coasts. Wrens, owls, hummingbirds, sparrows, woodpeckers, swallows, and finches appear in large numbers, along with the robin, cardinal, Baltimore oriole, and various blackbirds. Wild turkey, ruffed grouse, and ring-necked pheasant (introduced from Europe) are popular game birds.

Lakes, rivers, and streams are full of trout, bass, perch, carp, catfish, and pike. Sea bass, cod, snapper, and flounder are abundant along the coasts, along with such shellfish as lobster, shrimp, clams, oysters, and mussels. Four poisonous snakes survive, of which the rattlesnake is the most common. Alligators appear in southern waterways, and the Gila monster makes its home in the southwest.

5 ENVIRONMENTAL PROTECTION

The Environmental Protection Agency (EPA), created in 1970, is the main government agency responsible for control of air and noise pollution, water and waste management, and control of toxic substances.

Landmark federal laws protecting the environment include the Clean Air Act Amendments of 1970 and 1990, controlling automobile and electric utility emissions; and the Endangered Species Act of 1973, protecting wildlife near extinction.

Among the environmental movement's most notable successes have been the creation of recycling programs; the banning in the United States of the insecticide dichlorodiphenyltrichloroethane (DDT); the protection of more than 40 million hectares (100 million acres) of Alaska lands; and the gradual elimination of chlorofluorocarbon (CFC) production by 2000.

A continuing environmental problem is pollution of the nation's water by dumping of raw or partially treated sewage from major cities into United States waterways. In addition, runoffs of agricultural pesticides are deadly to fishing streams and very difficult to regulate. The amount of land suitable for farming has decreased due to erosion, depletion of the soil, and urbanization.

Facilities for solid waste disposal are still inadequate, and the United States nuclear industry has expanded without having a good way to dispose of radioactive wastes. Other environmental issues include acid rain (precipitation contaminated from burning coal); the contamination of homes by radon (a radioactive gas that is produced by the decay of underground deposits of radium and which can cause cancer); and the lack of available water in many western states due to overpopulation in naturally drier areas.

As of 1996, the United States Fish and Wildlife Service listed 751 endangered species in the United States (of which 432 were plant species) and 209 threatened species, including 94 plants. The agency listed another 522 endangered and 43 threatened foreign species by international agreement.

6 POPULATION

According to census figures for 2000, the population of the United States (including the 50 states and Washington, D.C.) was 281,421,906 (up from 248,709,873 in 1990), of whom 50.9% were female and 49.1% male. The median age of the population increased from 16.7 years in 1820 to 22.9 years in 1900, and to 35.3 years in 2000. The United States Bureau of the Census projected a population of 288.28 million for 2005. Population density varies greatly from region to region; the average is 79.6 persons per square kilometer (30.7 per square mile).

Suburbs have absorbed most of the shift in population distribution since 1950. In 2000 there were nine cities with more than 1 million population each. The country's largest city, New York City, has a population of over 8 million, a number approximately 55 times greater than the population of Tallahassee, Florida.

Photo credit: Oklahoma Tourism Photo by Fred W. Marvel.

American Indian Exposition, Anadarko, Oklahoma.

7 ETHNIC GROUPS

The majority of the population of the United States is of European origin. The largest groups in 1990 trace their ancestry to the United Kingdom (31,391,758), Germany (45,583,922), and Ireland (22,721,252). Many Americans have mixed ancestries. Major racial and national minority groups include blacks (either of United States or Caribbean parentage), Chinese, Filipinos, Japanese, Mexicans, and other Spanish-speaking peoples of the Americas. Whites comprised 75.1% of the United States population in 2000; blacks, 12.2%; Asians, 3.6%; Native Americans, 0.9%; and native Hawaiian and other Pacific islanders, 0.1%. The 2000 census reports that 2.4% of Americans claimed two or more races.

In 2000, 12.5% of Americans were of Hispanic origin: Mexican, 7.3%; Puerto Rican, 1.2%; Cuban, 0.4%; and other Hispanic or Latino, 3.6%. People of Hispanic origin can be of any race.

In 2000, there were 2.47 million Amerindians in the United States, found mostly in the southwestern states of Oklahoma, Arizona, New Mexico, and California. The black population in 2000 totaled 34.6 million. More than three out of four black Americans live in cities.

Included in the 2000 census of the United States were 10.2 million persons

State Areas, Entry Dates, and Populations

STATE	CAPITAL	ORDER OF ENTRY	DATE OF ENTRY	POPULATION AT ENTRY[†]	POPULATION CENSUS 1990	POPULATION CENSUS 2000
Alabama	Montgomery	22	14 December 1819	127,901	4,040,587	4,447,100
Alaska	Juneau	49	3 January 1959	226,167	550,043	626,932
Arizona	Phoenix	48	14 February 1912	204,354	3,665,228	5,130,632
Arkansas	Little Rock	25	15 June 1836	57,574	2,350,725	2,673,400
California	Sacramento	31	9 September 1850	92,597	29,760,021	33,871,648
Colorado	Denver	38	1 August 1876	39,864	3,294,394	4,301,261
Connecticut*	Hartford	5	9 January 1788	237,946	3,287,116	3,405,565
Delaware*	Dover	1	7 December 1787	59,096	666,168	783,600
Florida	Tallahassee	27	3 March 1845	87,445	12,937,926	15,982,378
Georgia*	Atlanta	4	2 January 1788	82,548	6,478,316	8,186,453
Hawaii	Honolulu	50	21 August 1959	632,772	1,108,229	1,211,537
Idaho	Boise	43	3 July 1890	88,548	1,006,749	1,293,953
Illinois	Springfield	21	3 December 1818	55,211	11,430,602	12,419,293
Indiana	Indianapolis	19	11 December 1816	147,178	5,544,159	6,080,485
Iowa	Des Moines	29	28 December 1846	192,214	2,776,755	2,926,324
Kansas	Topeka	34	29 January 1861	107,206	2,477,574	2,688,418
Kentucky	Frankfort	15	1 June 1792	73,677	3,685,296	4,041,769
Louisiana	Baton Rouge	18	30 April 1812	76,556	4,219,973	4,468,976
Maine	Augusta	23	15 March 1820	298,335	1,227,928	1,274,923
Maryland*	Annapolis	7	28 April 1788	319,728	4,781,468	5,296,486
Massachusetts*	Boston	6	6 February 1788	378,787	6,016,425	6,349,097
Michigan	Lansing	26	26 January 1837	212,267	9,295,297	9,938,444
Minnesota	St. Paul	32	11 May 1858	172,023	4,375,099	4,919,479
Mississippi	Jackson	20	10 December 1817	75,448	2,573,216	2,844,658,
Missouri	Jefferson City	24	10 August 1821	66,586	5,117,073	5,595,211
Montana	Helena	41	8 November 1889	142,924	799,065	902,195
Nebraska	Lincoln	37	1 March 1867	122,993	1,578,385	1,711,263
Nevada	Carson City	36	31 October 1864	42,491	1,201,833	1,998,257
New Hampshire*	Concord	9	21 June 1788	141,885	1,109,252	1,235,786
New Jersey*	Trenton	3	18 December 1787	184,139	7,730,188	8,414,350
New Mexico	Santa Fe	47	6 January 1912	327,301	1,515,069	1,819,046
New York*	Albany	11	26 July 1788	340,120	17,990,455	18,976,457
North Carolina*	Raleigh	12	21 November 1789	393,751	6,628,637	8,049,313
North Dakota	Bismarck	39	2 November 1889	190,983	638,800	642,200
Ohio	Columbus	17	1 March 1803[††]	43,365	10,847,115	11,353,140
Oklahoma	Oklahoma City	46	16 November 1907	657,155	3,145,585	3,450,654
Oregon	Salem	33	14 February 1859	52,465	2,842,321	3,421,399
Pennsylvania*	Harrisburg	2	12 December 1787	434,373	11,003,464	12,281,054
Rhode Island*	Providence	13	29 May 1790	68,825	1,003,464	1,048,319
South Carolina*	Columbia	8	23 May 1788	393,751	3,486,703	4,012,012
South Dakota	Pierre	40	2 November 1889	348,600	696,004	754,844
Tennessee	Nashville	16	1 June 1796	35,691	4,877,185	5,689,283
Texas	Austin	28	29 December 1845	212,592	16,986,510	20,851,820
Utah	Salt Lake City	45	4 January 1896	276,749	1,722,850	2,233,169
Vermont	Montpelier	14	4 March 1791	85,425	562,758	608,827
Virginia*	Richmond	10	25 June 1788	747,610	6,187,358	7,078,515
Washington	Olympia	42	11 November 1889	357,232	4,866,692	5,894,121
West Virginia	Charleston	35	20 June 1863	442,014	1,793,477	1,808,344
Wisconsin	Madison	30	29 May 1848	305,391	4,891,769	5,363,675
Wyoming	Cheyenne	44	10 July 1890	62,555	453,588	493,782

[†]Census closest to entry date.   [††]Date fixed in 1953 by congressional resolution.   *One of original 13 colonies.

United States Population by Race

Census 2000 was the first national census in which the instructions to respondents said, "Mark one or more races." This table shows the number of people who are of one, two, or three or more races. For those claiming two races, the number of people belonging to the various categories is listed. The U.S. government conducts a census of the population every ten years.

	Number	Percent
Total population	281,241,906	100.0
One race	274,595,678	97.6
Two races	6,368,075	2.3
White *and* Black or African American	784,764	0.3
White *and* American Indian/Alaska Native	1,082,683	0.4
White *and* Asian	868,395	0.3
White *and* Native Hawaiian/Pacific Islander	112,964	—
White *and* some other race	2,206,251	0.8
Black or African American *and* American Indian/Alaska Native	182,494	0.1
Black or African American *and* Asian	106,782	—
Black or African American *and* Native Hawaiian/Pacific Islander	29,876	—
Black or African American *and* some other race	417,249	0.1
American Indian/Alaska Native *and* Asian	52,429	—
American Indian/Alaska Native *and* Native Hawaiian/Pacific Islander	7,328	—
American Indian/Alaska Native *and* some other race	93,842	—
Asian *and* Native Hawaiian/Pacific Islander	138,802	—
Asian *and* some other race	249,108	0.1
Native Hawaiian/Pacific Islander *and* some other race	35,108	—
Three or more races	458,153	0.2

Source: U.S. Census Bureau. *Census 2000: Redistricting Data.* Press release issued by the Redistricting Data Office. Washington, D.C., March, 2001. A dash (—) indicates that the percent is less than 0.1.

who are of Asian descent, chiefly Chinese, Filipino, Japanese, Indian, Korean, and Vietnamese. Hawaii's proportion of Asians and Pacific Islanders was the highest in the country, making Hawaii the only state with an Asian and Pacific Islander majority. The Japanese population of Hawaii accounted in 2000 for 16.7% of the state's residents. As of 2000 there were 35.3 million Hispanic Americans.

8 LANGUAGES

The primary language of the United States is English, enriched by words borrowed from the languages of Indians and immigrants, mostly European.

The 1990 census recorded that of 229,875,493 Americans five years of age or over, 198,101,862 spoke only English at home; the remaining 31,773,631 spoke a language other than English. The principal foreign languages and their speakers were as follows: Spanish, 17,310,043; French, 1,920,621; German, 1,544,793; Chinese, 1,316,956; and Italian, 1,307,068. Refugee immigration has greatly increased the number of foreign-language speakers from Latin America and Asia.

Educational problems raised by the presence of large numbers of non-English speakers led to the passage in 1976 of the Bilingual Educational Act, allowing children to study basic courses in their first language while they learn English. A related school issue is that of black English, a Southern dialect variant that is spoken by many black students now in northern schools.

9 RELIGIONS

United States religious traditions are predominantly Judeo-Christian, and most Americans identify themselves as Protestants (of various denominations), Roman Catholics, or Jews. As of 1995, about 63% of all Americans reported affiliation with a religious group. About half of the total population belongs to a Judeo-Christian religious group.

The largest Christian denomination is the Roman Catholic Church, with 59.9 million members in 19,787 parishes in 1995. Immigration from western Europe and the Caribbean accounts for the large number of Roman Catholics in the Northeast, Northwest, and some parts of the Great Lakes region. Hispanic traditions and more recent immigration from Mexico and other Latin American countries account for the historical importance of Roman Catholicism in California and throughout the southwest. Jewish immigrants settled first in the Northeast, where the largest Jewish population remains; in 1994, 1.65 million Jews lived in New York out of an estimated total of 5.88 million American Jews.

As of 1992, Protestant groups in the United States had at least 94.6 million members. By far the nation's largest Protestant group, the Southern Baptist Convention, had 15.4 million members in 1992; the American Baptist Churches in the USA claimed a membership of some 1.5 million. A concentration of Methodist groups extends westward in a band from Delaware to eastern Colorado; the largest of these groups, the United Methodist Church, had 8.65 million members in 1992.

Lutheran groups, reflecting in part the patterns of German and Scandinavian settlement, are most highly concentrated in the north-central states, especially Minnesota and the Dakotas. Two Lutheran synods, the Lutheran Church in America and the American Lutheran Church merged in 1987 to form the Evangelical Lutheran Church in America, with 5.2 million members in 1992. In June 1983, the two major Presbyterian churches, the northern-based United Presbyterian Church in the USA and the southern-based Presbyterian Church in the US, formally merged as the Presbyterian Church (USA), ending a division that began with the Civil War; its membership in 1992 was 3.8 million.

Other Protestant denominations and their estimated memberships in 1992 were the Episcopal Church, 2.5 million; Churches of Christ, 1.65 million; and the United Church of Christ (Congregationalist), 1.5 million. One Christian group, the Church of Latter-day Saints (Mormon), which claimed 4.67 million members in 1992, was organized in New York in 1830 and, since migrating westward, has played a leading role in Utah's political, economic, and religious life. During the 1970s and early 1980s there was a rise in the fundamentalist, evangelical, and Pentecostal movements.

Photo credit: Delaware Tourism Office.

*Liberty bell in front of Legislator Hall, in Dover,
the state capital of Delaware.*

Many Native Americans continue to follow their traditional religions. Several million Muslims, Eastern Orthodox Christians, followers of various Asian religions, a number of small Protestant groups, and a sizable number of cults also participate in United States religious life. The 1980s and 1990s have seen the rise of feminist spirituality, New Age, earth-centered, and Neo-Pagan movements.

10 TRANSPORTATION

The United States has well-developed systems of railroads, highways, inland water-ways, oil pipelines, and domestic airways. Despite an attempt to encourage more people to travel by train through the development of a national network (Amtrak) in the 1970s, rail transport has continued to experience heavy financial losses. The United States had 541 freight railroads in 1995, with 146,785 rail miles (236,177 kilometers). Railroads carried 1.8 billion tons of cargo through 27.3 million rail-carloads handled in 1995.

The most widely used form of transportation is the automobile, and the extent and quality of the United States road-transport system are the best in the world. Over 204 million vehicles—a record number—were registered in 1997, including 128.5 million passenger cars. In 1995, 31% of the world's motor vehicles were registered in the United States, down from 36% in 1985. The United States has a vast network of public roads, whose total length as of 1998 was 3.99 million miles (6.42 million kilometers). About 179.54 million Americans were licensed drivers in 1995—88% of the population old enough to drive legally.

Major ocean ports or port areas are New York, Philadelphia, Baltimore, Norfolk, New Orleans, Houston, and the San Francisco Bay area. The inland port of Duluth on Lake Superior handles more freight than all but the top-ranking ocean ports. In 1998, the United States had a registered merchant shipping fleet of 385 vessels, with a total of 11.1 million gross registered tons.

Passengers carried by the airlines in 1997 totaled 590 million. The United

States in 1998 had 14,459 air facilities, of which 5,167 had paved runways. An estimated 187,312 general aviation aircraft flew a total of 26.1 million hours in 1996. As of 2000, the busiest airport was Hartsfield in Atlanta, finally surpassing Chicago's O'Hare.

11 HISTORY

Origins

The first Americans—distant ancestors of the American Indians—probably crossed the Bering Strait from Asia at least 12,000 years ago. By the time Christopher Columbus came to the New World (as America was known) in 1492 there were probably about 2 million Native Americans living in the land that was to become the United States.

The Spanish established the first permanent settlement at St. Augustine in the future state of Florida in 1565, and another in New Mexico in 1599. During the early seventeenth century, the English founded Jamestown in present-day Virginia (1607) and Plymouth Colony in present-day Massachusetts (1620). The Dutch and Swedish also established settlements in the seventeenth century, but the English eventually took over settlement of the east coast except for Florida, where the Spanish ruled until 1821. In the southwest, California, Arizona, New Mexico, and Texas also were part of the Spanish empire until the nineteenth century.

The American Revolution

The colonies enjoyed a large measure of self-government until the end of the French and Indian War (1745–63), which resulted in the loss of French Canada to the British. To prevent further troubles with the Indians, the British government in 1763 prohibited the American colonists from settling beyond the Appalachian Mountains. The British also enacted a series of tax measures which the colonists protested, setting off a struggle between colonial and British authority.

A series of conflicts led to the colonists' decision to separate from British rule and set up their own independent government. George Washington was appointed commander-in-chief of the new American army, and on 4 July 1776, the 13 American colonies adopted the Declaration of Independence. The American Revolution was officially begun.

British and American forces met in their first organized encounter near Boston on 17 June 1775. Numerous battles up and down the east coast followed. The entry of France into the war on the American side eventually tipped the balance. On 19 October 1781, the British commander, Charles Cornwallis, surrendered his army at Yorktown, Virginia. American independence was acknowledged by the British in a treaty of peace signed in Paris on 3 September 1783.

The Beginnings of American Government

The first constitution uniting the 13 original states—the Articles of Confederation—denied Congress power to raise taxes or regulate commerce, and many of its authorized powers required the approval of a minimum of nine states. In

1787 Congress passed the Northwest Ordinance, providing for the establishment of new territories on the frontier. In that same year, a convention assembled in Philadelphia to revise the articles. The convention adopted an altogether new document, the present Constitution of the United States, which greatly increased the powers of the central government at the expense of the states.

This document was ratified by the states with the understanding that it would be amended to include a bill of rights guaranteeing certain fundamental freedoms. These freedoms—including the rights of free speech, press, and assembly, freedom from unreasonable search and seizure, and the right to a speedy and public trial by an impartial jury—are assured by the first ten amendments to the constitution, known as the "Bill of Rights," adopted on 5 December 1791. The constitution did recognize slavery, and did not provide for universal suffrage. On 30 April 1789 George Washington was inaugurated as the first president of the United States.

The Federalist Party, to which Washington belonged, was opposed to the French Revolution (1789), while the Democratic-Republicans (an anti-Federalist party led by Thomas Jefferson) supported it. This division of the nation's leadership was the beginning of the two-party system, which has been the dominant characteristic of the United States political scene ever since.

Photo credit: Travel Montana/P. Fugleberg.

Lewis and Clark monument at Fort Benton in Montana.

Westward Expansion

In 1803, President Thomas Jefferson purchased the Louisiana Territory from France, including all the present territory of the United States west of the Mississippi drained by that river and its tributaries. Exploration and mapping of the new territory, particularly through the expeditions of Meriwether Lewis and William Clark, began almost immediately.

To make room for the westward expansion of European American settlement, the federal government in 1817 began a policy of forcibly resettling the Indians. They were moved to what later became known as Indian Territory (now Oklahoma); those Indians not forced to move were restricted to reservations. This "removal" of native Americans to make way for European American settlement was a form of genocide (the deliberate destruction of a whole race, culture, or group of people).

The Missouri Compromise (1820) provided for admission of Missouri into the Union as a slave state but banned slavery in territories to the west that lay north of 36°30′. And in 1823 President James Monroe declared the Western Hemisphere closed to further colonization by European powers.

Development of Farming and Industry

Farming expanded with westward migration. The cotton gin, invented by Eli Whitney in 1793, greatly simplified cotton production, and the growing textile industry in New England and Great Britain needed a lot of cotton. So the South remained an agricultural society based mostly on a one-crop economy. Large numbers of field hands were required for cotton farming, and black slavery became a significant part of the southern economy.

The successful completion of the Erie Canal (1825), linking the Great Lakes with the Atlantic, began a canal-building boom. Railroad building began in earnest in the 1830s, and by 1840 about 3,300 miles (5,300 kilometers) of track had been laid.

New States and the Slavery Question

In 1836, United States settlers in Texas revolted against Mexican rule and established an independent republic. Texas was admitted to the Union as a state in 1845. War with Mexico over a boundary dispute led in 1848 to the addition of California and New Mexico to the growing nation. A dispute with Britain over the Oregon Territory was settled in 1846 by a treaty that established the 49th parallel as the boundary with Canada.

Westward expansion increased the conflict over slavery in the new territories. The Kansas-Nebraska Act of 1854 repealed the Missouri Compromise and left the question of slavery in the territories to be decided by the settlers themselves. Finally, the election of Abraham Lincoln to the presidency in 1860 led strong supporters of slavery to decide to secede from the United States altogether.

The Civil War

Between December 1860 and February 1861, the seven states of the Deep South—South Carolina, Mississippi, Florida, Alabama, Georgia, Louisiana, and Texas—withdrew from the Union and formed a separate government, with a greater emphasis on individual states' rights. They were known as the Confederate States of America, under the presidency of Jefferson Davis. On 12 April 1861, the Confederates opened fire on Union troops at Fort Sumter in the harbor of Charleston, South Carolina, marking the beginning of war between the states. Arkansas, North Carolina, Virginia, and Tennessee quickly joined the Confederacy.

For the next four years, war raged between the Confederate and Union forces, largely in southern territories. An estimated 360,000 men in the Union forces lost their lives, including 110,000 killed in battle. Confederate dead were estimated at 250,000, including 94,000 killed in battle. The North, with more fighters and resources, finally won. With much of the South in Union hands, Confederate General Robert E. Lee surrendered to Union General Ulysses S. Grant at Appomattox Courthouse in Virginia on 9 April 1865.

The Post-Civil War Era

President Lincoln's Emancipation Proclamation of 1863 was the first step in freeing some four million black slaves. Their liberation was completed soon after the war's end by amendments to the Constitution. Five days after General Lee's surrender, Lincoln was assassinated by John Wilkes Booth. During the Reconstruction era (1865–77), the defeated South was governed by Union Army commanders. The resulting bitterness of southerners toward northern Republican rule, which gave blacks the rights of citizens, including the right to vote, lasted for years afterward. By the end of the Reconstruction era, whites had reestablished their political domination over blacks in the southern states and had begun to enforce rules of segregation that lasted for nearly a century.

Outside the South, the age of big business dawned. Pittsburgh, Chicago, and New York emerged as the nation's great industrial centers. The American Federation of Labor, founded in 1886, established a nationwide system of organized labor that remained dominant for many decades. During this period, too, the woman's rights movement began to organize to fight for the right to vote. It took women until 1920 to win their constitutional right of suffrage.

The 1890s marked the closing of the United States frontier for settlement and the beginning of United States overseas expansion. (Alaska had already been acquired from Russia for $7.2 million in 1867.) In 1898, at its own request, Hawaii was annexed as a territory by the United States. In the same year, as a result of the Spanish-American War, the United States added the Philippines, Guam, and Puerto Rico to its territories. A newly independent Cuba became a United States near-protectorate until the 1950s. In 1903, the United States leased the Panama Canal Zone and started construction of a 68-kilometer (42-mile) canal, completed in 1914.

World War I to World War II

United States involvement in World War I marked the country's emergence as one of the great powers of the world. By late 1917, when United States troops joined the Allied forces in the fighting on the western front, the European armies were approaching exhaustion. American intervention may well have been a key element in the eventual victory of the Allies. Fighting ended with the armistice (truce) of 11 November 1918. President Wilson played an active role in drawing up the 1919 Versailles peace treaty.

The 1920s saw a major business boom, followed by the great stock market crash of October 1929, which ushered in the longest and most serious economic depression the country had ever known. The election of Franklin D. Roosevelt, in March 1933, began a new era in United States history, in which the federal government took a much greater role in the nation's economic affairs. Relief measures were instituted, work projects established, and the federal Social Security program was set up. The National Labor Relations Act established the right of employees' organizations to bargain collectively with employers.

Following German, Italian, and Japanese aggression, World War II broke out in Europe during September 1939. In 1940, Roosevelt, ignoring a tradition dating back to Washington that no president should serve more than two terms, ran again for reelection. He easily defeated his Republican opponent, Wendell Willkie.

The United States was brought actively into the war by the Japanese attack on the Pearl Harbor naval base in Hawaii on 7 December 1941. United States forces waged war across the Pacific, in Africa, in Asia, and in Europe. Germany was successfully invaded in 1944 and conquered in May 1945. After the United States dropped the world's first atomic bombs on Hiroshima and Nagasaki in Japan, the Japanese surrendered in August.

Korean War and Civil Rights Movement

The United States became an active member of the new world organization, the United Nations, during President Harry S Truman's administration. In 1949 the North Atlantic Treaty Organization (NATO) established a defensive alliance among a number of West European nations and the United States. Following the North Korean attack on South Korea on 25 June 1950, the United Nations Security Council decided that members of the United Nations should go to the aid of South Korea. United States naval, air, and ground forces were immediately sent by President Truman. An undeclared war followed, which eventually was ended by a truce signed on 27 June 1953.

During President Dwight D. Eisenhower's administration, the United States Supreme Court's decision in *Brown v. Board of Education of Topeka* (1954) outlawed segregation of whites and blacks in public schools. In the early 1960s, sit-ins, freedom rides, and similar expressions of nonviolent resistance by blacks and their sympathizers—known collectively as the Civil Rights Movement—led to the end of some segregation practices.

In the early 1960s, during the administration of President Eisenhower's Democratic successor, John F. Kennedy, the Cold War heated up as Cuba, under the regime of Fidel Castro, aligned itself with the Soviet Union. In October 1962, President Kennedy successfully forced a showdown with the Soviet Union over Cuba in demanding the withdrawal of Soviet-supplied missiles from the nearby island. On 22 November 1963, President Kennedy was assassinated while riding in a motorcade through Dallas, Texas. Hours later, Vice President Lyndon B. Johnson was

Mount Rushmore, Black Hills, South Dakota.

inaugurated president. President Johnson's ambitious "Great Society" program sought to ensure black Americans' rights in voting and public housing, to give the underprivileged job training, and to provide persons 65 and over with hospitalization and other medical benefits.

The Vietnam War and Watergate

In 1965, President Johnson sent American combat troops to support anti-Communist forces in South Vietnam and ordered United States bombing raids on Communist North Vietnam. But American military might was unable to defeat the Vietnamese guerrillas, and the American people were badly divided over continuing the undeclared war.

Under President Richard M. Nixon (elected in 1968), the increasingly unpopular and costly war continued for four more years before a cease-fire was finally signed on 27 January 1973 and the last American soldiers were withdrawn. Two years later, the South Vietnamese army collapsed, and the North Vietnamese Communist regime united the country. In 1972, President Nixon opened up relations with the People's Republic of China, which had been closed to Westerners since 1949. He also signed a strategic arms limitation agreement with the Soviet Union. (Earlier, in July 1969, American technology had achieved a national triumph by landing the first astronaut on the moon.)

The Watergate scandal began on 17 June 1972 with the arrest of five men associated with Nixon's reelection campaign during a break-in at Democratic Party headquarters in the Watergate office building in Washington, D.C. Although Nixon was reelected in 1972, further investigations by the press and by a Senate investigating committee revealed a pattern of political "dirty tricks" and illegal wiretapping and other methods of spying on his opponents throughout his first term. The House voted to begin impeachment proceedings. On 9 August 1974, Nixon became the first president to resign the office. The American people's trust in their government leaders was seriously damaged.

The Reagan Era

Gerald R. Ford was appointed in October 1973 to succeed ousted Vice President Spiro T. Agnew. Less than a month after taking office, President Ford granted a full pardon to Nixon for any crimes he may have committed as president. Ford's pardon of Nixon probably contributed to his narrow defeat by a Georgia Democrat, Jimmy Carter, in 1976. During 1978–79, President Carter convinced the Senate to pass treaties ending United States sovereignty over the Panama Canal Zone. He also mediated a peace agreement between Israel and Egypt, signed at the Camp David, Maryland, retreat in September 1978. But an economic recession and a prolonged quarrel with Iran over more than 50 United States hostages seized in Tehran on 4 November 1979 caused the American public to doubt his leadership. Exactly a year after the hostages were

taken, former California governor Ronald Reagan defeated Carter in the 1980 presidential election. The hostages were released on 20 January 1981, the day of Reagan's inauguration.

President Reagan used his popularity to push through significant policy changes. He made cuts in income tax and more than doubled the military budget between 1980 and 1989, which resulted in a doubling of the national debt. In an effort to balance the federal budget, Reagan cut welfare and Medicare benefits, reduced allocations for food stamps, and slashed the budget of the Environmental Protection Agency.

Reagan's appointment of Sandra Day O'Connor as the first woman justice of the Supreme Court was widely praised and won unanimous confirmation from the Senate. Protests were raised, however, about his decisions to help the government of El Salvador in its war against leftist rebels, to aid groups in Nicaragua trying to overthrow the leftist Sandinista government in their country, and to send American troops to Grenada in October 1983 to overthrow a leftist government there.

Presidents Bush and Clinton

Reagan was succeeded in 1988 by his vice president, George Bush. President Bush used his personal relationships with foreign leaders to bring about peace talks between Israel and its Arab neighbors, to encourage a peaceful unification of Germany, and to negotiate significant arms cuts with the Russians. Bush sent 400,000 American soldiers to lead the way in forming a multinational coalition to oppose Iraq's invasion of Kuwait in 1990. The multinational forces destroyed Iraq's main force within seven months.

One of the biggest crises that the Bush administration encountered was the collapse of the savings and loan industry in the late 1980s. The federal government was forced by law to rescue the savings and loan banks, under the Federal Savings and Loan Insurance Corporation (FSLIC), costing taxpayers over $100 billion.

In the 1992 presidential election, Democrat Bill Clinton, governor of Arkansas, defeated Bush. Clinton was elected to a second term in 1996. Under Clinton, the United States economy prospered with unemployment reaching a 30-year low and the Dow Industrial Average topping 10,000. In his second term, however, he was impeached by the House of Representatives on charges that he obstructed justice and lied in a court proceeding to cover-up an extramarital affair with a White House intern. A trial was held in the Senate, but there were not enough votes to remove him from office.

The 2000 Presidential Election

In 2000, President Clinton's vice president Al Gore and former President George Bush's son George W. Bush (the governor of Texas) engaged in an election unlike any seen in modern history. As the polls closed the race was neck and neck as the states reported their results. As the night wore on, the state of Florida held the key to the White House. When the votes were counted, Bush's margin of victory was less than 2000 votes. Gore immediately challenged the results and asked for a recount. The votes across the state were recounted first by machine and then, in selected counties, by hand. With each count Gore gained ground, but not enough to take the lead. Voting irregularities were claimed by both sides. Gore argued that some ballots were confusing and that many people who thought they were voting for Gore ended up voting for someone else. Bush argued that the absentee ballots of American service men and women were being unfairly rejected on technicalities. Both parties blanketed the state, and courts, with teams of lawyers. The spectacle peaked as teams of weary election officials under the constant gaze of the nation via television hand counted ballots. Ultimately, the election was decided by a closely divided US Supreme Court. The court found that the process for counting the ballots was flawed and that there wasn't enough time to fix the problem. The ruling secured the election for Bush.

George W. Bush assumed the office of the presidency with the Republican Party in control of both house of Congress, but just barely. The Senate was evenly divided 50–50 with the vice president providing the tie-braking vote. Bush immediately pushed for, and won, a massive $1.35 trillion tax cut. His victory, however, was marred by the defection of Vermont senator Jim Jefford from the Republican party. Jefford chose to become an independent, thereby shifting control of the Senate to the Democrats.

[12] FEDERAL GOVERNMENT

The Constitution of the United States, signed in 1787, is the nation's governing document. In the first ten amendments to the Constitution, ratified in 1791 and known as the Bill of Rights, certain rights are guaranteed to United States citizens. In all, there have been 27 amendments to the Bill of Rights, including the 13th Amendment (1865) which banned slavery, and the 19th (1920), which gave women the right to vote. Suffrage is universal beginning at age 18.

The United States has a federal form of government, with the distribution of powers between federal and state governments constitutionally defined. The legislative powers of the federal government rest in Congress, which consists of the House of Representatives and the Senate. There are 435 members of the House of Representatives. Each state is given a number of representatives in proportion to its population. Representatives are elected for two-year terms in every even-numbered year. The Senate consists of two senators from each state, elected for six-year terms. One-third of the Senate is elected in every even-numbered year.

A bill that is passed by both houses of Congress in the same form is then given to the president, who may sign it or veto (reject) it. The president must be a citizen born in the United States, at least 35 years old, and must have been a resident of the United States for 14 years. Under the 22nd Amendment to the Constitution, adopted in 1951, a president may not be elected more than twice.

The vice president, elected at the same time and on the same ballot as the president, serves as president of the Senate. The vice president assumes the power and duties of the presidency on the president's removal from office or as a result of the president's death, resignation, or inability to perform his duties. Both the president and the vice president can be removed from office after impeachment by the House and conviction at a Senate trial for "treason, bribery, or other high crimes and misdemeanors."

The president nominates and, with the approval of the Senate, appoints ambassadors, consuls, and all federal judges, including the justices of the Supreme Court. As commander in chief, the president is ultimately responsible for the management of the land, naval, and air forces, but the power to declare war belongs to Congress. The president conducts foreign relations and makes treaties with the advice and consent of the Senate. No treaty is binding unless it wins the approval of two-thirds of the Senate. The president's independence is also limited by the House of Representatives, where all money bills originate.

The president also appoints his cabinet, subject to Senate confirmation. The cabinet consists of the secretaries who head the departments of the executive branch. As of 1997, the executive branch included the following cabinet departments: Agriculture, Commerce, Defense, Education, Energy, Health and Human Services, Housing and Urban Development, Interior, Justice, Labor, State, Transportation, Treasury, and Veterans' Affairs.

Each state is divided into counties, municipalities, and special districts such as those for water, education, sanitation, highways, parks, and recreation. There were 3,043 counties in the United States in 1997 and 19,372 municipalities, including cities, villages, towns, and boroughs.

13 POLITICAL PARTIES

Two major parties, Democratic and Republican, have dominated national, state, and local politics since 1860. Minority parties have been formed at various periods in American political history, but none has had any significant national impact. The most successful minority party in recent decades was that of Texas billionaire Ross Perot in 1992. Independent candidates have won state and local office, but no candidate has won the presidency without major party backing.

Traditionally, the Republican Party is more sympathetic to business interests and gets greater support from business than does the Democratic Party. A majority of industrial workers, by contrast, have generally supported the Democratic Party, which favors more lenient labor laws, particularly as they affect labor unions. Republicans promote private business and an increased role for state government, while Democrats generally support greater federal government participation and regulatory authority.

14 STATE AND LOCAL GOVERNMENT

Governmental units within each state comprise counties, municipalities, and such special districts as those for water, sanitation, highways, parks, and recreation. In 1997, there were 3,043 counties in the US; 19,372 municipalities, including cities, villages, towns, and boroughs; 13,726 school districts; and 34,683 special districts. Additional townships, authorities, commissions, and boards make up the rest of the 87,453 local governmental units.

The states are autonomous within their own spheres of government, and their autonomy is defined in broad terms by the 10th Amendment to the US Constitution, which reserves to the states such powers as are not granted to the federal government and not denied to the states. The states may not, among other restrictions, issue paper money, conduct foreign relations, impair the obligations of contracts, or establish a government that is not republican in form. Subsequent amendments to the Constitution and many Supreme Court decisions added to the restrictions placed on the states. The 13th Amendment prohibited the states from legalizing the ownership of one person by another (slavery); the 14th Amendment deprived the states of their power to determine qualifications for citizenship; the 15th Amendment prohibited the states from denying the right to vote because of race, color, or previous condition of servitude; the 16th Amendment gave the federal government the authority to tax personal income; the 17th Amendment allowed for the direct election of Senators; and the 19th Amendment granted women the right to vote. The 18th Amendment (1919), which banned the manufacture, sale, and transportation of liquor, was repealed by the 21st Amendment in 1933.

Each state is headed by an elected governor. State legislatures have two houses except Nebraska's, which has had just one since 1934. Generally, the upper house is called the senate, and the lower house the house of representatives or the assembly. Bills must be passed by both houses, and the governor has a suspensive veto, which usually may be overridden by a two-thirds vote.

The number, population, and geographic extent of the more than 3,000 counties in the US—including the analogous units called boroughs in Alaska and parishes in Louisiana—show no uniformity from state to state. The county is the most conspicuous unit of rural local government and has a variety of powers, including location and repair of highways, county poor relief, determination of voting precincts and of polling places, and organization of school and road districts. City governments, usually headed by a mayor or city manager, have the power to levy taxes; to borrow; to pass, amend, and repeal local ordinances; and to grant franchises for public service corporations. Township government through an annual town meeting is an important New England tradition.

15 JUDICIAL SYSTEM

The Supreme Court, established by the United States Constitution, is the nation's highest judicial body, consisting of the chief justice of the United States and eight associate justices. All justices are appointed for life by the president with the approval of the Senate.

The Supreme Court acts as an appeals court for federal district courts, circuit courts of appeals, and the highest courts in the states. The Supreme Court also exercises the power of judicial review, determining the constitutionality of any state laws, state constitutions, congressional statutes, and federal regulations that are specifically challenged.

The United States Congress establishes all federal courts lower than the Supreme Court. On the lowest level and handling the most federal cases are the district courts, including one each in Puerto Rico, Guam, the Virgin Islands, the Northern Mariana Islands, and the District of Columbia. District courts have no appeals jurisdiction; their decisions may be carried to the courts of appeals, organized into 13 circuits. For most cases, this is usually the last stage of appeal, except where the court rules that a statute of a state conflicts with the Constitution of the United States, with federal law, or with a treaty. Special federal courts include the Court of Claims, Court of Customs and Patent Appeals, and Tax Court.

State courts operate independently of the federal judiciary. Most states have a court system that begins on the lowest level with a justice of the peace and includes courts of general trial jurisdiction and appeals courts. At the highest level of the system is a state supreme court. The court of trial jurisdiction (sometimes called the county or superior court) has both original and appeals jurisdiction; all criminal cases and some civil cases are tried in this court. The state supreme court interprets the constitution and the laws of the state.

16 MIGRATION

Between 1840 and 1930, some 37 million immigrants, most of them Europeans, arrived in the United States. In 1924 a quota system was established that favored immigrants from northern and western Europe. The quota system was radically reformed in 1965 and abandoned in 1978, when all specific limits by nationality were replaced by a simple total limit of 290,000. A major 1990 overhaul of immigration laws raised the annual ceiling to 700,000 (675,000 in 1995).

Between 1990 and 1997, international migration increased the country's population by an estimated 5.63 million. In 1997 alone, about 827,000 immigrants entered the United States. In 1994, some 36.4% came from Asia, 39.8% from the Americas, 20% from Europe, 3.3% from Africa, and 0.5% from Pacific Island nations. The changes in immigration law have resulted in a sharp rise in the number of Asian immigrants (primarily Chinese, Filipinos, Indians, Japanese, and Koreans).

Between 1975 and 1978, following the defeat of the American-backed Saigon government in South Vietnam, several hundred thousand Vietnamese refugees came to the United States. Under the Refugee Act of 1980, a limit to the number of refugees allowed to enter the United States is set annually. In 1995, 99,490 refugees were admitted into the United States.

In November 1986, Congress passed a bill allowing illegal aliens who had lived and worked in the United States since 1982 the opportunity to become permanent residents. By the end of fiscal year 1992, 2,650,000 persons had become permanent residents under this bill. In 1996 the number of illegal alien residents was estimated at 5 million, of whom 2 million were believed to be in California.

The major migratory trends within the United States in the twentieth century have been an exodus of southern blacks to the cities of the north and midwest, especially after World War I (1914–18); a shift of whites from central cities to surrounding suburbs since World War II (after 1945); and, also during the post–World War II period, a massive shift from the north and east to the south and southwest.

17 ECONOMY

The United States probably has a greater variety and quantity of natural resources than any other single nation. However, because of its vast economic growth, the United States depends increasingly on foreign sources for a long list of raw materials. American dependence on oil imports was dramatically demonstrated during the 1973 Arab oil embargo, when serious fuel shortages developed in many sections of the country.

Industrial activity within the United States has been expanding southward and westward for much of the twentieth century, most rapidly since World War II. Louisiana, Oklahoma, and especially Texas are centers of industries based on petroleum refining; aerospace and other high technology industries are the basis of the new wealth of Texas and California, the nation's leading manufacturing state. The industrial heartland of the United States consists of Ohio, Indiana, Illinois, Michigan, and Wisconsin, with steelmaking and automobile manufacturing among the leading industries. The Middle Atlantic states (New Jersey, New York, and Pennsylvania) and the Northeast are also highly industrialized.

Foreign Trade

The United States led the world in value of exports and imports in 1995. Exports of domestic merchandise, raw materials, agricultural and industrial products, and military goods amounted in 1995 to $584.7 billion. General imports were valued at over $771 billion, leaving a trade deficit of over $100 billion. A rapidly growing export category was computers, which rose from $1.2 billion in 1970 to $33.5 billion in 1995.

Principal purchasers of United States exports in 1995 were Canada, Japan, Mexico, the United Kingdom, South Korea, Germany, Taiwan, the Netherlands, and Singapore. Principal suppliers of imports to the United States were Canada, Japan, Mexico, China, Germany, Taiwan, the United Kingdom, and South Korea.

18 INCOME

The median household income in 1995 was $34,076, and the average annual pay was $28,940 per worker. Some 13.5% of all Americans lived below the United States federal poverty level in 1996–97, far below the 1959 level of 22.4%. By race, 28% of blacks in the United States were below the federal poverty level, comprising 28% of the total number of impoverished United States citizens. Some 11% of whites lived in poverty, accounting for 66% of all Americans living in poverty.

19 INDUSTRY

Although the United States remains one of the world's top industrial powers, manufacturing no longer plays as dominant a role in the economy as it once did. Between 1979 and 1995, manufacturing employment fell from 21.8% to 14.8% of national employment. In 1996, industry accounted for about 23% of the domestic economy. The Midwest leads all other regions in heavy industry, including the manufacturing of automobiles, trucks, and other vehicles.

Leading manufacturing industries of durable goods include non-electrical machinery, electric and electronic equipment, motor vehicles and equipment, and other transportation equipment. The principal manufacturing industries of nondurable goods are chemicals and allied products, food, printing and publishing, and petroleum and coal products. Large corporations are dominant especially in areas such as steel, automobiles, pharmaceuticals, aircraft, petroleum refining, computers, soaps and detergents, tires, and communications equipment. In 1996, the 500 largest American corporations, as ranked by *Fortune* magazine, had over $5.1 trillion in sales and $301 billion in profits.

Advances in chemistry and electronics have revolutionized many industries through new products and methods.

Industries that have been best able to make use of new technology have done well, and the economies of some states—in particular California and Massachusetts—are largely based on it. On the other hand, certain industries—especially clothing and steelmaking—have suffered from outmoded facilities that force the price of their products above the world market level.

The United States is typically the world's second- or third-leading steel producer, but also the world's second-largest steel importer. Automobile manufacturing was another industry suffering in the 1980s: passenger car production fell from 7.1 million in 1987 to 5.4 million in 1991, but rose to 8.3 million by 1999.

20 LABOR

The country's civilian and military labor force in 1999 numbered about 139 million persons. During 1992, a recession year, the unemployment rate reached 7.4%; in 1997 it was 4.9%. As of 1997, services employed 46.07 million people; retail trade, 21.07 million; manufacturing, 20.59 million; finance, insurance and real estate, 8 million; wholesale trade, 4.82 million; transportation and public utilities, 8.72 million; construction, 7.79 million; and agriculture 3.04 million. As of 1995, federal, state, and local governments employed 19.52 million persons.

Earnings of workers vary considerably with type of work and section of country. The national average wage was $13.24 per hour for non-agricultural workers in 1999. There were 39 national labor unions with over 100,000 members, the largest being the National Educational Association with 2 million members, as of 2000. In 1995, 14.9% of the work force belonged to labor unions, down from 20.1% in 1983. The most important federation of organized workers in the United States is the American Federation of Labor–Congress of Industrial Organizations (AFL–CIO), whose affiliated unions had 13 million members in 1995. In the mid-1990s, 19 states had right-to-work laws, forbidding forced union membership as a condition of employment.

21 AGRICULTURE

In 1998, the United States produced a huge share of the world's agricultural commodities, including soybeans, 47%; corn for grain (maize), 41%; cotton, 16%; wheat, 12%; and tobacco, 10%.

About 19% of the total United States land area is used for crops; another 25% is grassland pasture. The total amount of farmland declined from 1.18 billion acres (479 million hectares) in 1959 to 954 million acres (386 million hectares) in 1998. The farm population, which comprised 35% of the total United States population in 1910, declined to 25% during the Great Depression of the 1930s and dwindled to less than 2% by 1998.

Substantial quantities of corn, the most valuable crop produced in the United States, are grown in almost every state. Its yield and price are important factors in the economies of the regions where it is grown.

Photo credit: Candace Cochrane, State of New Hampshire Tourism.

Maple sugaring is a popular activity as the sap begins to run in New Hampshire.

22 DOMESTICATED ANIMALS

The livestock population in 1998 included an estimated 98.5 million head of cattle (approximately 9% were milk cows), 62.2 million hogs, 7.2 million sheep and lambs, 1.77 billion chickens, and 95 million turkeys. The value of cattle production in 1995 was $24.82 billion; hog production, $5.28 billion; and sheep and lambs, $412 million.

Milk production totaled 70.6 million metric tons in 1995. United States butter production totaled 1.26 billion metric tons in 1995; in that year, the United States was the world's largest producer of cheese,

with more than 3.15 million metric tons (28% of the world's total).

23 FISHING

The United States, which ranked fifth in the world in volume of its commercial fishing catch in 1994, nevertheless imports far more fish and fishery products than it exports. The 1997 commercial catch was 5.5 million tons. Fish for food make up 78% of the catch, and nonfood fish (processed for fertilizer and oil), 22%. Alaska accounted for 48% of 1997 commercial fish caught.

Alaska pollock is the most important species in terms of quantity, followed by salmon, crab, flounder, cod, and shrimp. Per person finfish and shellfish consumption (edible meat basis) is 6.7 kilograms (14.8 pounds).

24 FORESTRY

United States forest and woodlands covered about 212.5 million hectares (525 million acres) in 1995, or 23% of land area. Major forest regions include the eastern, central hardwood, southern, Rocky Mountain, and Pacific coast areas. The National Forest System accounts for approximately 19% of the nation's forestland. There are large tracts of forested land owned by private lumber companies in Alabama, Arkansas, Florida, Georgia, Maine, Oregon, and Washington.

Domestic production of roundwood during 1997 amounted to 490.7 million cubic meters, of which softwoods accounted for roughly 60%. The United States, the world's second-leading producer of newsprint, produced 7 million metric tons in 1995. Other forest products in 1995 included 66 million metric tons of pulp for paper, 58.9 million metric tons of wood pulp, 17.1 million cubic meters (604 million cubic feet) of plywood, and 15.4 million cubic meters (544 million cubic feet) of particleboard. Rising petroleum prices in the late 1970s caused an increase in the use of wood as home heating fuel, especially in the Northeast. Fuelwood production amounted to 14.8 million cubic meters (523 million cubic feet) in 1995.

25 MINING

Rich in a variety of mineral resources, the United States is a world leader in the production of many important mineral commodities such as aluminum, cement, copper, pig iron, lead, molybdenum, phosphates, potash, salt, sulfur, uranium, and zinc. The leading mineral-producing states are: Texas, Louisiana, Oklahoma, and New Mexico, which are important for petroleum and natural gas; and Kentucky, West Virginia, and Pennsylvania, important for coal. Iron ore supports the nation's most basic nonagricultural industry, iron and steel manufacture.

The United States typically mines more salt, phosphate, and elemental sulfur than any other country; it is also usually second in lead, gold, and silver. The United States is also a world leader in mining uranium, nitrogen in ammonia, potash, and iron ore.

26 ENERGY AND POWER

The United States, with about 4.6% of the world's population, consumed 24.3% and produced 19.1% of the world's energy in 1995. The United States produced 14% of the world's coal in 1995, 25% of its natural gas, and 10% of its crude oil. Coal supplied about 23.9% of primary energy in 1995; nuclear sources, 8.8%; natural gas, 27%; waterpower, 1.2%; petroleum, 39%; and geothermal, wood, waste, wind, photovoltaic, and solar thermal energy, 0.1%.

In 1999 proved recoverable reserves of crude oil totaled an estimated 22.5 billion barrels; reserves of natural gas were about 167 trillion cubic feet (4.7 trillion cubic meters) in 1996; and recoverable coal reserves amounted to 275.1 billion tons (44% anthracite and bituminous) at the end of 1998. Mineral fuel production in 1995 included an estimated 636.1 million tons of hard coal (second after China) and 393.5 million tons of lignite (first); 18.9 trillion cubic feet (538.5 billion cubic meters) of natural gas (second after Russia); and 382.5 million tons of crude oil (second after Saudi Arabia).

In 1998, public utilities and private industrial plants generated 3.62 trillion kilowatt hours of electricity. That year, coal-fired generation produced 50.9% of the electricity generated, and natural gas, 14.8%. Because of cost and safety concerns, the growth of the nuclear power industry in the United States slowed in the late 1980s.

27 COMMERCE

Retail sales in the US exceeded $2.99 trillion in 1999, with California, Texas, Florida, and New York, leading in volume. The growth of great chains of retail stores, particularly in the form of the supermarket, was one of the most conspicuous developments in retail trade following the end of World War II. Nearly 100,000 single-unit grocery stores went out of business between 1948 and 1958; the independent grocer's share of the food market dropped from 50% to 30% of the total in the same period.

Multiunit chain stores account for over one-third of the total retail trade, but in certain kinds of retail business (variety and department store trade) the chain is the dominant mode of business organization. The leading retail chains in 1996 were Wal-Mart, Sears, and Dayton Hudson (owner of the Target chain). With the great suburban expansion of the 1960s emerged the planned shopping center, usually designed by a single development organization and intended to provide different kinds of stores in order to meet all the shopping needs of the particular area.

Installment credit is a major support for consumer purchases in the US. Most US families own and use credit cards. Credit cards accounted for 36% of consumer debt in 1996.

The US advertising industry is the world's most highly developed. Particularly with the expansion of television audiences, spending for advertising has increased almost annually to successive record levels.

28 PUBLIC FINANCE

Under the Budget and Accounting Act of 1921, the president is responsible for preparing the federal government budget. In fact, the budget is prepared by the Office of Management and Budget (established in 1970), based on requests from the heads of all federal departments and agencies and advice from the Board of Governors of the Federal Reserve System, the Council of Economic Advisers, and the Treasury Department. The president submits a budget message to Congress in January.

The public debt, subject to a statutory debt limit, rose from $43 billion in 1940 to more than $3.3 trillion in 1993. In fiscal year 1991/92, the federal deficit reached $290 million, a record high. President Clinton introduced a taxing and spending plan to reduce the rate of growth of the federal deficit when he began his term in 1993. Sustained economic growth and restraint on public spending in the mid-1990s enabled the government to reduce its deficit so that by 1997/98 the federal budget had its first surplus since 1969.

29 TAXATION

Measured as a proportion of the GDP, the total US tax burden is less than that in most industrialized countries. Federal, state, and local taxes are levied in a variety of forms. The greatest source of revenue for the federal government is the personal income tax, which is paid by citizens and resident aliens on their worldwide income. Most states and many local governments also impose taxes on personal income.

Other federal taxes are imposed on the sale of certain motor vehicles, personal air transportation, some motor fuels, alcoholic beverages, tobacco products, tires, telephone charges, and gifts and estates.

30 HEALTH

The United States health care system is among the most advanced in the world. In 1995, health expenditures reached $988.4 billion, equivalent to 14% of gross domestic product (GDP). Medical facilities in the United States included 6,097 hospitals in 1997, with 1.03 million beds. In 1996, there was 1 doctor for about every 268 people in the United States. During 1994, the United States Census Bureau estimated that 15.2% of the population was without any form of health insurance.

Life expectancy in 1998 was a record high 76.8 years. Males could expect to live 73.5 years, females 80.2 years. By race and gender, white females had the highest average expected lifespan, with 79.7 years; next came black females, 74.2; white males, 73.9; and black males, 66.1.

Leading causes of death (with percent of total deaths) in 1996 were: heart disease (31.7%); cancer (23.3%); cerebrovascular diseases (6.9%); chronic obstructive pulmonary diseases (4.6%); accidents and adverse effects (4.1%); pneumonia and influenza (3.6%); diabetes mellitus (2.7%); human immunodeficiency virus (HIV) infection (1.3%); suicide (1.3%); and chronic liver disease and cirrhosis (1.1%).

Other leading causes of death in 1996 included nephritis, septicemia, Alzheimer's disease, homicide and legal intervention, and arteriosclerosis. About 20% of all deaths in the United States are attributed to cigarette smoking. First identified in 1981, HIV infection and AIDS (acquired immune deficiency syndrome) have spread rapidly; by 1995, over 573,000 AIDS cases had been reported in the United States.

31 HOUSING

The housing resources of the United States far exceed those of any other country, with 102.3 million housing units as of 1990, 91.9 million of which were occupied. Construction of housing following World War II (1939–45) set a record-breaking pace; 1986 was the 38th successive year during which construction of more than one million housing units was begun. After 1986, housing starts dropped for five years in succession, hitting 946,000 in 1991 and then climbing back to 1.43 million by 1996. Most dwellings are one-family houses. Half of all the housing structures in the country were built before 1965. Perhaps the most significant change in the housing scene has been the shift to the suburbs made possible by the widespread ownership of automobiles.

32 EDUCATION

The literacy rate is estimated to be 98% (males, 97% and females, 98%). Education is compulsory in all states and a responsibility of each state and local government. Generally, formal schooling begins at the age of 6 and continues up to age 17. Spending on education accounts for one-third of all expenditures by state and local governments.

Elementary schooling is from grade 1 to grade 8. High schools cover grades 9 through 12. Colleges include junior or community colleges, offering two-year associate degrees; regular four-year colleges and universities; and graduate or professional schools.

In 1996, public elementary and middle schools had 45.8 million students, while private schools had 8.9 million. High schools had 14.4 million students. In the same year, colleges had 14.4 million students, with 11.3 million in public and 3.1 million in private colleges. In 1995, there were 3,688 two-year and four-year colleges and universities.

33 ARTS

The nation's arts centers are emblems of the importance of the performing arts in US life. New York City's Lincoln Center for the Performing Arts, whose first concert hall opened in 1962, is now the site of the Metropolitan Opera House, three halls for concerts and other musical performances, two theaters, the New York Public Library's Library and Museum of the Performing Arts, and The Juilliard School. The John F. Kennedy Center for the Performing Arts in Washington, D.C., opened in 1971; it comprises two main theaters, two smaller theaters, an opera house and a concert hall.

The New York Philharmonic, founded in 1842, and conducted by Kurt Masur in 2000, is the nation's oldest professional musical ensemble. Other leading orchestras include those of Boston (conducted by Seiji Ozawa), Chicago (Daniel Barenboim), Cleveland (Christoph von Dohnanyi), Los Angeles (Esa-Pekka Salonen), Philadelphia (Wolfgang Sawallisch), Pittsburgh (Mariss Jansons), and Washington, D.C. (the National Symphony, led by Leonard Slatkin). Particularly renowned for artistic excellence are the Lyric Opera of Chicago, San Francisco Opera, Opera Company of Boston, Santa Fe Opera, New York City Opera, and Metropolitan Opera.

The recording industry is an integral part of the music world. The US accounts for fully one-third of the global total of $40 billion in sales. Popular music (mostly rock), performed in halls and arenas in every major city and on college campuses throughout the US, dominates record sales. In 2000, the Internet website Napster challenged the recording industry's copyright privileges by offering free downloads of popular music.

Though still financially insecure, dance still has a wide following. The American Ballet Theater, founded in 1940, is the nation's oldest dance company still active today; the New York City Ballet is equally acclaimed. Other important companies include those of Martha Graham, Merce Cunningham, Alvin Ailey, Paul Taylor, and Twyla Tharp, as well as the Feld Ballet, Joffrey Ballet, and Pilobolus.

Drama remains a principal performing art, not only in New York City's renowned theater district but also in regional, university, summer, and dinner theaters throughout the US. Television and the motion picture industry have made film the dominant modern medium. The motion picture industry had receipts of $7.5 billion in 1999.

34 LIBRARIES AND MUSEUMS

Of the 32,852 libraries in the US in 2000, 9,837 were public, with 6,376 branches; 4,723 were academic; 1,874 were government; 1,906 were medical; and over 8,000 were religious, military, legal, and specialized independent collections.

The foremost library in the country is the Library of Congress, with holdings of more than 80 million items (including more than 26 million books and pamphlets) in 2000. Other great libraries are the public libraries in New York, Philadelphia, Boston, and Baltimore, and the John Crerar and Newberry libraries in Chicago. Noted special collections are those of the Pierpont Morgan Library in New York; the Huntington Library in San Marino, Calif.; the Folger Shakespeare Library in Washington, D.C.; the Hoover Library at Stanford University; and the rare book divisions of Harvard, Yale, Indiana, Texas, and Virginia universities. Among the leading university libraries, as judged by the extent of their holdings in 1993, are those of Harvard, Yale, Illinois (Urbana-Champaign), Michigan (Ann Arbor), California (Berkeley), Columbia, Stanford, Cornell, California (Los Angeles), Chicago, Wisconsin (Madison), and Washington (Seattle)—each having more than 4 million bound volumes.

There are about 5,000 nonprofit museums in the US. The most numerous type is the historic building, followed in descending order by college and university museums, museums of science, public museums of history, and public museums of art. Eminent US museums include the American Museum of Natural History, the Metropolitan Museum of Art, and the Museum of Modern Art, all in New York City; the National Gallery of Art and the Smithsonian Institution in Washington, D.C.; the Boston Museum of Fine Arts; the Art Institute of Chicago and the Chicago Museum of Natural History; the Franklin Institute and Philadelphia Museum of Art, both in Philadelphia; and the M. H. de Young Memorial Museum in San Francisco.

35 COMMUNICATIONS

All major electric communications systems are privately owned but regulated by the Federal Communications Commission. The US uses wire and radio services for communications more extensively than any other country in the world. In 1997, 93.9% of all US households had telephone service.

Radio serves a variety of purposes other than broadcasting. It is widely used by ships and aircraft for safety; it has become an important tool in the movement of buses, trucks, and taxicabs. Forest conservators, fire departments, and the police operate with radio as a necessary aid; it is used in logging operations, surveying, construction work, and dispatching of repair crews. In 1999, broadcasting stations on the air comprised over 10,000 radio stations and more than 1,500 television stations. Over 98% of all US households own at least one TV set. The cable television industry, with 9,000 cable systems in 1997, served 60.5 million subscribers.

The Post Office Department of the US was replaced on 1 July 1971 by the US Postal Service (USPS), a financially autonomous federal agency. In 1995, the USPS handled 180.7 billion pieces of mail. Since the 1970s, numerous privately owned overnight mail and package delivery services have been established.

36 PRESS

In 1995 there were 1,586 daily newspapers in the US, with a combined circulation of over 60 million. Circulation has hovered around the 60 million mark since the early 1980s. Twenty large newspaper chains account for nearly 60% of the total daily circulation. The US book-publishing industry consists of the major book companies (mainly in the New York metro area), nonprofit university presses distributed throughout the US, and numerous small publishing firms. In 1994, 51,863 book titles were published in the US. Among computer users, the Internet rapidly gained popularity in the mid-1990s; in 1998, there were over 976 Internet hosts for every 1,000 population, as well as some 85 million personal computers.

37 TOURISM AND RECREATION

Foreign visitors to the United States numbered approximately 46.3 million in 1998. Of these visitors, 33% came from Canada, 25% from Mexico, 19% from Europe, and 14% from Eastern Asia and the Pacific. In 1997, travelers to the United States from all foreign countries spent $73.3 billion. With a few exceptions, such as Canadians entering from the Western Hemisphere, all visitors to the United States are required to have passports and visas.

The United States had a total of 48.1 million acres (19.5 million hectares) of national parks as of 1994. Among the most striking scenic attractions in the United States are the Grand Canyon in Arizona; Carlsbad Caverns in New Mexico; Yosemite National Park in California; Yellows tone National Park in Idaho, Montana, and Wyoming; Niagara Falls, partly in New York; and the Everglades in Florida.

Historical attractions include the Liberty Bell and Constitution Hall in Philadelphia; the Statue of Liberty in New York City; the White House, the Capitol, and the monuments to Washington, Jefferson, and Lincoln in Washington, D.C.; the Williamsburg historical restoration in Virginia; the Alamo in San Antonio, Texas; and Mount Rushmore in South Dakota.

Among many other popular tourist attractions are the movie and television studios in Los Angeles; the cable cars in San Francisco; casino gambling in Las Vegas, Nevada, and in Atlantic City, New Jersey; the Grand Ole Opry in Nashville, Tennessee; the many jazz clubs of New Orleans; and such amusement parks as Disneyland (Anaheim, California) and Walt Disney World (near Orlando, Florida). For amount and variety of entertainment—theater, movies, music, dance, and sports—New York City has few rivals.

Photo credit: The Wagner Perspective.

Bullriding at The Cheyenne Frontier Days rodeo in Wyoming, the largest professional outdoor rodeo in the world.

Americans' recreational activities range from the major spectator sports—professional baseball, football, basketball, ice hockey, soccer, horse racing, and college football and basketball—to home gardening. Participant sports are a favorite form of recreation, including jogging, tennis, and golf. Skiing is a popular recreation in New England and the western mountain ranges. Sailing, power boating, and rafting are popular water sports. In 1994, the United States hosted the World Cup Soccer Championship. A number of Winter and Summer Olympics have been held in the United States in the past, most recently the 1996 Summer Olympics, held in Atlanta, Georgia.

38 SPORTS

Baseball, long honored as the national pastime, is the nation's leading professional team sport, with two major leagues having 30 teams (2 in Canada); in the 1998 season, over 63 million attended major league games. In 1992, the Toronto Blue Jays became the first non-US team to win the World Series. In addition, there is an extensive network of minor league baseball teams, each of them related to a major league franchise. The National Basketball Association, created in 1946, include 29 teams, which drew nearly 21.8 million fans during the 1995/96 season. In 2000, the 19 teams of the Women's National Basketball Association played to almost 2 million fans. In 2000, millions of Americans attended regular season games of the National football League's 31 teams. Attendance at National Hockey League (NHL) games exceeded 15.7 million in 1997. Of the 30 NHL teams, 6 are Canadian, as are most of the players. The North American Soccer League (NASL), popular in the late 1970s, discontinued outdoor play in 1985. The Major Indoor Soccer League played from 1978 until 1992, and the National Professional Soccer League (also indoor) has played since 1983. Professional outdoor soccer returned to the United States in 1996, after a successful World Cup soccer Tour in the US in 1994. Major League Soccer had 12 teams in 3 divisions in 2000. Radio and television contracts are integral to the popular and financial success of all professional team sports. In 1994, a strike by baseball players caused the World Series to be canceled for the first time since 1904; hockey players also held a strike in 1992 and were locked out by owners in 1994; a dispute between owners and players in 1998 shortened the basketball season.

Several other professional sports are popular nationwide. Horse racing is among the nation's most popular spectator sports—in 1996, thoroughbred racing lured some 34.6 million Americans to the track. Annual highlights of thoroughbred racing are the three jewels of the Triple Crown—Kentucky Derby, Preakness, and Belmont Stakes. In 1993, nearly $9.4 billion was legally wagered on thoroughbred horse racing. Harness racing is also popular; in 1996, attendance was over 8.9 million and involved over $1.5 billion in wagering. Attendance at greyhound race-tracks in 15 states exceeded 9.3 million in 1996; legal wagering on greyhound racing totaled $1.5 billion. The prize money that Henry Ford won on a 1901 auto race helped him start his now-famous car company two years later; since then, automobile manufacturers have backed sports car, stock car, and motorcycle racing at tracks throughout the US. From John L. Sullivan to Muhammad Ali, the personality and power of the great boxing champions have drawn millions of spectators to ringside. Glamour and top prizes also draw national followings for tennis and golf, two professional sports in which women are nationally prominent. Other professional sports include bowling and rodeo.

Football has been part of US college life since the game was born on 6 November 1869 with a New Jersey match between Rutgers and Princeton. The National Collegiate Athletic Association (NCAA) and National Association of Intercollegiate Athletics (NAIA) coordinate collegiate football and basketball. Colleges recruit top athletes with sports scholarships in order to win media attention, and to keep the loyalty of the alumni, thereby boosting fund-raising. Baseball, hockey, swimming, gymnastics, crew (rowing), lacrosse, track and field, and a variety of other sports also fill the intercollegiate competitive program.

The Amateur Athletic Union (AAU), a national nonprofit organization founded in 1888, conducts the AAU/USA Junior Olympics, offering competition in 22 sports in order to help identify candidates for international Olympic competition. St. Louis hosted the 1904 summer Olympics; Los Angeles was home to the games in 1932 and 1984; Atlanta was host in 1996. The winter Olympic games were held in Squaw Valley, Calif., in 1960, and at Lake Placid, N.Y., in 1932 and 1980, and will be held in Salt Lake City in 2002.

39 FAMOUS AMERICANS

Political and Military Figures

Printer, inventor, scientist, and statesman, Benjamin Franklin (1706–90) was America's outstanding figure of the colonial period. George Washington (1732–99), military leader in the American Revolution and first president of the United States, is known as the father of his country. Chief author of the Declaration of Independence and third president was Thomas Jefferson (1743–1826). His lead-

UNITED STATES OF AMERICA

Presidents of the US, 1789–2001

	NAME (BIRTH–DEATH)	OTHER MAJOR OFFICES HELD	RESIDENCE AT ELECTION	PARTY
1	George Washington 22 February 1732–14 December 1799	Commander in Chief, Continental Army (1775–83)	Mt. Vernon, Va.	Federalist
2	John Adams 30 October 1735–4 July 1826	Representative, Continental Congress (1774–77); US vice president (1797–97)	Quincy, Mass.	Federalist
3	Thomas Jefferson 13 April 1743–4 July 1826	Representative, Continental Congress (1775–76); governor of Virginia (1779–81); secretary of state (1790–93); US vice president (1797–1801)	Monticello, Va.	Dem.–Rep.
4	James Madison 16 March 1751–28 June 1836	Representative, Continental Congress (1780–83; 1786–88); US representative (1789–97); secretary of state (1801–9)	Montpelier, Va.	Dem.–Rep.
5	James Monroe 28 April 1758–4 July 1831	US senator (1790–94); governor of Virginia (1799–1802); secretary of state (1811–17); secretary of war (1814–15)	Leesburg, Va.	Dem.–Rep.
6	John Quincy Adams 11 July 1767–23 February 1848	US senator (1803–8); secretary of state (1817–25); US representative (1831–48)	Quincy, Mass.	National Republican
7	Andrew Jackson 15 March 1767–8 June 1845	US representative (1796–97); US senator (1797–98)	The Hermitage, Tenn.	Democrat
8	Martin Van Buren 5 December 1782–24 July 1862	US senator (1821–28); governor of New York (1829); secretary of state (1829–31); US vice president (1833–37)	New York	Democrat
9	William Henry Harrison 9 February 1773–4 April 1841	Governor of Indiana Territory (1801–13); US representative (1816–19); US senator (1825–28)	North Bend, Ohio	Whig
10	John Tyler 29 March 1790–18 January 1862	US representative (1816–21); governor of Virginia (1825–27); US senator (1827–36); US vice president (1841)	Richmond, Va.	Whig
11	James K. Polk 2 November 1795–15 June 1849	US representative (1825–39); governor of Tennessee (1839–41)	Nashville, Tenn.	Democrat
12	Zachary Taylor 24 November 1784–9 July 1850	—	Louisiana	Whig
13	Millard Fillmore 7 January 1800–8 March 1874	US representative (1833–35; 1837–43); US vice president (1849–50)	Buffalo, N.Y.	Whig
14	Franklin Pierce 23 November 1804–8 October 1869	US representative, (1833–37); US senator (1837–43)	Concord, N.H.	Democrat
15	James Buchanan 23 April 1791–1 June 1868	US representative (1821–31); US senator (1834–45); secretary of state (1845–49)	Lancaster, Pa.	Democrat
16	Abraham Lincoln 12 February 1809–15 April 1865	US representative (1847–49)	Springfield, Ill.	Republican

TERMS IN OFFICE[1]	VICE PRESIDENTS	NOTABLE EVENTS	
30 April 1789–4 March 1793	John Adams	Federal government organized; Bill of Rights enacted (1791); Whiskey Rebellion suppressed (1794); North Carolina, Rhode Island, Vermont, Kentucky, Tennessee enter Union.	1
4 March 1797–4 March 1801	Thomas Jefferson	Alien and Sedition Acts passed (1798); Washington, D.C., becomes US capital (1800)	2
4 March 1801–4 March 1805	Aaron Burr George Clinton	Louisiana Purchase (1803); Lewis and Clark Expedition (1803–6); Ohio enters Union.	3
4 March 1809–4 March 1813 4 March 1813–4 March 1817	George Clinton Elbridge Gerry	War of 1812 (1812–14); protective tariffs passed (1816); Louisiana, Indiana enter Union.	4
4 March 1817–4 March 1821 4 March 1821–4 March 1825	Daniel D. Tompkins Daniel D. Tompkins	Florida purchased from Spain (1819–21); Missouri Compromise (1820); Monroe Doctrine (1823); Mississippi, Illinois, Alabama, Maine, Missouri enter Union.	5
4 March 1825–4 March 1829	John C. Calhoun	Period of political antagonisms, producing little legislation; road and canal construction supported; Erie Canal opens (1825).	6
4 March 1829–4 March 1833	John C. Calhoun Martin Van Buren	Introduction of spoils system; Texas Republic established (1836); Arkansas, Michigan enter Union.	7
4 March 1837–4 March 1841	Richard M. Johnson	Financial panic (1837) and subsequent depression.	8
4 March 1841–4 April 1841	John Tyler	Died of pneumonia one month after taking office.	9
4 April 1841–4 March 1845	—	Monroe Doctrine extended to Hawaiian Islands (1842); Second Seminole War in Florida ends (1842).	10
4 March 1845–4 March 1849	George M. Dallas	Boundary between US and Canada set at 49th parallel (1846); Mexican War (1846–48), ending with Treaty of Guadalupe Hidalgo (1848); California gold rush begins (1848); Florida, Texas, Iowa, Wisconsin enter Union.	11
4 March 1849–9 July 1850	Millard Fillmore	Died after 16 months in office.	12
9 July 1850–4 March 1853	—	Fugitive Slave Law (1850); California enters Union.	13
4 March 1853–4 March 1857	William R. King	Gadsden Purchase (1853); Kansas–Nebraska Act (1854); trade opened with Japan (1854).	14
4 March 1857–4 March 1861	John C. Breckinridge	John Brown's raid at Harpers Ferry, Va. (now W. Va.; 1859); South Carolina secedes (1860); Minnesota, Oregon, Kansas enter Union.	15
4 March 1861–4 March 1865 4 March 1865–15 April 1865	Hannibal Hamlin Andrew Johnson	Confederacy established, Civil War begins (1851); Emancipation Proclamation (1863); Confederacy defeated (1865); Lincoln assassinated (1865); West Virginia, Nevada attain statehood.	16

Presidents of the US, 1789–2001 (Continued)

	NAME (BIRTH–DEATH)	OTHER MAJOR OFFICES HELD	RESIDENCE AT ELECTION	PARTY
17	Andrew Johnson 29 December 1808–31 July 1875	US representative (1843–53); governor of Tennessee (1853–57; 1862–65); US senator (1857–62); US vice president (1865)	Greeneville, Tenn.	Republican
18	Ulysses S. Grant 27 April 1822–23 July 1885	Commander, Union Army (1864–65); secretary of war (1867–68)	Galena, Ill.	Republican
19	Rutherford B. Hayes 4 October 1822–17 January 1893	US representative (1865–67); governor of Ohio (1868–72; 1876–77)	Fremont, Ohio	Republican
20	James A. Garfield 19 November 1831–19 September 1881	US representative (1863–80)	Mentor, Ohio	Republican
21	Chester A. Arthur 5 October 1829–18 November 1886	US vice president (1881)	New York, N.Y.	Republican
22	Grover Cleveland 18 March 1837–24 June 1908	Governor of New York (1882–84)	Albany, N.Y.	Democrat
23	Benjamin Harrison 20 August 1833–13 March 1901	US senator (1881–87)	Indianapolis, Ind.	Republican
24	Grover Cleveland 18 March 1837–24 June 1908	Governor of New York (1882–84)	New York, N.Y.	Democrat
25	William McKinley 29 January 1843–14 September 1901	US representative (1877–83; 1885–91); governor of Ohio (1892–96)	Canton, Ohio	Republican
26	Theodore Roosevelt 27 October 1858–6 January 1919	Governor of New York (1899–1900); US vice president (1901)	Oyster Bay, N.Y.	Republican
27	William H. Taft 15 September 1857–8 March 1930	Governor of Philippines (1901–4); secretary of war (1904–8); chief justice of the US (1921–30)	Washington, D.C.	Republican
28	Woodrow Wilson 28 December 1856–3 February 1924	Governor of New Jersey (1911–13)	Trenton, N.J.	Democrat
29	Warren G. Harding 2 November 1865–2 August 1923	US senator (1915–21)	Marion, Ohio	Republican
30	Calvin Coolidge 4 July 1872–5 January 1933	Governor of Massachusetts (1919–20); US vice president (1921–23)	Boston, Mass.	Republican
31	Herbert Hoover 10 August 1874–20 October 1964	Secretary of commerce (1921–29)	Stanford, Calif.	Republican
32	Franklin D. Roosevelt 30 January 1882–12 April 1945	Governor of New York (1929–1933)	Hyde Park, N.Y.	Democrat

TERMS IN OFFICE[1]	VICE PRESIDENTS	NOTABLE EVENTS	
15 April 1865–4 March 1869	—	Reconstruction Acts (1867); Alaska purchased from Russia (1867); Johnson impeached but acquitted (1868); Nebraska enters Union.	17
4 March 1869–4 March 1873 4 March 1873–4 March 1877	Schuyler Colfax Henry Wilson	Numerous government scandals; financial panic (1873); Colorado enters Union.	18
4 March 1877–4 March 1881	William A. Wheeler	Federal troops withdrawn from South (1877); civil service reform begun.	19
4 March 1881–19 Sept. 1881	Chester A. Arthur	Shot after 4 months in office, dead 2½ months later.	20
19 Sept. 1881–4 March 1885	—	Chinese immigration banned despite presidential veto (1882); Civil Service Commission established by Pendleton Act (1883).	21
4 March 1885–4 March 1889	Thomas A. Hendricks	Interstate Commerce Act (1887)	22
4 March 1889–4 March 1893	Levi P. Morton	Sherman Silver Purchase Act (1890); North Dakota, South Dakota, Montana, Washington, Idaho, Wyoming enter Union.	23
4 March 1893–4 March 1897	Adlai E. Stevenson	Financial panic (1893); Sherman Silver Purchase Act repealed (1893); Utah enters Union.	24
4 March 1897–4 March 1901	Garret A. Hobart Theodore Roosevelt	Spanish–American War (1898); Puerto Rico, Guam, Philippines ceded by Spain; independent Republic of Hawaii annexed; US troops sent to China to suppress Boxer Rebellion (1900); McKinley assassinated.	25
14 Sept. 1901–4 March 1905 4 March 1905–4 March 1909	Charles W. Fairbanks	Antitrust and conservation policies emphasized; Roosevelt awarded Nobel Peace Prize (1906) for mediating settlement of Russo–Japanese War; Panama Canal construction begun (1907); Oklahoma enters Union.	26
4 March 1909–4 March 1913	James S. Sherman	Federal income tax ratified (1913); New Mexico, Arizona enter Union.	27
4 March 1913–4 March 1917 4 March 1917–4 March 1921	Thomas R. Marshall Thomas R. Marshall	Clayton Antitrust Act (1914); US Virgin Islands purchased from Denmark (1917); US enters World War I (1917); Treaty of Versailles signed (1919) but not ratified by US; constitutional amendments enforce prohibition (1919), enfranchise women (1920).	28
4 March 1921–2 Aug. 1923	Calvin Coolidge	Teapot Dome scandal (1923–24).	29
3 Aug. 1923–4 March 1925 4 March 1925–4 March 1929	Charles G. Dawes	Kellogg–Briand Pact (1928).	30
4 March 1929–4 March 1933	Charles Curtis	Stock market crash (1929) inaugurates Great Depression.	31
4 March 1933–20 Jan. 1937 20 Jan. 1937–20 Jan. 1941 20 Jan. 1941–20 Jan. 1945 20 Jan. 1945–12 April 1945	John N. Garner John N. Garner Henry A. Wallace Harry S Truman	New Deal social reforms; prohibition repealed (1933); US enters World War II (1941)	32

Presidents of the US, 1789–2001 (Continued)

NAME (BIRTH–DEATH)	OTHER MAJOR OFFICES HELD	RESIDENCE AT ELECTION	PARTY
33 Harry S Truman 8 May 1884–26 December 1972	US senator (1935–45); US vice president (1945)	Independence, Mo.	Democrat
34 Dwight D. Eisenhower 14 October 1890–28 March 1969	Supreme allied commander in Europe (1943–44); Army chief of staff (1945–48)	New York	Republican
35 John F. Kennedy 29 May 1917–22 November 1963	US representative (1947–52); US senator (1953–60)	Massachusetts	Democrat
36 Lyndon B. Johnson 27 August 1908–22 January 1973	US representative (1937–48); US senator (1949–60); US vice president (1961–63)	Johnson City, Tex.	Democrat
37 Richard M. Nixon 9 January 1913–22 April 1994	US representative (1947–51); US senator (1951–53); US vice president (1953–61)	New York, N.Y.	Republican
38 Gerald Rudolph Ford 14 July 1913	US representative (1949–73); US vice president (1973–74)	Grand Rapids, Mich.	Republican
39 James Earl Carter, Jr. 1 October 1924	Governor of Georgia (1951–75)	Plains, Ga.	Democrat
40 Ronald Wilson Reagan 6 February 1911	Governor of California (1967–76)	Los Angeles, Calif.	Republican
41 George Herbert Walker Bush 12 June 1924	US representative (1967–71); Vice president (1981–88)	Houston, Texas	Republican
42 William Jefferson Clinton 19 August 1946	Attorney general of Arkansas (1977–79); Governor of Arkansas (1979–81; 1983–92)	Little Rock, Arkansas	Democrat
43 George Walker Bush 6 July 1946	Governor of Texas (1994–2000)	Midland, Texas	Republican

[1]In the event of a president's death or removal from office, his duties are assumed to devolve immediately upon his successor, even if he does not immediately take the oath of office.

ing political opponents were John Adams (1735–1826), second president; and Alexander Hamilton (b.West Indies, 1755–1804), first secretary of the treasury. James Madison (1751–1836), a leading figure in drawing up the United States Constitution, served as fourth president.

Abraham Lincoln (1809–65) led the United States through its most difficult period, the Civil War, in the course of which he issued the Emancipation Proclamation. Jefferson Davis (1808–89) served as the only president of the short-lived Confederacy. Among the foremost presidents of the 20th century have been Nobel Peace Prize winner Theodore Roosevelt (1858–1919); Woodrow Wilson (1856–1924), who led the nation during World

TERMS IN OFFICE[1]	VICE PRESIDENTS	NOTABLE EVENTS	
12 April 1945–20 Jan. 1949 20 Jan. 1949–20 Jan. 1953	Alben W. Barkley	United Nations founded (1945); US nuclear bombs dropped on Japan (1945); World War II ends (1945); Philippines granted independence (1946); Marshall Plan (1945); Korean conflict begins (1950); era of McCarthyism.	33
20 Jan. 1953–20 Jan. 1957 20 Jan. 1957–20 Jan. 1961	Richard M. Nixon Richard M. Nixon	Korean conflict ended (1953); Supreme Court orders school desegregation (1954); Alaska, Hawaii enter Union.	34
20 Jan. 1961–22 Nov. 1963	Lyndon B. Johnson	Conflicts with Cuba (1961–62); aboveground nuclear test ban treaty (1963); Kennedy assassinated.	35
22 Nov. 1963–20 Jan. 1965 20 Jan. 1965–20 Jan. 1969	Hubert H. Humphrey	Great Society programs; Voting Rights Act (1965); escalation of US military role in Indochina; race riots, political assassinations.	36
20 Jan. 1969–20 Jan. 1973 20 Jan. 1973–9 Aug. 1974	Spiro T. Agnew Spiro T. Agnew Gerald R. Ford	First lunar landing (1969); arms limitation treaty with Soviet Union (1972); US withdraws from Viet–Nam (1973); Agnew resigns in tax scandal (1973); Nixon resigns at height of Watergate scandal (1974).	37
9 Aug. 1974–20 Jan. 1977	Nelson A. Rockefeller	First combination of unelected president and vice president; Nixon pardoned (1974).	38
20 Jan. 1977–20 Jan. 1981	Walter F. Mondale	Carter mediates Israel-Egypt peace accord (1978); Panama Canal treaties ratified (1979); tensions with Iran (1979–81).	39
20 Jan. 1981–20 Jan. 1985 20 Jan. 1985–20 Jan. 1989	George H. Bush George H. Bush	Defense buildup; social spending cuts; rising trade and budget deficits; tensions with Nicaragua.	40
20 Jan. 1989–20 Jan. 1993	J. Danforth Quayle	Multi-national force repelled Iraqi invaders from Kuwait; savings and loan crisis; 1991 recession.	41
20 Jan. 1993–20 Jan. 1997 20 Jan. 1997–20 Jan. 2001	Albert Gore, Jr. Albert Gore, Jr.	North American Free Trade Agreement (1993); sent troops to Haiti to restore elected president deposed by a military coup (1994); Dayton Accords (1995); Whitewater and FBI files scandals (1995–96); rapid stock market growth (1995–97); balanced federal budget plan (1997); Clinton impeached (1998).	42
20 Jan. 2001–	Richard Bruce Cheney	$1.35 trillion tax cut through 2010.	43

War I; and Franklin Delano Roosevelt (1882–1945), elected to four terms spanning the Great Depression and World War II.

Outstanding military leaders of the Civil War were Union general Ulysses Simpson Grant (1822–85), who later served as the eighteenth president; and Confederate general Robert Edward Lee (1807–70). Douglas MacArthur (1880–1964) commanded the United States forces in Asia during World War II, oversaw the postwar occupation and reorganization of Japan, and directed United Nations forces in the first year of the Korean conflict. Dwight D. Eisenhower (1890–1969) served as supreme Allied commander during World War II, later becoming the thirty-fourth president.

John Marshall (1755–1835), chief justice of the United States from 1801 to 1835, established the power of the

Supreme Court through the principle of judicial review. Other important chief justices included Earl Warren (1891–1974), whose period as chief justice from 1953 to 1969 saw important decisions on desegregation, reapportionment, and civil liberties. Prominent associate justices included Oliver Wendell Holmes (1841–1935) and Louis Dembitz Brandeis (1856–1941).

Native American chiefs renowned for their resistance to white invasion were Tecumseh (1768–1813), Geronimo (1829?–1909), Sitting Bull (1831?–90), and Crazy Horse (1849?–77). Historical figures who have become part of American folklore include pioneer Daniel Boone (1734–1820); silversmith, engraver, and patriot Paul Revere (1735–1818); frontiersman David "Davy" Crockett (1786–1836); scout and Indian agent Christopher "Kit" Carson (1809–68); William Frederick "Buffalo Bill" Cody (1846–1917); and the outlaws Jesse Woodson James (1847–82) and Billy the Kid (William H. Bonney, 1859–81).

Inventors and Scientists

Outstanding inventors were Robert Fulton (1765–1815), who developed the steamboat; Samuel Finley Breese Morse (1791–1872), who invented the telegraph; and Elias Howe (1819–67), who invented the sewing machine. Alexander Graham Bell (b.Scotland, 1847–1922) invented the telephone. Thomas Alva Edison (1847–1931) was responsible for hundreds of inventions, among them the incandescent electric lamp, the phonograph, and a motion picture camera and projector. Two brothers, Wilbur Wright (1867–1912) and

Orville Wright (1871–1948), designed, built, and flew the first successful motor-powered airplane. Amelia Earhart (1898–1937) and Charles Lindbergh (1902–74) were aviation pioneers. Pioneers in the space program include John Glenn (b.1921), the first American astronaut to orbit the earth; and Neil Armstrong (b.1930), the first man to set foot on the moon.

Outstanding botanists and naturalists include George Washington Carver (1864–1943), known especially for his work on industrial applications for peanuts; and John James Audubon (1785–1851) who won fame as an ornithologist and artist.

Albert Abraham Michelson (b.Germany, 1852–1931) measured the speed of light and became the first of a long line of United States Nobel Prize winners. The theory of relativity was conceived by Albert Einstein (b.Germany, 1879–1955), generally considered one of the greatest minds in the physical sciences. Enrico Fermi (b.Italy, 1901–54) created the first nuclear chain reaction and contributed to the development of the atomic and hydrogen bombs. Also prominent in the splitting of the atom were J. Robert Oppenheimer (1904–67) and Edward Teller (b.Hungary, 1908). Jonas Edward Salk (1914–95) developed an effective vaccine for polio, and Albert Bruce Sabin (1906–93) contributed oral, attenuated live-virus polio vaccines.

Noah Webster (1758–1843) was the outstanding American dictionary author, and Melvil Dewey (1851–1931) was a leader in the development of library science. Also important in the social sciences has been anthropologist Margaret Mead (1901–78).

Social Reformers

Social reformers of note include Frederick Douglass (Frederick Augustus Washington Bailey, 1817–95), a prominent abolitionist; Elizabeth Cady Stanton (1815–1902) and Susan Brownell Anthony (1820–1906), leaders in the women's suffrage movement; Clara Barton (1821–1912), founder of the American Red Cross; Eugene Victor Debs (1855–1926), labor leader and an outstanding organizer of the Socialist movement in the United States; Jane Addams (1860–1935), a pioneer in settlement house work; Margaret Higgins Sanger (1883–1966), pioneer in birth control; and Martin Luther King, Jr. (1929–68), a central figure in the black civil rights movement and winner of the Nobel Peace Prize in 1964.

Religious leaders include Roger Williams (1603–83), an early advocate of religious tolerance in the United States; Jonathan Edwards (1703–58), New England preacher and theologian; Joseph Smith (1805–44), founder of the Church of Jesus Christ of Latter-day Saints (Mormon), and his chief associate, Brigham Young (1801–77); and Mary Baker Eddy (1821–1910), founder of the Christian Science Church.

Literary Figures

The first American author to be widely read outside the United States was Washington Irving (1783–1859). James Feni-more Cooper (1789–1851) was the first popular American novelist. The writings of two men of Concord, Massachusetts—Ralph Waldo Emerson (1803–82) and Henry David Thoreau (1817–62)—influenced philosophers, political leaders, and ordinary men and women in many parts of the world. The novels and short stories of Nathaniel Hawthorne (1804–64) explore New England's Puritan heritage. Herman Melville (1819–91) wrote the novel *Moby Dick,* a symbolic work about a whale hunt that has become an American classic. Mark Twain (Samuel Langhorne Clemens, 1835–1910) is the best-known American humorist.

Other leading novelists of the later 19th and early 20th centuries were Henry James (1843–1916), Edith Wharton (1862–1937), Stephen Crane (1871–1900), Willa Cather (1873–1947), and Sinclair Lewis (1885–1951), first American winner of the Nobel Prize for literature (1930). Later Nobel Prize–winning United States novelists include William Faulkner (1897–1962) in 1949; Ernest Hemingway (1899–1961) in 1954; John Steinbeck (1902–68) in 1962; Saul Bellow (b.Canada, 1915), in 1976; and Isaac Bashevis Singer (b.Poland, 1904–91) in 1978.

Noted American poets include Henry Wadsworth Longfellow (1807–82), Edgar Allan Poe (1809–49), Walt Whitman (1819–92), Emily Dickinson (1830–86), and Robert Frost (1874–1963). Allen Ginsberg (1926–97), Maya Angelou (b. 1928), and Sylvia Plath (1932–63) are among the best-known poets since World War II. Carl Sandburg (1878–1967) was a noted poet, historian, novelist, and folklorist. The foremost United States playwrights include Eugene (Gladstone) O'Neill (1888–1953), who won the Nobel Prize for literature in 1936; Tennessee Williams (Thomas Lanier Williams, 1911–83); and Arthur Miller (b.1915). Neil Simon (b.1927) is among the nation's most popular playwrights.

Artists

Two renowned painters of the early period were John Singleton Copley (1738–1815) and Gilbert Stuart (1755–1828). Outstanding 19th-century painters were James Abbott McNeill Whistler (1834–1903) and John Singer Sargent (b.Italy, 1856–1925). More recently, Edward Hopper (1882–1967), Georgia O'Keeffe (1887–1986), Norman Rockwell (1894–1978), and Andrew Wyeth (b.1917) have achieved wide recognition.

Sculptors of note include Alexander Calder (1898–1976), Louise Nevelson (b.Russia, 1899–1988), and Isamu Noguchi (1904–88). Frank Lloyd Wright (1869–1959) was the country's most famous architect. Contemporary architects of note include Richard Buckminster Fuller (1895–1983) and Ieoh Ming Pei (b.China, 1917). The United States has produced many fine photographers, notably Mathew B. Brady (1823?–96), who documented the Civil War in pictures; Alfred Stieglitz (1864–1946); and Margaret Bourke-White (1904–71).

Entertainment Figures

The first great American "showman" was Phineas Taylor Barnum (1810–91). Outstanding figures in the motion picture industry are Sir Charles Spencer "Charlie" Chaplin (b.England, 1889–1978), Walter Elias "Walt" Disney (1906–66), and George Orson Welles (1915–85). Sir Alfred Hitchcock (b.England, 1899–1980) was a famous motion picture director; George Lucas (b.1944), Steven Spielberg (b.1947), and Spike Lee (b.1957) have achieved remarkable popular success with their films, as has Woody Allen (Allen Konigsberg, b.1935).

World-famous American actors and actresses include Humphrey Bogart (1899–1957); Clark Gable (1901–60); Cary Grant (Alexander Archibald Leach, b.England, 1904–86); John Wayne (Marion Michael Morrison, 1907–79); Judy Garland (Frances Gumm, 1922–69); Marlon Brando (b.1924); Marilyn Monroe (Norma Jean Mortenson, 1926–62); Dustin Hoffman (b.1937), and Harrison Ford (b.1942). Among other great entertainers are W. C. Fields (William Claude Dukenfield, 1880–1946); Jack Benny (Benjamin Kubelsky, 1894–1974); Fred Astaire (Fred Austerlitz, 1899–1987); Bob (Leslie Townes) Hope (b.England, 1903); Frank (Francis Albert) Sinatra (1915–98); Elvis Aaron Presley (1935–77); and Barbra (Barbara Joan) Streisand (b.1942).

Composers and Musicians

The songs of Stephen Collins Foster (1826–64) have achieved folk-song status. Among the foremost composers are Edward MacDowell (1861–1908), Aaron Copland (1900–90), and Leonard Bernstein (1918–90). Leading composers of popular music are John Philip Sousa

(1854–1932), George Michael Cohan (1878–1942), George Gershwin (1898–1937), Woody Guthrie (1912–67). Prominent in the blues tradition are Leadbelly (Huddie Ledbetter, 1888–1949), Bessie Smith (1898?–1937), and Muddy Waters (McKinley Morganfield, 1915–83). Leading jazz figures include the composers Scott Joplin (1868–1917), Edward Kennedy "Duke" Ellington (1899–1974), and William "Count" Basie (1904–84), and performers Louis Armstrong (1900–71), Billie Holiday (Eleanora Fagan, 1915–59), John Birks "Dizzy" Gillespie (1917–93), and Charlie "Bird" Parker (1920–55).

Sports Figures

Among the many noteworthy sports stars are baseball's Tyrus Raymond "Ty" Cobb (1886–1961) and George Herman "Babe" Ruth (1895–1948); football's Jim Brown (b.1936); and golf's Mildred "Babe" Didrikson Zaharias (1914–56). Billie Jean (Moffitt) King (b.1943) starred in tennis; Joe Louis (Joseph Louis Barrow, 1914–81) and Muhammad Ali (Cassius Marcellus Clay, b.1942) in boxing; Wilton Norman "Wilt" Chamberlain (1936–99) and Michael Jordan (b.1963) in basketball; Mark Spitz (b.1950) in swimming; Eric Heiden (b.1958) in speed skating; and Jesse Owens (1913–80) in track and field.

40 BIBLIOGRAPHY

Barone, Michael. *The Almanac of American Politics.* Washington, D.C.: National Journal, 1992.

Bennett, Lerone. *Before the Mayflower: A History of Black America.* 6th ed. New York: Penguin, 1993.

Frank, Nicole. *Welcome to the USA.* Milwaukee, WI: Gareth Stevens, 2000.

Hart, James David, ed. *Oxford Companion to American Literature.* New York: Oxford University Press, 1983.

Josephy, Alvin M., Jr. *Now that the Buffalo's Gone: A Study of Today's American Indians.* Norman, Okla.: Univ. of Oklahoma Press, 1984.

Morison, Samuel Eliot. *The Oxford History of the American People.* New York: New American Library, 1972.

Nagel, Rob, and Anne Commire. "Abraham Lincoln." In *World Leaders, People Who Shaped the World.* Volume III: North and South America. Detroit: U*X*L, 1994.

———. "Benjamin Franklin." In *World Leaders, People Who Shaped the World.* Volume III: North and South America. Detroit: U*X*L, 1994.

———. "Crazy Horse." In *World Leaders, People Who Shaped the World.* Volume III: North and South America. Detroit: U*X*L, 1994.

———. "Franklin D. Roosevelt." In *World Leaders, People Who Shaped the World.* Volume III: North and South America. Detroit: U*X*L, 1994.

———. "Frederick Douglas." In *World Leaders, People Who Shaped the World.* Volume III: North and South America. Detroit: U*X*L, 1994.

———. "George Washington." In *World Leaders, People Who Shaped the World.* Volume III: North and South America. Detroit: U*X*L, 1994.

———. "Harriet Tubman." In *World Leaders, People Who Shaped the World.* Volume III: North and South America. Detroit: U*X*L, 1994.

———. "John F. Kennedy." In *World Leaders, People Who Shaped the World.* Volume III: North and South America. Detroit: U*X*L, 1994.

———. "Malcolm X." In *World Leaders, People Who Shaped the World.* Volume III: North and South America. Detroit: U*X*L, 1994.

———. "Martin Luther King, Jr." In *World Leaders, People Who Shaped the World.* Volume III: North and South America. Detroit: U*X*L, 1994.

———. "Robert E. Lee." In *World Leaders, People Who Shaped the World.* Volume III: North and South America. Detroit: U*X*L, 1994.

———. "Sitting Bull." In *World Leaders, People Who Shaped the World.* Volume III: North and South America. Detroit: U*X*L, 1994.

———. "Susan B. Anthony." In *World Leaders, People Who Shaped the World.* Volume III:

North and South America. Detroit: U*X*L, 1994.

————. "Thomas Jefferson." In *World Leaders, People Who Shaped the World*. Volume III: North and South America. Detroit: U*X*L, 1994.

————. "Thurgood Marshall." In *World Leaders, People Who Shaped the World*. Volume III: North and South America. Detroit: U*X*L, 1994.

Stein, R. *The United States of America*. Chicago: Children's Press, 1994.

Tocqueville, Alexis de. *Democracy in America*. New York: A. Knopf, 1994.

Travis, George. *State Facts*. Vero Beach, Fla.: Rourke Press, 1999.

Webb, Marcus. *The United States of America*. San Diego: Lucent Books, 2000.

Glossary

ALPINE: generally refers to the Alps or other mountains; can also refer to a mountainous zone above the timberline.

ANCESTRY: based on how people refer to themselves, and refers to a person's ethnic origin, descent, heritage, or place of birth of the person or the person's parents or ancestors before their arrival in the United States. The Census Bureau accepted "American" as a unique ethnicity if it was given alone, with an unclear response (such as "mixed" or "adopted"), or with names of particular states.

ANTEBELLUM: before the US Civil War.

AQUEDUCT: a large pipe or channel that carries water over a distance, or a raised structure that supports such a channel or pipe.

AQUIFER: an underground layer of porous rock, sand, or gravel that holds water.

BLUE LAWS: laws forbidding certain practices (e.g., conducting business, gaming, drinking liquor), especially on Sundays.

BROILERS: a bird (especially a young chicken) that can be cooked by broiling.

BTU: The amount of heat required to raise one pound of water one degree Fahrenheit.

CAPITAL BUDGET: a financial plan for acquiring and improving buildings or land, paid for by the sale of bonds.

CAPITAL PUNISHMENT: punishment by death.

CIVILIAN LABOR FORCE: all persons 16 years of age or older who are not in the armed forces and who are now holding a job, have been temporarily laid off, are waiting to be reassigned to a new position, or are unemployed but actively looking for work.

CLASS I RAILROAD: a railroad having gross annual revenues of $83.5 million or more in 1983.

COMMERCIAL BANK: a bank that offers to businesses and individuals a variety of banking services, including the right of withdrawal by check.

COMPACT: a formal agreement, covenant, or understanding between two or more parties.

CONSOLIDATED BUDGET: a financial plan that includes the general budget, federal funds, and all special funds.

CONSTANT DOLLARS: money values calculated so as to eliminate the effect of inflation on prices and income.

CONTERMINOUS US: refers to the "lower 48" states of the continental US that are enclosed within a common boundary.

CONTINENTAL CLIMATE: the climate typical of the US interior, having distinct seasons, a wide range of daily and annual temperatures, and dry, sunny summers.

COUNCIL-MANAGER SYSTEM: a system of local government under which a professional administrator is hired by an elected council to carry out its laws and policies.

CREDIT UNION: a cooperative body that raises funds from its members by the sale of shares and makes loans to its members at relatively low interest rates.

CURRENT DOLLARS: money values that reflect prevailing prices, without excluding the effects of inflation.

DEMAND DEPOSIT: a bank deposit that can be withdrawn by the depositor with no advance notice to the bank.

ELECTORAL VOTES: the votes that a state may cast for president, equal to the combined total of its US senators and representatives and nearly always cast entirely on behalf of the candidate who won the most votes in that state on Election Day.

ENDANGERED SPECIES: a type of plant or animal threatened with extinction in all or part of its natural range.

FEDERAL POVERTY LEVEL: a level of money income below which a person or family qualifies for US government aid.

FISCAL YEAR: a 12-month period for accounting purposes.

FOOD STAMPS: coupons issued by the government to low-income persons for food purchases at local stores.

GENERAL BUDGET: a financial plan based on a government's normal revenues and operating expenses, excluding special funds.

GENERAL COASTLINE: a measurement of the general outline of the US seacoast. See also TIDAL SHORELINE.

GREAT AWAKENING: during the mid–18th century, a Protestant religious revival in North America, especially New England.

GROSS STATE PRODUCT: the total value of goods and services produced in the state.

GROWING SEASON: the period between the last 32°F (0°C) temperature in spring and the first

32°F (0°C) temperature in autumn.

HISPANIC: a person who originates from Spain or from Spanish-speaking countries of South and Central America, Mexico, Puerto Rico, and Cuba.

HOME-RULE CHARTER: a document stating how and in what respects a city, town, or county may govern itself.

HUNDREDWEIGHT: a unit of weight that equals 100 pounds in the US and 112 pounds in Britain.

INPATIENT: a patient who is housed and fed—in addition to being treated—in a hospital.

INSTALLED CAPACITY: the maximum possible output of electric power at any given time.

MASSIF: a central mountain mass or the dominant part of a range of mountains.

MAYOR-COUNCIL SYSTEM: a system of local government under which an elected council serves as a legislature and an elected mayor is the chief administrator.

MEDICAID: a federal-state program that helps defray the hospital and medical costs of needy persons.

MEDICARE: a program of hospital and medical insurance for the elderly, administered by the federal government.

METRIC TON: a unit of weight that equals 1,000 kilograms (2,204.62 pounds).

METROPOLITAN AREA: in most cases, a city and its surrounding suburbs.

MONTANE: refers to a zone in mountainous areas in which large coniferous trees, in a cool moist setting, are the main features.

NO-FAULT INSURANCE: an automobile insurance plan that allows an accident victim to receive payment from an insurance company without having to prove who was responsible for the accident.

NONFEDERAL PHYSICIAN: a medical doctor who is not employed by the federal US government.

NORTHERN, NORTH MIDLAND: major US dialect regions.

OMBUDSMAN: a public official empowered to hear and investigate complaints by private citizens about government agencies.

PER CAPITA: per person.

PERSONAL INCOME: refers to the income an individual receives from employment, or to the total incomes that all individuals receive from their employment in a sector of business (such as personal incomes in the retail trade).

PIEDMONT: refers to the base of mountains.

POCKET VETO: a method by which a state governor (or the US president) may kill a bill by taking no action on it before the legislature adjourns.

PROVED RESERVES: the quantity of a recoverable mineral resource (such as oil or natural gas) that is still in the ground.

PUBLIC DEBT: the amount owed by a government.

RELIGIOUS ADHERENTS: the followers of a religious group, including (but not confined to) the full, confirmed, or communicant members of that group.

RETAIL TRADE: the sale of goods directly to the consumer.

REVENUE SHARING: the distribution of federal tax receipts to state and local governments.

RIGHT-TO-WORK LAW: a measure outlawing any attempt to require union membership as a condition of employment.

SAVINGS AND LOAN ASSOCIATION: a bank that invests the savings of depositors primarily in home mortgage loans.

SECESSION: the act of withdrawal, such as a state that withdrew from the Union in the US Civil War.

SERVICE INDUSTRIES: industries that provide services (e.g., health, legal, automotive repair) for individuals, businesses, and others.

SHORT TON: a unit of weight that equals 2,000 pounds.

SOCIAL SECURITY: as commonly understood, the federal system of old age, survivors, and disability insurance.

SOUTHERN, SOUTH MIDLAND: major US dialect regions.

SUBALPINE: generally refers to high mountainous areas just beneath the timberline; can also more specifically refer to the lower slopes of the Alps mountains.

SUNBELT: the southernmost states of the US, extending from Florida to California.

SUPPLEMENTAL SECURITY INCOME: a federally administered program of aid to the aged, blind, and disabled.

TIDAL SHORELINE: a detailed measurement of the US seacoast that includes sounds, bays, other outlets, and offshore islands.

TIME DEPOSIT: a bank deposit that may be withdrawn only at the end of a specified time period or upon advance notice to the bank.

VALUE ADDED BY MANUFACTURE: the difference, measured in dollars, between the value of finished goods and the cost of the materials needed to produce them.

WHOLESALE TRADE: the sale of goods, usually in large quantities, for ultimate resale to consumers.

Abbreviations & Acronyms

AD—Anno Domini
AFDC—aid to families with dependent children
AFL–CIO—American Federation of Labor–Congress of Industrial Organizations
AI—American Independent
AM—before noon
AM—amplitude modulation
American Ind.—American Independent Party
Amtrak—National Railroad Passenger Corp.
b.—born
BC—Before Christ
Btu—British thermal unit(s)
bu—bushel(s)
c.—circa (about)
C—Celsius (Centigrade)
CIA—Central Intelligence Agency
cm—centimeter(s)
Co.—company
comp.—compiler
Conrail—Consolidated Rail Corp.
Corp.—corporation
CST—Central Standard Time
cu—cubic
cwt—hundredweight(s)
d.—died
D—Democrat
e—evening
E—east
ed.—edition, editor
e.g.—exempli gratia (for example)
EPA—Environmental Protection Agency
est.—estimated
EST—Eastern Standard Time
et al.—et alii (and others)
etc.—et cetera (and so on)
F—Fahrenheit
FBI—Federal Bureau of Investigation
FCC—Federal Communications Commission
FM—frequency modulation
Ft.—fort
ft—foot, feet
GDP—gross domestic products
gm—gram
GMT—Greenwich Mean Time
GNP—gross national product
GRT—gross registered tons
Hist.—Historic
I—interstate (highway)
i.e.—id est (that is)

in—inch(es)
Inc.—incorporated
Jct.—junction
K—kindergarten
kg—kilogram(s)
km—kilometer(s)
km/hr—kilometers per hour
kw—kilowatt(s)
kwh—kilowatt-hour(s)
lb—pound(s)
m—meter(s); morning
m^3—cubic meter(s)
mi—mile(s)
Mon.—monument
mph—miles per hour
MST—Mountain Standard Time
Mt.—mount
Mtn.—mountain
mw—megawatt(s)
N—north
NA—not available
Natl.—National
NATO—North Atlantic Treaty Organization
NCAA—National Collegiate Athletic Association
n.d.—no date
NEA—National Education Association or National Endowment for the Arts
N.F.—National Forest
N.W.R.—National Wildlife Refuge
oz—ounce(s)
PM—after noon
PST—Pacific Standard Time
r.—reigned
R—Republican
Ra.—range
Res.—reservoir, reservation
rev. ed.—revised edition
s—south
S—Sunday
Soc.—Socialist
sq—square
St.—saint
SRD—States' Rights Democrat
UN—United Nations
US—United States
USIA—United States Information Agency
w—west

NAMES OF STATES AND OTHER SELECTED AREAS

	Standard Abbreviation(s)	Postal Abbreviation
Alabama	Ala.	AL
Alaska	*	AK
Arizona	Ariz.	AZ
Arkansas	Ark.	AR
California	Calif.	CA
Colorado	Colo.	CO
Connecticut	Conn.	CN
Delaware	Del.	DE
District of Columbia	D.C.	DC
Florida	Fla.	FL
Georgia	Ga.	GA
Hawaii	*	HI
Idaho	*	ID
Illinois	Ill.	IL
Indiana	Ind.	IN
Iowa	*	IA
Kansas	Kans. (Kan.)	KS
Kentucky	Ky.	KY
Louisiana	La.	LA
Maine	Me.	ME
Maryland	Md.	MD
Massachusetts	Mass.	MA
Michigan	Mich.	MI
Minnesota	Minn.	MN
Mississippi	Miss.	MS
Missouri	Mo.	MO
Montana	Mont.	MT
Nebraska	Nebr. (Neb.)	NE
Nevada	Nev.	NV
New Hampshire	N.H.	NH
New Jersey	N.J.	NJ
New Mexico	N.Mex.(N.M.)	NM
New York	N.Y.	NY
North Carolina	N.C.	NC
North Dakota	N.Dak. (N.D.)	ND
Ohio	*	OH
Oklahoma	Okla.	OK
Oregon	Oreg. (Ore.)	OR
Pennsylvania	Pa.	PA
Puerto Rico	P.R.	PR
Rhode Island	R.I.	RI
South Carolina	S.C.	SC
South Dakota	S.Dak. (S.D.)	SD
Tennessee	Tenn.	TN
Texas	Tex.	TX
Utah	*	UT
Vermont	Vt.	VT
Virginia	Va.	VA
Virgin Islands	V.I.	VI
Washington	Wash.	WA
West Virginia	W.Va.	WV
Wisconsin	Wis.	WI
Wyoming	Wyo.	WY

*No standard abbreviation

Index

This index contains terms from all four volumes of this encyclopedia. The number of the volume is enclosed in brackets. The volume number is followed by the page number. For example, the reference [2]73 means that the indexed term can be found in volume 2 on page 73.

Tennessee

Texas

Utah

Vermont

Virginia

Washington

West Virginia

Wisconsin

Wyoming

District of Columbia

Puerto Rico

United States